Nudge+

AF736727

Sanchayan Banerjee • Peter John

Nudge+

Think, Before You Nudge

palgrave
macmillan

Sanchayan Banerjee
School for Government,
The Policy Institute
King's College London
London, UK

Peter John
Department of Political Economy
King's College London
London, UK

ISBN 978-3-032-13260-4 ISBN 978-3-032-13261-1 (eBook)
https://doi.org/10.1007/978-3-032-13261-1

© The Editor(s) (if applicable) and The Author(s), under exclusive license to Springer Nature Switzerland AG 2026

This work is subject to copyright. All rights are solely and exclusively licensed by the Publisher, whether the whole or part of the material is concerned, specifically the rights of translation, reprinting, reuse of illustrations, recitation, broadcasting, reproduction on microfilms or in any other physical way, and transmission or information storage and retrieval, electronic adaptation, computer software, or by similar or dissimilar methodology now known or hereafter developed.
The use of general descriptive names, registered names, trademarks, service marks, etc. in this publication does not imply, even in the absence of a specific statement, that such names are exempt from the relevant protective laws and regulations and therefore free for general use.
The publisher, the authors and the editors are safe to assume that the advice and information in this book are believed to be true and accurate at the date of publication. Neither the publisher nor the authors or the editors give a warranty, expressed or implied, with respect to the material contained herein or for any errors or omissions that may have been made. The publisher remains neutral with regard to jurisdictional claims in published maps and institutional affiliations.

This Palgrave Macmillan imprint is published by the registered company Springer Nature Switzerland AG.
The registered company address is: Gewerbestrasse 11, 6330 Cham, Switzerland

If disposing of this product, please recycle the paper.

To Maa, Baba, and Saranya—for being by my side and tolerating me in this endless academic hustle – Sanchayan Banerjee. For Mike, my husband and true love, whose death in 2025 leaves me so forlorn – Peter John

"Nudge changed how we think about policy. Nudge+ changes how we think about nudge. Banerjee and John brilliantly bridge the gap between the subtle power of nudges and the deeper engagement of reflective thinking, creating a hybrid approach that's both practical and ethically sound. Drawing on rigorous experiments and real-world insights, this book challenges us to rethink how we design interventions that truly empower citizens. As someone who's spent decades testing what works at scale, I see Nudge+ as the next evolution in thought. Smarter, more inclusive, and ready to tackle today's biggest policy challenges. A must-read."

—John A. List, *Kenneth C. Griffin Distinguished Service Professor of Economics, University of Chicago, USA*

"Sanchayan Banerjee and Peter John have broken new ground for years with their unique perspective that we need "nudge+". Now, they've collected these insights to provide a deep, accessible and practical account of how behavioral science can go further by getting people to step back and reflect. This is essential reading to understand the next generation of behavioral science."

—Michael Hallsworth, *Chief Behavioural Scientist at the Behavioural Insights Team*

"This book challenges some of the practical and ethical weaknesses of earlier Nudge style behavioural change and offers an exciting alternative that respects people's autonomy and capacity to think for themselves. It will be of great value to both academics and policymakers."

—Gerry Stoker, OBE, *Professor, University of Southampton, UK*

"The book positions nudge+ as a practical response to ongoing ethical and implementation debates—it is useful to researchers and practitioners seeking a systematic, policy-facing discussion of how reflective elements might be incorporated into behavioural interventions."

— Lucia Reisch, *El-Erian Professor of Behavioural Economics and Policy, Director of the El-Erian Institute of Behavioural Economics and Policy, Cambridge Judge Business School, UK*

"Sanchayan Banerjee & Peter John are two leading thinkers in the space of applied behavioural science - this book promises to elucidate one of the most important questions for the field - how do we move beyond nudging?"

—Michael Sanders, *Professor of Public Policy, Director of the School for Government, King's College London, UK*

Preface

The antecedents of nudge+ go back to the early 2010s. Rooted in the political philosophy of libertarian paternalism (Sunstein and Thaler 2003; Thaler and Sunstein 2003), nudge was then making its way into public policies. Peter John, then Professor of Governance at the University of Manchester, along with Gerry Stoker, Alice Moseley, Sarah Cotterill, Liz Richardson, and Graham Smith, was working on the competing idea of think—bottom-up deliberative policies—to achieve prosocial behaviour change. A think encourages citizens to reflect widely about big issues in society. In contrast to nudge, think was designed to promote citizen engagement and agency. A think for the wider population was believed to deliver long-lasting and meaningful behaviour change, one that a nudge alone might fail to do. As they tested out these ideas, Peter and others came to realise that scaling up think can be hard to achieve whereas nudge often worked well on its own terms. Think was often just too difficult to implement successfully in the public policy context. Organising citizen-wide engagement for behaviour changes at the same time as needing to fit into the everyday lives of citizens was not usually possible.

Somewhat later, Gerry and Peter asked whether think could be embedded into nudge. Gerry named the new hybrid 'nudge plus' (there was no '+' at this stage: we replaced the plus with + later in a totally agonised almost non-decision (Banerjee and John 2022)). He suggested that there is something more than a nudge in a nudge+. Only if citizens could be encouraged to deliberate before being nudged, they would be more adept at navigating nudge. Later, these ideas appear in Peter's *How Far to Nudge?* (John 2018). Sanchayan Banerjee, then a doctoral student at LSE, read this book, which inspired his experiment—a test of think delivered to people before they were nudged (Banerjee 2019). The difference to prior tests was that think was no longer designed for a group as a whole. Instead, it was targeted to individuals as a prompt that enables them to think just before they were given a nudge. It was in effect a mini-think (John and Stoker 2019).

Experimental findings from Sanchayan's first experiment showed that when people were encouraged to think individually about nudge, they could commit to more sustainable life choices. Joining forces in 2019, we mapped out the cognitive underpinnings of nudge+ and set out its workings and testable hypothesis (Banerjee and John 2024). The relevance of this individual thinking before nudging became clearer, more so over the last few years as we engaged in multiple trials which showed there were demonstrable merits to an approach whereby the policy-maker encourages free thought on the part of citizens that they nudged. The title of our book reflects this important takeaway: before nudging people, policy-makers should pause and think. But this title is not only for policy-makers who ought to do the thinking before nudging. Citizens should also think about a nudge that is delivered to them, whether that nudge sits well with their own goals, preferences, and values. Our plea is to develop 'Think, before you nudge' into a mantra that allows people to own behaviour changes by becoming quick thinkers who can conveniently use nudge to get them to where they want to be. This aim fulfils the true purpose of libertarian paternalism: we encourage people to decide for themselves but with some guidance along the way. We propose that the benefits of thinking and nudging can be realised jointly in a programme of nudge+.

The time is now right to set out nudge+ in much more detail to engage with key debates in the field and to draw implications for public policy. This book aims to be the building block that establishes the research programme of nudge+, locating it within social science debates and theory. It asks what a modified form of behavioural public policy can and should be and draws on experimental studies to validate its claims.

In this book, we review what it is to become a reflective person, and how thinking helps us in taking charge and maintaining our autonomy as we navigate through some of the most pressing public policy challenges of our time. We explore the idea of perspective transformation and the ethical challenges of nudging, giving a large number of examples along the way. We hope this book makes you believe in nudge+ as much as we do!

London, UK Sanchayan Banerjee
London, UK Peter John

References

Banerjee, Sanchayan. 2019. Going beyond classic nudges: Comparing the effectiveness of information nudges combined with commitment devices in lowering meat consumption. *Available at SSRN 3493588*. https://doi.org/10.2139/ssrn.3493588.

Banerjee, Sanchayan, and Peter John. 2022. To nudge plus or to nudge+: A dilemma. https://bppblog.com/2022/02/18/to-nudge-plus-or-nudge-a-dilemma/.

Banerjee, Sanchayan, and Peter John. 2024. Nudge plus: Incorporating reflection into behavioral public policy. *Behavioural Public Policy* 8 (1): 69–84. https://doi.org/10.1017/bpp.2021.6.

John, Peter. 2018. *How far to nudge?: Assessing behavioural public policy*. Edward Elgar Publishing.

John, Peter, and Gerry Stoker. 2019. Rethinking the role of experts and expertise in behavioural public policy. *Policy & Politics* 47 (2): 209–225. https://doi.org/10.1332/030557319X15526371698257.

Sunstein, Cass R, and Richard H. Thaler. 2003. Libertarian paternalism is not an oxymoron. *The University of Chicago Law Review* 1159–1202. https://doi.org/10.2307/1600573.

Thaler, Richard H, and Cass R Sunstein. 2003. Libertarian paternalism. *American Economic Review* 93 (2): 175–179. https://doi.org/10.1257/000282803321947001.

Acknowledgements

We thank our extended nudge+ team, especially those who led this idea from the days of *Nudge Nudge, Think Think* namely Gerry Stoker, Alice Moseley, and Liz Richardson. We also thank Susana Mourato and Matteo Galizzi who were a major part of Sanchayan's intellectual journey of discovering nudge+ during his doctoral research at the London School of Economics. We thank many colleagues and friends from the BPP community but mainly Cass Sunstein, Ralph Hertwig, and Till Grüne-Yanoff for the different conversations on tools of behaviour change and its related effects on human autonomy and agency, which inspired nudge+ and this book in many ways. We are grateful to Liam Delaney, Patrik Michaelsen, Michael Sanders, and Leonie Peiffer who gave us their invaluable feedback and comments during the writing of this book which enabled us to refine the argument. We thank our editor Stewart Beale for believing in our book, the editorial team at Palgrave Macmillan, and the anonymous reviewers who helped us refine our work. We also thank Saranya Mukherjee and Philipp Thamer for reading and providing us with comments on the final draft of our manuscript. We thank AI-assisted large language models (GPT4o) for helping us proofread and copyedit our text in various chapters.

Setting the Scene

Today it seems normal for policy-makers to consider a wide array of human behaviours. Decision-makers at all levels of government regularly use their understandings of human cognition and habits to design public policies. As a result, encouraging prosocial behaviour change has become a routine occurrence for most agencies and public bodies today. The main example of these behaviourally informed policies is a nudge, which is a light-touch prompt designed to encourage citizens to do what, ideally they and society want to achieve (Thaler and Sunstein 2008). Nudge is based on the idea that public policies should take account of human heuristics and biases, which are ways in which people process information and come to decisions using traits and habits rather than a strict rational weighing up of costs and benefits. It operates by appealing to people's use of rules of thumb and short-cuts when they make decisions, such as choosing a pension scheme if it is offered as a default or donating organs or paying taxes on time if people get a signal that everyone else is doing these activities at the same time (John 2018; Banerjee and John 2024).

This shift in emphasis was very important for public policy. If public policy is based on correct assumptions about what people are going to do in response to changes in the tools of government to achieve a public end, such as a new budget incentive to get people to save or change in the law to stop them doing something like smoking in confined public places, it is more likely that the new policy will be complied with in the expected manner than if the wrong theory was used. Nudge seeks to ensure that public policy operates with the correct model of individual motivation thereby promoting collective welfare much more than if an incorrect or less realistic model was used. People change their behaviour in the intended direction when the communication signal they receive works along the grain of their preferences and is customised to how they see the world. Using the right theory of human nature also puts the policy-maker closer to where the citizen is in terms of how they normally think. The citizen-centred focus makes it more likely that policies that emerge are realistic in terms of what citizens are expected to do as well as being a more legitimate form of intervention.

The behavioural approach seems like common-sense today, but it was an innovative idea two decades ago, largely because of the dominance of instrumental rational actor models in the design of public policies, which assume that individuals maximise benefits and reduce costs when deciding to comply with government policies or when acting in the collective interest. The advice to policy-makers was to design instruments or tools of government, such as taxes and laws, that affect the costs and benefits individual and group face, with the idea that socially-beneficial activities become the preferred option because costs are reduced and benefits maximised (and vice versa for socially undesirable actions). Such cost-benefit calculation was the conventional way in which policy was designed and evaluated prior to the late 2000s and is still highly influential today (Boardman et al. 2018). Nudge implies that policies are based on more rounded accounts of human nature that encompass the wide variety of human behaviours. People react to policies in terms of their priors and biases and policy-makers need to understand how citizens approach their actions if they are to calibrate effective policies that cause them to act in prosocial ways.

We propose to deepen and extend this citizen-friendly form of governance. We intend to show a new way in which we can involve citizens much more in terms of shaping and driving these very policies designed to influence them. The result reduces the distance between the citizen and the policy-maker. This idea has been promoted by nudge, but there is an opportunity to move to the next, more radical stage. Even though nudge continues to offer prosocial benefits, now is the time to make the extra step in including citizens more actively when seeking to nudge them. The result of this deepening and democratisation of nudge is a step-change for behavioural public policy. There is a need for a radical set of proposals for policy change and institutional reform that in many ways can challenge the conservatism of the nudge programme itself. We, along with several other colleagues who have worked with us to develop these ideas (John and Richardson 2012; John and Stoker 2019; Banerjee 2021), have called this programme nudge+. As the name suggests, the *plus* alongside nudge indicates that there is something more than just a nudge. This is both the claim that a nudge does more than simply tapping into one's biases, for example, where it engages people to think about a way of life they want to build when they encounter a nudge; but it also conveys the idea that given current global challenges, we need more than a simple nudge. A modified form of behavioural public policy puts citizens at the heart of policy-making, so they can be empowered to move forward with the behaviour changes that are needed to tackle the many challenging policy problems of today. This is what we set out to do in this book as we outline the research programme of nudge+.

The next chapter (Chapter 1) will provide the necessary context for our approach, which situates our work within the broader field of behavioural economics and public policy. In that chapter, we will discuss the background and origins of behavioural economics and behavioural public policy, much of which has been a discussion around nudge and nudging in public policy mainly for the last few years. We will critically examine this consensus around the nudge. While we remain highly sympathetic to the enormous task that nudge had set out to achieve, we will highlight the many ways in which the nudge programme has fallen short in empowering citizens. Then we will propose a way to move forward radically by encouraging citizen reflection as part of the nudge. We will discuss nudges with the possibilities of reflection embedded into them. Our idea of empowering citizens to think while actively making the most of the nudge programme is core to nudge+ which will combine the best of these both worlds. The chapter will prepare the reader to think more radically about the endless possibilities of thinks. When delivered alongside the nudge, they can deliver a radical form of behavioural public policy that is not only ethically sound and legitimate but also effective and persistent so tasked to deal with the big problems of today.

Then, in Chapter 2, we turn our attention to the role of automatic processes in public policy and personal life. This chapter will show that much of what shapes our behaviour relies on habits and signals, from paying taxes to recycling. Yet, we can be both automatic and reflective: we can pause to see the bigger picture even as we act automatically. This chapter highlights the missed opportunities in everyday signals, showing how small moments of reflection can scale up to meaningful, long-term behaviour change. We explore why nudge+ is more than an occasional, large-scale deliberation. It seeks to achieve sustainable, self-reflective changes in citizens' behaviour, combining reflection and nudge for greater legitimacy and autonomy.

Chapter 3 delves deeper into reflection itself. We ask what it means to reflect: is it passive or active, individual or collective, or costly or natural? We argue that true reflection transforms perspective by changing or building on current views rather than simply adding mental effort. The chapter examines how reflection can be supported by tools like nudges yet must remain autonomous to be effective. Here, we prepare the groundwork for understanding how thinking humans can take an active role in shaping nudges using nudge+.

Chapter 4 brings together nudge and its reflective plus, showing how they complement and strengthen each other. We discuss the ways reflective prompts can enhance conventional nudges, and the different roles reflection can play—from transparency to self-examination, to understanding the source and goals of a nudge. The chapter also considers the limits of reflection, including cognitive burdens, attention constraints, and the risk of echo chambers, stressing the importance of structured reflection for meaningful behaviour change.

In Chapter 5, we explore the apparent paradox of combining fast and slow thinking within nudge+. Thinking requires slowing down, evaluating pros and cons, whereas nudges leverage automatic responses. We show how these forms of cognition can work together naturally, allowing citizens to monitor fast responses while cueing slower, reflective thinking when needed. This chapter grounds nudge+ in contemporary cognitive models and highlights its potential as a hybrid framework for behaviour change.

Chapter 6 shifts the focus to the ethical dimension of reflection. We argue for the value of agency. We need interventions that enable citizens to reflect and act thoughtfully, which are ethically preferable to those that manipulate unconsciously. While people may sometimes make choices that are suboptimal, the capacity to reflect and learn from experience supports long-term self-determination. Reflection, in this sense, is a moral as well as practical improvement over conventional nudges.

Chapter 7 examines scale and participation in nudge+. Ethical reflection depends not only on the individual but also on how interventions engage citizens and who delivers them. Traditional deliberative mechanisms have limited reach, whereas nudge+ can involve large numbers at scale while tackling complex social and policy issues. We also consider the possibility of reversing the traditional nudge relationship, giving citizens a role in influencing policy-makers and establishing a more balanced interaction between those who nudge and those who are nudged.

Finally, Chapter 8 pulls together the insights of the book to present nudge+ as an integrated project. We summarise the preceding chapters, address common criticisms, and discuss the future potential of nudge+ for researchers, policy-makers, and citizens alike. This chapter summarises the benefits and challenges of combining reflection and nudging to achieve meaningful, persistent, and ethically grounded behaviour change.

With this roadmap at hand, we now invite the reader to explore what it means to nudge+ and how to do it, and hope that at the end of it, we will have convincingly defended our mantra of 'Think, before you nudge'!

References

Banerjee, Sanchayan. 2021. Rethinking the origin of the behavioural policy cube with nudge plus. In *Behavioral-based interventions for improving public policies*, 1–16. IGI Global Scientific Publishing.

Banerjee, Sanchayan, and Peter John. 2024. Nudge plus: Incorporating reflection into behavioral public policy. *Behavioural Public Policy* 8 (1): 69–84. https://doi.org/10.1017/bpp.2021.6.

Boardman, Anthony E., David H. Greenberg, Aidan R. Vining, and David L. Weimer. 2018. *Cost-benefit analysis: Concepts and practice*. Cambridge University Press.

John, Peter. 2018. *How far to nudge?: Assessing behavioural public policy*. Edward Elgar Publishing.

John, Peter, and Liz Richardson. 2012. *Nudging citizens towards localism*. The British Academy.

John, Peter, and Gerry Stoker. 2019. Rethinking the role of experts and expertise in behavioural public policy. *Policy & Politics* 47 (2): 209–225. https://doi.org/10.1332/030557319X15526371698257.

Thaler, Richard H, and Cass R Sunstein. 2008. *Nudge: Improving decisions about health, wealth, and happiness*. Penguin.

Contents

About the Authors

Sanchayan Banerjee is Associate Professor of Economics and Public Policy and Director of the Behavioural Public Policy Lab in the School for Government at Policy Institute in King's College London. He is a visiting fellow of the London School of Economics and Political Science and affiliate of Vrije Universiteit Amsterdam. His research focuses on developing citizen-oriented, participatory behavioural public policies and testing them in areas of food and energy policy, public health, and charitable donations. He sits on the editorial boards of Nature Scientific Reports, PLoS One, Frontiers in Behavioral Economics, and Humanities and Social Sciences Communications. Previously he was the editor of New Voices section of Behavioural Public Policy. Sanchayan is the founding chair of Behavioural Insights for Policy (BiP) network at King's and Behavioural Transformations, which lead knowledge-exchange workshops on BPP globally.

Peter John is Professor of Public Policy at King's College London. He is known for his work on behavioural interventions and randomised controlled trials. He is author of *Analyzing Public Policy* (2013), *Nudge, Nudge, Think, Think: Experimenting with Ways to Change Civic Behaviour* (Manchester University Press, 2019), *Field Experiments in Political Science and Public Policy* (Routledge, 2017), *Political Turbulence: How Social Media Shape Collective Action* (Princeton University Press, 2015), *Making Policy Work* (Routledge, 2011), *How Far to Nudge: Assessing Behavioural Public Policy* (Edward Elgar, 2018), and *British Politics An Analytical Approach* (Oxford University Press 2022).

List of Tables

CHAPTER 1

Challenging the Behavioural Economics Consensus

Background and Origins

The idea of taking account of human psychology into decision-making, especially economic decisions, has a long pedigree. Oliver (2013, 6) and others (Ashraf et al. 2005) regard the theory of Adam Smith as an example of behaviourally-inspired economic thinking which is at odds (or complementary) with the conventional perception of Smith as the justifier of market economics. In his *Theory of Moral Sentiments* (1759), Adam Smith said that market arrangements need a social support structure to survive, and that there are several motivations in human nature, some selfish while some not; moreover, habit and fashion play a role just as they do in behavioural economics (Smith 1759).

Despite these honourable antecedents, economists since the late nineteenth century largely worked within a rational-actor model of decision-making, inspired by the work of Alfred Marshall (1890; see republished 2009 version), who set out the basic theory of marginal costs and benefits (Marshall 1890). Even now many economists assume that individuals can and do maximise their personal utility when choosing between alternatives. The power and predictions of economics come from these axioms or micro-foundations that then can be used to build more general models of the economy and show how politics, institutions, and public policies interact with these incentives.

© The Author(s), under exclusive license to Springer Nature Switzerland AG 2026

S. Banerjee, P. John, *Nudge+*,
https://doi.org/10.1007/978-3-032-13261-1_1

Even within mainstream economics there are problems with this approach. Oliver (2017) writes about how a later generation of economists explored the anomalies within formal or rational actor theory that indicate a more psychologically plausible route to understanding decision-making. Important is the work of Allais (1953) who pointed out common inconsistencies in typical choices of individuals, which arise partly from the way these choices are arranged. There was a gradual reaction against founding economic theory in the fully rational actions of the individuals. If people do not often act according to the rational-actor model, then it becomes hard to make these cost-benefit calculations, at least in a proportionate way.

The tweaking rather than challenging the assumptions of mainstream economics is the reason for the success of behavioural economics. Some accounts of nudge make it read like attacks on economically rational decision-making (sometimes called 'homo economicus') and make it seem like behavioural economics is setting off on a completely new approach to mainstream economics (Thaler 2015). But the study of economics has always involved some degree of behavioural inquiry (noted by Richard Thaler who calls behavioural economics a 'pleonasm'). Further, many of the familiar tools of modern neoclassical economics, such as mathematical modelling, are still in place within behavioural economics, as Thaler's earlier work on commitment devices illustrates (Thaler and Shefrin 1981). In fact, between 1987 and 1990, Thaler was invited to write a regular column in the mainstream *Journal of Economic Perspectives*, which eventually was collected into a book (Thaler 1992). This viewpoint of behavioural economics as an extension of mainstream economics appears in more radical accounts, such as from geographers seeing behavioural public policies as part of standard model of neo-liberal decision-making (Jones et al. 2013). These critics believe that it offers nothing new except a re-tread of orthodox ideas, and there are strong links between behavioural and more mainstream versions of economics.

While some of the work that moved towards behavioural economics came from within economics, with economists becoming aware of the difficulties that standard models created, the main impetus came from pioneering work in psychology, especially from the ground-breaking experiments of Kahneman and Tversky (Tversky and Kahneman 1974; Kahneman et al. 1982). Such concerns about the limitations of rational-actor models have been expressed outside mainstream economics for many decades, such as the claim from the public administration scholar Herbert

Simon that people satisfice (Simon 1955). People choose solutions from rules of thumb rather than calculate the costs and benefits of all the available options, partly to reduce the search costs of reviewing the options for often little relative gain. What Kahneman and Tversky did was to test in a series of famous experiments the claim that people use shortcuts, such as status quo bias, preferring to keep the current choice in place rather than give full weight to a range of alternatives, or availability, the idea that people choose options that are easy for them to take, so creating biases. Another is anchoring, which is where a particular number or figure is introduced as part of a calculation unduly influencing the decision. Overconfidence is where too much early gain is expected out of optimism rather than calculation. These biases mean that people choose options that have fewer tangible benefits than had they weighed up the costs and benefits. It was a remarkable research programme, based on a fruitful intellectual partnership (see Lewis 2016), which had a wide influence, partly because of the way in which economists took great interest in these findings, and how they disseminated these ideas in an elite community of scholars (Thaler 2015), so becoming the mainstream rather than a challenge to the orthodoxy. This joins with work in political science and public policy that takes a broad approach to human behaviour with many motivations at work. Rather than just behavioural economics as the new subdiscipline, we should think of the political economy of behavioural sciences and public policy as the encompassing project (Oliver 2023; John 2025b).

From Behavioural Economics to Behavioural Public Policy

These early contributions in behavioural economics were revisions to theory and often done as laboratory experiments. But it did not take long for economists, who have always been interested in public policy, to see the relevance of their findings for the wider world. By considering human psychology as well as costs and benefits of government interventions, it might be possible to help individuals get to socially desirable ends and outcomes that benefit themselves too, which are important policy matters. By framing information in ways that appeal to these traits and biases, it may be possible to encourage people to choose better options. This is where behavioural science comes in to understand these behaviours more closely and to guard against occasions where the imposition of a law or a costly policy has the opposite of intended effect because it encourages people to resent the policy through reactance, or signal that other people are evading it too, so emboldening people showing the role of social norms. Overall, behavioural science recognises how people are motivated and offers redesign of policy instruments accordingly. Questioning the rational actor model does not overthrow cost-benefit analysis or other rational-actor approaches to understanding decision-making; what research on behavioural public polices does is to add more information about what individuals are likely to do in response to a change in use of the tools of government.

While behavioural economics considers biases as a deviation from rational choices of people, behavioural science is a much wider, applied discipline that relies on data-driven analyses of human behaviour (Banerjee and Veltri 2024). Behavioural science can be interpreted as a broader attempt of viewing humans from different lenses: neurosciences for how the brain reacts, sociology for how people behave with others in the society, psychology to model these behaviours at face value without expectations of making optimal choices, and economics which assumes at the end people do what is best for them, albeit at times, with certain limitations. This inductive approach generates behavioural insights which then feed into making public policies—a field, which is more recently termed as behavioural public policy. Although owing much to behavioural economics (Oliver 2017), behavioural public policy is interdisciplinary, using insights and research from applied psychology, social policy, social marketing, environmental studies, political science, and health policy, to name a few fields (Banerjee et al. 2024b). Many scholars in these fields had been studying the psychological dimension to decision-making and public policy long before it became more fashionable as behavioural public policy. Now they have a common language that connects these previously disparate areas of study.

Using the insights of behavioural economics and psychology, the various tools in behavioural public policy are designed to move individuals closer to where economic theory thinks they ought to be in terms of personal decisions, such as to nudge someone to engage in more rational pension investing. Hence, nudge is designed to correct human bias so that the individual can get back on track as a rational actor even if it does not involve weighing up decisions as a rational actor would need to do.

The first prominent example of nudge was over pensions where people had failed to opt into employer pension schemes even when there are large contributions made by the employer, and where the monthly costs are low. People do not choose them because they want to avoid a short-term loss. In terms of rational-actor theory, people are overweighting the present costs and not giving enough consideration to the future benefits, which is a case of what is called inconsistent time discounting. To get people to select pensions that would benefit them, Thaler and Benartzi proposed the use of defaults whereby employees are assumed to have joined the pension scheme as well as using the timing of a pay rise to introduce the default taking advantage of their status-quo bias (Thaler and Benartzi 2004). Recent work has shown that such default nudges have not only shifted savings but led to an overall increase in total savings of employees (Benartzi and Thaler 2013; Chetty et al. 2014).

The other early example was about organ donation whereby experimental evidence suggested that defaults or at least prompted choice versus active choice could lead people to choose the more social-beneficial option of committing to leave their organs to another person on their death (Johnson and Goldstein 2003). There followed a large policy interest in redesigning information on defaults for organ donation on car registration websites and other places where choice options (architectures) could be altered and messages reframed (Sallis et al. 2018).

By the mid-2000s, policy-makers had started taking much more notice of behavioural economics and behavioural science, particularly as outward-facing think tanks and foundations were championing behavioural interventions and were interested in fashionable new tools of applied economics, as emphasised in many popular books, such as *Freakonomics* (Levitt and Dubner 2014). In 2008, ideas42, a consultancy, was set up in the USA to encourage the diffusion of behavioural insights, led by prominent behavioural economists (Mullainathan and Shafir 2013). In the UK, the New Economics Foundation was an early promoter (Dawnay and Shah 2005). David Halpern pioneered behavioural economics ideas when he was working for the Prime Minister's Strategy Unit under Tony Blair in the second New Labour government from 2001, coauthoring an influential report (Halpern et al. 2004). The official interest led to the commissioning of MINDSPACE which was a scheme that simplified behavioural insights into the letters of the acronym (Dolan et al. 2012) and became the UK's Institute for Government's most downloaded paper (Dolan et al. 2010).

These developments coincided with the publication of *Nudge* by Richard Thaler and Cass Sunstein (Thaler and Sunstein 2008). This book drew together the main insights from the behavioural economics literature in a lively and accessible way conveyed with gentle humour from both authors. The title encapsulated the basic approach, which then became the catchword for the whole phenomenon. The main innovation was to stress that nudge can be carried out in a way that retains the freedom of the individual because these tools are not compulsory, usually very low cost, and be easily opted out of. They write that 'a nudge, as we will use the term, is any aspect of the choice architecture that alters people's behaviour in a predictable way without forbidding any options or significantly changing their economic incentives. To count as a mere nudge, the intervention must be easy and cheap to avoid. Nudges are not mandates' (Thaler and Sunstein 2008, 6). This definition highlights nudge as a subset of behavioural public policies, as kinds of psychologically-designed, low-cost, and non-compulsory tools rather than commands (e.g., laws) or strong incentives (e.g., taxes). A nudge is thus a central part of this larger field of behavioural public policy which can also accommodate other forms of public policies, such as behaviourally-informed tax changes (Chetty et al. 2009).

The nudge book was a considerable success, generating much comment in the media, from op eds in influential newspapers, such as *The New York Times*, as well as current affairs radio and TV programmes and podcasts. The links to policy were very clear as it implied that governments and other actors could redesign the tools of government or change what they called choice architectures to get better public policy outcomes. In the wake of these developments, was the setting up of the UK's Behavioural Insights Team (BIT). Called the nudge unit, BIT was set up at the start of the former Prime Minister David Cameron-led coalition government in 2010, with just seven personnel located in the Cabinet Office with Halpern directly working in No. 10 Downing Street. But it was the start of something big as the unit championed pioneering new innovations in government with political support and cover (John 2014; Halpern 2015). The unit expanded quickly, eventually becoming detached from government, first as co-owned non-profit company, then in 2021 as the wholly-owned subsidiary of Nesta (the innovation organisation that spends lottery funds on public purpose projects). Similar innovations occurred in the USA with one of the authors of *Nudge*, Cass Sunstein, working for the federal government under President Obama, and the creation of the Social and Behavioral Sciences Team (SBST) based in the White House. From these two pioneers, the use of nudge diffused rapidly across the world, with other nudge units, consultancies, and research units geared up to market nudge to governments and agencies interested in the practice (John 2018, 2019), helped by programmes/reviews commissioned by international agencies, such as OECD (2017) and the World Bank (2014). Today there are more than 650 nudge units or their equivalents around the world (Naru 2024; Varazzani and Hubble 2025). Through these nudge units and other innovations, there was the widespread uptake of behavioural insights in public policy. Governments lauded this behavioural toolkit because of the low-cost wins it offered. It was novel as an idea at the time and was successful in changing many human behaviours in a range of domains. One prominent example is increasing tax compliance (Kettle et al. 2016); another is reducing energy consumption (Allcott and Kessler 2019). These successes lent nudge a cost-effective status, favourable when compared with traditional tools of government (Benartzi et al. 2017), responding to the preferences of citizens (Sunstein 2016a), albeit only when they want to be nudged. Studies showed that nudge backfired or failed to work typically when citizens disagreed with the nudger (Sunstein 2017; Sunstein et al. 2019).

The early days also saw a critical backlash against nudge, such as a prominent UK House of Lords report criticising the claims of nudge as overblown and leading to a down-prioritisation of standard policy tools (House of Lords 2011). Similarly, there have been criticisms of overclaiming from more conventional academic sources and fears about the sustainability of these interventions (Marteau et al. 2011). From more critical perspectives, nudge has been seen to be representing a more authoritarian and less consultative form of government by experts (Goodwin 2012; Jones et al. 2013; Leggett 2014; Mols et al. 2015; Ball and Head 2021), leading to the rise of the so-called psychological state, even the neuroliberal state (Whitehead et al. 2017). More recently, some scholars have claimed that too much focus on individual-driven (i-frame) interventions has led the field of behavioural public policy astray and there is a need to introduce more systemic (s-frame) interventions and policies (Chater and Loewenstein 2023). There is a line of critical work, such as by Rebonato (2014) and Leggett (2014). They worry about loss of autonomy and excessive manipulation, seeing nudging in a wider political context. As a result of these critiques, several authors suggest new approaches for behavioural public policy (Ewert et al. 2023; Straßheim 2020), which move away from what are seen as neo-liberal assumptions of nudge to a fuller and more rounded form of behavioural public policy.

Although many of these criticisms are conceptual and concerned about the very nature of nudge and its dominance in public policy, they did not deter governments from using nudge as a useful policy tool. Governments discovered that nudge improved policy outcomes across a range of fields such as education, finance, health, and the environment as well as welfare policies and development programmes. Governments adopted many of the recommendations of the early trials, with pension defaults now a requirement in most countries and the introduction of new ways to frame appeals to donate organs. Behavioural science predictions (and to some extent the role of nudging), for example, in tackling the COVID-19 pandemic have been validated by a large team of cross-national experts (Ruggeri et al. 2023). Reviews of overall policy effectiveness show a positive impact (Benartzi et al. 2017; Loewenstein and Chater 2017). But this evidence is mixed and the review of nudges is still ongoing. For example, a meta-analysis of RCTs carried out by the two biggest nudge units respectively in the US and UK shows an average treatment effect of 8.1 per cent (DellaVigna and Linos 2022) which decreased when considering field studies versus those in academic samples. Another review by Beshears and Kosowsky (2020) of 174 articles calculated positive treatment effects (mean Cohen's *d* of 0.405), with higher effects for the automatic processes, the classic nudge. Then another meta-analysis, making corrections for publication bias, says that the effects are null (Maier et al. 2022, 2): 'our Bayesian analysis indicates that, after correcting for this bias, no evidence remains that nudge is effective as tools for behaviour change'. Meta-analyses of specific nudge types are also increasingly common, such as that on labelling for sustainability choices, which suggests that: 'although labelling may indirectly influence long-term behaviours and institutional purchasing decisions, more ambitious initiatives are required to meaningfully shift consumer behaviours toward sustainability at scale' (Ding et al. 2025). The debate continues. While these critiques do not demolish the nudge agenda entirely, they do suggest that it may be time for something more—an approach that builds on, rather than replaces, what has come before, and that is better equipped to address today's complex policy challenges. We believe this is an opportune moment for a new research programme to emerge, as the initial enthusiasm around nudging gives way to space for more mature and pluralistic approaches.

Moving Beyond Nudge

It might be thought that the main lesson of the last 15 years or so of nudging is to continue on the path of more testing and greater diffusion of nudge as there is more knowledge to be gained about their use. This is the classic phase of bedding down and learning of a new programme, focusing on comprehensive evaluations as policies are rolled out and tweaked. Of course, this development depends on stable pattern of diffusion and of agencies learning knowledge gradually, which is not strictly true from research on innovations. Innovation is always patchy and dependent on chance encounters and bursts of interest from political and bureaucratic entrepreneurs (John 2013). There is a danger that the energy beyond new policies might be lost as normalisation takes place. Such ideas about renewing nudge or behavioural public policy have informed a recent manifesto by Hallsworth (2023), with concrete proposals to improve the science and policy practice, including some bottom-up, decentralist recommendations. This manifesto has sparked a lot of attention in the field and has led to extensive debate, such as around the need for a cultural lens (John 2025a), alternative narratives (Dold 2025), and addressing other challenges for governments (Varazzani and Hubble 2025).

Many concerns are designed to counter some weaknesses to the nudge agenda. The very easiness of nudge and its low-cost nature present dangers. Nudge relies on the triggering of automatic processes that cause people to behave in different ways. This account of nudge appeared in Kahneman (2011), in particular in his view of two systems theory. This is the idea in psychological science that there are two parts of the brain: the fast-thinking automatic system 1 and the slow-thinking system 2. While there is little evidence that the brain is distinctly segmented into two independent parts, as the dual systems theory neatly describes, there is value in the idea that there are two types of brain processes, one that is quick and intuitive, and the other that is slow and reasoned. If many kinds of nudge are tapping into the automatic processes, such as a default that does not need much thinking about just choosing because it is easy and unproblematic to do, just like driving a car, then it is easy to see there are large advantages in such an approach linked to the success of nudge. It does not impose costs on the individual, nor much for the implementing agency that rolls out the policy, in contrast to a strong (dis)incentive, or getting an unpopular law enforced. These are the advantages of going with the grain of preferences, which means that individuals do not need to think much and just get on with the new behaviour. They are less likely to kick off and be a problem for public agencies, which reduces the financial and political costs of implementing a policy. For example, Lohmann et al. (2025) show that system 1 nudges (which rely on these type 1 processes), such as menu repositioning, are effective for promoting climate-friendly choices when decisions are made quickly, but this effect fades out with extended deliberation. On the other hand, in their experiment, carbon labels which require more engagement show minimal effects and tend to be effective only for those who are more educated.

But there are some limitations of the automatisation of citizen responses to policy instruments. The first is about the efficacy of relying on automatic reactions (Brandon et al. 2017). Here the action is guided by the instrument only and is not necessarily internalised. A default only works when it is in operation, so the question is what happens long term. For some decisions the default can be very powerful long term as when the default changes the behaviour from a new choice architecture, then it may become the new default once switched over. This is the basis of many business models, such as banking or even airline loyalty schemes. The decision to default into a pensions scheme continues because the default renews each month and is hard to get out of. The person must write to their own employer to say they want to discontinue, which many people cannot be bothered to do, and agencies can make it procedurally difficult. But think how bad that would be if it was a bad financial product or even a good one but it was not tailored to the personal needs. What if the policy-maker made it very hard to change options, creating a lot of difficulties in signing out of a commitment? This is the concept of sludge (Sunstein 2019). It is standard practice among commercial companies to make opting out very difficult, or for consumers to do things that cost the company money, such as complain, though of course many companies know the advantages of good practice and making things easy as it leads to better customer relations in the long term. But this is more controversial in the public sector, because it could be claimed that making opting out hard is good for someone. Most nudgers believe sludge to be bad overall and recommend its removal (Thaler 2018). Today there are standard practices in place to recognise sludges in the form of audits (Mills et al. 2023). Even without sludge and just a default, it is easy to see how the individual is very dependent on the policy-maker getting it right in general and tailoring it precisely.

Moreover, policy-makers and politicians suffer from the same biases as citizens, as shown in many tests comparing choices made by citizens and politicians (Linde and Vis 2017; Sheffer et al. 2018), and citizens and bureaucrats (Wittels 2023). Rather than having the capacity to design rational policies, despite having the backup of researcher and information-gathering units, they are like the citizens they are trying to regulate. There have been many decades of work in public policy that shows that policy-makers depart from the ideal of rational decision-making and rely on cues and shortcuts (Lindblom 1959; Allison and Zelikow 1971; Baumgartner and Jones 2010). So there just can't be a perfect nudger who gets it right all the time. In this way, a more active role of the citizen, as a checker on the policy-maker might be more appropriate in many cases than just accepting the policy. This can be turned into more general advice in life, as it is always good to both take expert advice and respect the default, for example, over a new pension scheme, but to read the small print as well. The nudgee should check if the default option is the right one for them.

Nudges can have unintended consequences, some of which can be negative. Returning to savings once again linked to pensions, Andrieş and Walker (2023) find the messages in their experiment reduced people's willingness to save when they had set a goal. The nudges here may have induced a boomerang effect highlighting the difficulty of attaining goals. In some cases, classic norm-based nudges can backfire, such as for littering where the norm conveyed actually encourages non-compliance (Cialdini 2003) and for electricity consumption where norm messages can increase usage for low consumption households (Allcott 2011). Even though norms to encourage tax compliance generally work, there are studies showing a backfire (John and Blume 2018), which again may be connected to the perception of the norm. In the environmental domain, Hagmann et al. (2019) show that a green energy default nudge decreases support for a carbon tax, partly because they offer an unplausible quick fix to complex problems. There are negative spillovers, where being nudged to do one beneficial activity can increase a less desirable behaviour, such as water conservation spillover to increased electricity consumption (Tiefenbeck et al. 2013). Osman (2020) reviews 65 studies where there are backfires suggesting there is much to be learnt from these relatively frequent negative effects that appear in the literature.

These backfires often illustrate the danger of reactance (Brehm and Brehm 1981), once citizens find out they have been encouraged to do something without their consent (Gerver et al. 2024). Once they realise they have been in a non-optimal scheme, they might react negatively to the whole decision-making process that they did not consent to thinking that all government decision-making has tricked them. Sometimes nudges can also fail to work in transparent contexts (Just and Gabrielyan 2025). Long-term automaticity might in the end lead to anger on the part of individuals once they realise that they did not fully consent into an arrangement, even if it is a long-term benefit for them, so undermining the legitimacy needed of public policy and the consent that is needed for policy implementation. Belardinelli finds that the manipulative nature of nudges can affect the trust and legitimacy of governments (Belardinelli 2024, Chapter 5), writing that 'nudging holds the potential to erode the trust in public institutions' (82).

Such findings link to the loss of trust in government in recent decades (Dalton 2004; Pew Research Centre 2023), often stemming from citizens realising the failures of government and politicians following their short-run electoral interests rather than the public good. Along with a critical media and the diffusion of distrust in the social media, many countries have seen the rise of anti-politics (Hay 2007; Clarke et al. 2016) whereby citizens are suspicious of politicians. Even though anti-politics sometimes means that citizens prefer independent scientists to make policy in place of politicians, it can also lead to a more general populist suspicion of experts and of making policy behind the scenes. Anti-politics has helped cause a backlash against established politicians, like former prime minister David Cameron who commissioned the nudge unit, but who was the target of the criticism that the public has had enough of experts in the Brexit referendum campaign (Shipman 2016). There is a risk that non-consenting nudge policies reinforce the more general criticism of lack of engagement with politics and governments who treat citizens like children who need to be guided. So far, the public seem fine with nudge and trust government to implement these policies (Sunstein 2016a; Sunstein et al. 2019), but maybe this could change as these interventions become more routine, and people find out more about them through media reporting. During the COVID crisis, some people became critical of government policies and the use of behavioural science (IJzerman and Lewis Jr 2020), reflecting the persistence of these anti-government and anti-science ideas, which are not helped by the relative secrecy in which they are designed and implemented.

Moreover, the continuous use of nudge is also problematic. Many behaviours need renewing all the time, daily or weekly even, such as pro-environmental behaviours of recycling or volunteering; or financial behaviours like pension plans, especially when someone's financial situation changes. But the effects of nudge might wear off. Repeating a nudge has declining effects because people get used to the nudge or they find out about its purpose. For example, the meta-evaluation by DellaVigna and Linos (2022) finds that the nudge effects wear off by 8.7 percentage points every day after the intervention was discontinued. Such habits do not apply to all nudges, with recycling or voting falling off about 50 per cent a year later (Gerber et al. 2003; Cutts et al. 2009), which is good value for money for nudge but imply there are limitations to automaticity. More policy-orientated nudges can have promising effects, such as introducing a default of standing at desks rather than sitting, which lasted at 90 per cent two months later (Venema et al. 2018). About 30 to 55 per cent of the reduction from an energy nudge persists (Brandon et al. 2017). It is important to observe change at more than a few months, which is often beyond the scope of most evaluations. Many policy challenges need behaviour change for the long term (i.e., years), but nudge is not well suited to deliver on this essential need in public policy or at least we do not know this from the stock of current research knowledge.

Of course, people associate nudges with correcting minor human behaviours and improving transactional process of government, such as tax collection. But there are larger policy problems to solve, such as climate change, poverty, misinformation, and intolerance, which require more profound changes in behaviours, mindsets, and values. The question is whether unconscious nudges are up to the task of addressing these long-term challenges. Moreover, people might revert to their old behaviours once the novelty of nudges wears off. Better that people are nudged knowing why rather than finding out later they had been manipulated. It would be preferable for the nudge to be seen as signal from those in power that a partnership is needed between citizens and the state to solve these problems. Governments and private companies need to do their bit but so do citizens in going along with regulation and changing their consumer habits. This approach needs citizens to reflect on what the government is doing and to help inform government about how to best do it. This is particularly important because societies cannot just rely on the citizens acting on their own, they need to see themselves acting in partnership with others. It is not just that citizens face high perceived costs of acting with long-term benefits that are not obviously of personal values, that they may have inertia and habits that are hard to break, it is that if they act on their own, they bear the costs but may get no action if other citizens do not contribute. It becomes rational not to contribute when anticipating the non-contributions of others, for fear of being left bearing the costs of climate change when others freeride. This is the classic collective action problem that affects the public goods that many policy-makers care about, particularly the environment (Ostrom 1986). But what if citizens could be made to think when nudges were delivered? Thinking at the time of being nudged can help citizens to take charge and allow them to see the signals to others to act. We will say more about this later in the book.

The next limitation, which is linked to the efficacy of nudge in the long term, is normative: it is wrong for policy-makers to rely heavily on automatic processes because it involves the individual complying with the intentions of the policy-maker but not realising it, so appearing to be manipulated even when it is in the best interests of the individual to comply. This is the attack of paternalism: replacing the preferences or wishes of the citizen in favour of those of the policy-maker who justifies it that the policy is in the best interests of the person and/or society. Paternalism is not necessarily wrong, and some theorists defend it (Conly 2014); but most liberals believe that it is important to protect agency (Banerjee et al. 2024a), even if it ends up as a balancing exercise, seeking to protect autonomy where possible (Dworkin 1972). Nudge theorists have argued that nudge is not paternalist in the conventional sense of the state taking decisions for the individual for their and society's benefit. It gives the individual a choice not to follow the officially mandated policy (Sunstein and Thaler 2003). What Sunstein and Thaler term as libertarian paternalism has caused a vigorous debate on the ground of internal inconsistency (Anderson 2010; Rebonato 2012), by claiming to be both paternalist, that is taking choice away from someone, and libertarian which means respecting freedom of choice, at the same time. How can it be both? If behaviour is known to alter in response to the nudge in advance and the individual is not aware of the nudge, then that is loss of liberty just as much as compulsion, as the end result of a centrally guided change in behaviour is the same with both paternalist and libertarian paternalist policies. Nudging may even be worse than conventional paternalism as someone who disagrees with a law at least has the luxury of resentful compliance, but the nudgee is not given the chance of realising whether the nudge is good for them or not. Maybe the term soft paternalism is better than libertarian paternalism (Kirchgässner 2017).

Nudge theorists have been aware of this problem for some time, believing that publicity is enough to deal with the potential lack of consent as policy-makers can ensure that citizens can find the information if they look for it or become aware of it by publicising it. Of course, the average citizen does not go searching for the minutes of nudge units to see if they have been nudged, nor are usually aware of the vast amount of official information that is produced by government agencies. The other approach is to make the citizen aware of the nudge after it happened on the ground that much survey evidence shows that citizens approve of nudging (Sunstein 2016b), which implies that an after-the-event justification is not problematic. By letting in this argument about implied consent, nudge authors are admitting that citizens being aware of nudge is a good thing ethically, that consent is good as it is with ethical approval of ethics projects at universities. Researchers do not like doing things to people without their consent and debriefing after deception is only a second-best outcome. It is important in a democracy that people own decisions, that is they have agency. Citizens vote and take part in politics as autonomous actors rather than as manipulated subjects as would appear to be the case in autocracies, subject to political propaganda and manipulation. As the policy-maker takes instructions from citizen-voters, it follows that active consent should also be sought in between elections. That is the theory and aspirations of democratic citizenship as understood today, where there is a broadening of understanding about how representative institutions should operate (Hirst 2013). Even if reality does not always live up to this ideal, political institutions are there to protect autonomy, for example in forms of legal redress, so that people can have agency, despite the difficulties of achieving it.

Nudgers are often prone to resist consent while the nudge is being delivered because they believe that it works 'better in the dark' (Bovens 2009). Automatic processes are powerful as they are triggered without reflection, relying on the power of a cue to its secret work. Once people become aware of a nudge they can modify their action, either not agreeing with it, or even having to think it through clumsily, or being aware they are manipulated, so they react against this loss of autonomy, causing the reactance discussed earlier. But some experiments show that being aware of being nudged does not reduce effectiveness (Loewenstein et al. 2015; Bruns et al. 2018; Michaelsen 2024). In fact, the argument could work in the opposite way: a nudge could be more effective when people are made aware because they have had a chance to own the nudge and to consider the preferences of the policy-maker in relation to their life projects. Reflection allows for the nudge to bed down into people's everyday routines. People can actively choose to change their behaviour and stick with it, rather than having to rely on continuous nudging to get to a socially-beneficial outcome. Recent research also shows how transparency improves the reputation of the policy-maker (Michaelsen et al. 2021; Michaelsen 2024). The analogy would be a religious person needing an official of their religion to keep on reminding them to attend a service; but the more thinking disciple goes of their own accord not needing this prompt or reminder. This form of self-regulation is more efficient as reminders do not need to be done but is more dignified as it is the individual doing the choosing in an active way (though subtle reminders are not a bad thing once in a while). However, research on transparency reveals mixed findings as there is evidence that some nudges fail when made transparent, and can also induce reactance, as discussed earlier (Just and Gabrielyan 2025).

The argument of the previous section implies that there needs to be more than just automatisation. People should be encouraged to think before they are nudged. There are two main grounds for letting citizens think rather than nudge. First, thinking is more sustainable and makes it more likely that the individual is going to internalise the idea behind a policy, if the policy is the right one and where any reasonable person would get to after thinking about the problem the policy is aiming to fix. They agree with the policy so they are more likely to change their behaviour in the long term rather than have the artificial stimulation of nudge that might wear off after a few doses. This is also what was envisioned with the nudge's 'as judged by themselves' criterion—which is to say, the nudge will steer people towards welfare-improving behaviours, which people would agree with upon reflection. The second reason is that it is ethically better that someone has consented to a policy followed by government rather than doing it unknowingly, as it shows governments respecting people as autonomous agents capable of reasoning and owning their own agency. Getting someone to think about the options is more consistent with a responsive and democratic government. In this way, policy is led by the citizens rather than experts and politicians telling the citizens what to do or ensuring they comply with subliminal messages and hidden default options.

If these arguments are accepted then it might be thought that a full-on think strategy should be pursued where government decisions and citizens roles are guided by a set of think tools that allows conscious thought, as collectively gathered from citizens, to emerge. The strategy of think is the goal of deliberative democrats (Saward 2003; Neblo 2015; see review in Bächtiger et al. 2018; Curato et al. 2022), who wish to enhance democracy. They highlight the limitations of liberal democracy whereby decisions are aggregated upwards in voting and oversimplified and distorted in the decision-making process. They believe that citizens are effectively taken away from decisions between elections which are implemented by expert bureaucracies without much citizens' involvement, much like the nudge units deciding policies as described in the previous section. The alternative is a more direct form of democracy and popular control as envisaged in classical account in ancient Greek times, whereby citizen responsibility is encouraged in return for their involvement. The attraction of deliberative democracy is that it provides either an alternative or complement to contemporary forms of decision-making, expert procedures that are often closed to the citizen or just instrumental forms of consultation, with a more open form of democracy as a better outcome. As a result of this desire to transform democracy there are a number of democratic innovations which may be adopted, which can help and even challenge more conventional decision-making mechanisms or at least work alongside them (Smith 2009), such as citizens juries/citizen assemblies or mini-publics (small selected groups of citizens debating a specific topic facilitated by experts) and deliberative polls (survey polling that simulates a deliberation with randomly selected citizens) (Fishkin 2009). The idea is that opinion shifts occur in these forums that flow from more reasoned forms of decision-making that citizens are freely engaged in.

Do these acts work as much as their protagonists say, as most evaluations are based on case studies of successful initiatives (e.g., Fung 2004)? There are only a few experimental evaluations of these deliberative mechanisms, and these show only a weak impact compared to a control group (John et al. 2009). The other issue is the potential for scaling up in that think tends to be small scale, based on small groups of people interacting as in the citizens jury, so there is the danger of self-selection and lack of representativeness despite attempts to recruit citizens from all walks of life (that needs to be more than statistical representativeness as there is self-selection to participate within each category of person). It is harder to encourage people to think large scale as in online deliberations which can involve more people. The logistics of managing such large-scale exercises and a natural reluctance people have from participating limit the impact of these activities. Face-to-face interactions, using facial expressions or gentle prompts, encourage people to participate directly where they can hide online, what are called the 'lurkers'. Online cues and forms of human understanding are not so salient (higher education teachers faced this problem in the COVID era when encouraging students to turn on their cameras in an online seminar!).

Another issue is how to connect reflective thinking to actual policy choices that require behaviour change on the part of individuals, as well as their active participation with policy-makers. This is coproduction, which involves a process of continuous consultation, which has had some success in the form of local projects working with community groups and local governments (Durose and Richardson 2015); but they tend to be hard to do needing high commitment from local entrepreneurs and partners to keep going. It is much harder to design stand-alone think tools to get citizens to think in their own time and alongside their everyday lives and linked to their own behaviour change.

In a series of randomised controlled trials (RCTs) and qualitative experiments (called design experiments), a team of researchers tested a more customised think alongside more conventional nudge (John 2013, 2019). The results were that the nudges (such as door knocks for household recycling, smileys for food waste, and publicity for volunteering) worked with decent-sized treatment effects. But the think, such as coproduction exercises with local citizens, was much harder to do, and suffered from implementation problems and lack of engagement of those canvassed (while of course realising that not everyone who is nudged responds, but at least they do on average). The attempt to scale up think in an online deliberation was challenging to get many people to post online, and then to deliberate, so suffering from the same self-selection problem as more small-scale face-to-face deliberations. In one experiment comparing think with nudge to encourage young people for donating organs online, the think did worse, even than the placebo or distractor treatment, possibly because it caused worry among the young people whereas the nudge pointed more clearly to the socially desired outcome. Perhaps the young people were right to reject the paternalistic encouragement when they had a chance to debate it. Or maybe that debate needs supporting?

Deliberative theorists have become more aware of the similarities of nudging and thinking. That often the deliberative forum itself is full of cues and prompts, so subject to bias and manipulation, which means that designers of deliberative forums need to be aware of cognitions when they set up deliberative forums (Ryfe 2005). In a similar way, nudgers can become more aware of the thinking that goes on when there is nudging. Often nudge needs what is called policy thinking, which is an understanding of the policy process and the expected role of the citizens to carry out the nudge, which means the nudge only works when the citizens can see its purpose (John 2018). For example, study of defaults of organ donation showed that if people become aware of the purpose of a default and know why it has been chosen, they are more likely to support it (McKenzie et al. 2006). These are the 'recommendations implicitly in defaults', the title of their paper. In the field, policy-makers are likely to make people aware of defaults, which affects why people adopt them. The study authors conclude that 'implicit recommendations could therefore have large effects on decisions about being an organ donor and saving for retirement' (p. 419). More recently, in a large meta-analysis of defaults, Jachimowicz et al. (2019) show that endorsement remains one of the main reasons why default nudges are effective.

In any case the results from the *Nudge, Nudge, Think, Think* project suggest that think alone does not work in a straightforward way, whereas nudge can. One reaction is to say that only a nudge is worth investing. Another is that the think might need adjusting and to be made more meaningful for citizens. And this is where the hybrid nudge+ comes in to use the best in nudge, and to enhance it with a more feasible think that helps citizens own where they may want to go. This is especially true over the bigger problems we face like climate change, where there may be a case for both thinking and nudging at the same time: 'While nudging can be utilised in paternalistic and undemocratic ways, combining nudging with deliberation promises a timelier and more effective response to climate change' (Lenzi 2019). As Belardinelli (2024, 81) reports in his work with Martin Lodge, think is associated with higher trust, such as for public officials.

Nudging with Possibilities of Thinking in Them

We have discussed the limitations of forums beloved by deliberative democrats. These tools suffer from the sheer difficulty of scaling them up for enough citizens who are also representative of the general population. An alternative to using possibly cumbersome deliberative institutions to effectuate behaviour change is to deliver nudge that is deliberative in nature, so they become a kind of thinking nudge. This is what Sunstein has called a system 2 nudge (Sunstein 2016b). A system 2 nudge is aimed to 'target or benefit from deliberative processing' (p. 1) and is often seen as an educative nudge. It appeals to system 2 processes (to use again the term from cognitive science, popularised for behavioural public policy by

Kahneman, as discussed earlier). This deliberative nudge has the advantage of a think, but more focused on the one-off delivery instrument which is the standard nudge, with some similarity also to an educational boost that aims to equip people with better rules for decision making.[1] Examples of such system 2 educative nudges are the provision of information designed to provoke thought, such as about the risks of smoking or informative policies about water conservation, as with the invitation to participate in recycling of hotel towels, which comes with an explanation of the purpose or the scheme. Another example of the system 2 nudge is to encourage slow thinking, such as through Cognitive Behavioural Therapy (CBT), such as over employment decisions (Blattman et al. 2017; Heller et al. 2017) also designed to reduce crime. Sunstein presents evidence of conditional support for such policies (Sunstein 2016b; Jung and Mellers 2016).

The advantage of the system 2 nudge as opposed to the full-on deliberation is that it can promote the benefits of deliberation, such as thinking about the other side of the argument without undermining more mainstream democratic processes of engagement, which is the fear invoked by Mutz (2006). Contributing to the debate about deliberative versus participatory democracy, Mutz celebrates the everyday contribution of people in their networks and organisations, who make deliberative contributions. Nudge+ fits right into this defence of the everyday practice of democratic politics, where much is built up from low-cost interactions.

Moreover, there is also evidence that the system 2 nudges work, albeit with smaller effect sizes than standard nudges. They still show respectable effect sizes with a Cohen's *d* of 0.346 (Beshears and Kosowsky 2020, 10), with the example of reflection on pension decisions. This relates to McKenzie and Liersch's (2011) study encouraging employees at a company to think about their future retirement savings plan and introducing them to the concept of exponential growth, core to pension benefits. Beshears and Kosowsky conclude 'that 14.7% of the treatment effect estimates in our data set are associated with a nudge that inspires broader thinking' (p. 10).

[1] Earlier accounts of boosting compare a short-term boost with an educative nudge (see Grüne-Yanoff and Hertwig 2016). However, this claim has been recently withdrawn in newer accounts of boosting for example as the Grüne-Yanoff (2025) remarks: 'Boosts are not educative or System-2 nudges'.

These system 2 nudges, especially with their focus on education, have since then also inspired a new kind of behavioural public policy, a boost (Grüne-Yanoff and Hertwig 2016; Hertwig and Grüne-Yanoff 2017; Hertwig 2017; Paunov and Grüne-Yanoff 2023) (also see fn. 1 above). But boosts go further than system 2 educative nudges as boosting is about strategies and resources that can increase the capacity of individuals to approach decisions smartly. This comes from the problem identified in the behavioural economics literature that individuals have great difficulty making calculations to inform decisions, and in many cases a grasp of statistics needed say to make an informed choice about a medical treatment, which means that people are subject to framing of the information and receptive to many biases. To avoid this, a boost would train individuals with the essential message of Bayesian statistics, so people can follow with some easy ('frugal') rules. This has now been the subject of greater testing comparing nudge with boost, as with tests over flood insurance, for example (Bradt 2022). In our own research (Banerjee et al. 2023), we have engaged in more systematic testing of nudges with boosts, thinking, and nudge+ interventions,[2] which we introduce next. To summarise, we have seen a gradual shift away from automatic nudges towards nudges that have the possibilities of reflection in them. This has come in different forms, with earlier accounts simply being modifications of the standard nudge as system 2 nudges to more recent inspirations such as the boost. Nudge+ builds on these innovations and takes the next step in making deliberation a key aspect of behavioural public policy.

Putting Citizens into the Heart of BPP with Nudge+

By now, it should be clear where this chapter is heading with the discussion of nudge, boost, think, transparent nudge, and system 2 nudge: there is a potential for a modified form of behavioural public policy that seeks to leverage nudge's efficiency and ease of introduction at the same time as introducing the legitimacy of reflection (avoiding the costs of a full-on deliberation). All the toolkits introduced so far have the limitation that

[2] While these labels are core to advancing much of the conceptual discussion around the future of nudging, some scholars have lamented on the need for such a discussion on semantics, with the suggestion that behavioural public policy should drop buzzwords and simply assess all policy interventions using a normative benchmark (Oliver 2025).

they either harness the benefits of automatisation or that of deliberation and capacity building but not both. The nudge+ research programme fills this gap.

A nudge+ builds on recent developments in behavioural public policy to modify the nudge such that it has both the nudge and think incorporated into its mechanism, with the nudge running alongside the think, either as part of it, or the think just before or after the nudge (John and Stoker 2019; Banerjee and John 2023, 2024). This takes advantage of what has been learned from nudge in the past 15 years or so, but offers additional traction, and most importantly legitimacy. It embodies and exemplifies the 'as judged by themselves' criterion of the nudge literally, for the *plus* involves a prompt to think, very much like a knee-jerk reaction when the nudge is delivered, in an attempt to make people think explicitly if that what is aspired by the nudge is in line with what people want to achieve themselves and by using those means as is suggested by the nudge. A nudge+, therefore, is best understood as any nudge that is combined with an active reflection prompt, such as one that asks, 'Do you think this is the best way to nudge you towards your goals?'. Of course, just like nudging and its types, this reflective prompt can be designed in manifold ways and to suit many objectives, but at the heart of nudge+ is always an active reflection exercise that enables citizens to break the mould of unconsciousness when under the influence of a nudge, take active control of whether they want to be nudged, and consequently switch off once again and let the nudging do all the work (or not), depending on what they decide.

Some nudge+ mechanisms may be quite close to an existing nudge that has reflection already embedded into them, such as the commitment contract, making the task of nudge+ designers to improve the hybrid that is already there, such as a dual-self pledge card where a person makes two commitments one for the present and the other for future self. In other cases, something new is required, such as adding a cool-off prompt just after the nudge is in place to slow people down to think more consciously or introduce a pop-up prompt that verifies one's preferences and encourages them to assess if the nudge works in their favour and so on. In this book, we explore this idea of the nudge+ in much more detail.

Throughout this book, we acknowledge that nudges are both needed and justified. However, we argue that they are not always sufficient on their own. Nudging requires a citizen component—one that invites people to engage actively with the intervention. This not only fosters greater acceptance but also strengthens the ethical justification for using behavioural tools, particularly in today's world where behavioural science is widespread and nudges have become the norm. In such a context, the early easy wins of nudging are harder to come by, as people are now more aware of these techniques.

To sustain effectiveness and legitimacy, we believe citizens should be encouraged to think before responding to a nudge. For instance, a classic nudge might set pension enrolment as the default. A nudge+, however, would go further: it might include a prompt such as, 'We are defaulting you into a pension plan', highlighting transparency. But transparency alone is not enough. A true nudge+ would, therefore, also include a reflective prompt like, 'Take a moment to consider: What do you think about having a pension?' This creates space for authentic thought, allowing individuals to form their own views. So, one person might respond: 'This nudge helps me achieve my long-term goals. I can save a little each month, and my employer contributes too. Over time, this adds up to a secure income in retirement.' Another might think differently: 'I'm not sure I want this pension. It ties up my money for too long and depends on investments that may not be reliable. I'd rather keep the money available for my family or to pay energy bills.'

As policy designers with some degree of paternalism, we might prefer the first response. After all, it aligns with the intended outcome of the nudge. But as freedom-respecting, human-centred thinkers, we must also respect the second view. It reflects a considered position and may be entirely reasonable, depending on individual circumstances. People's needs vary, and some may legitimately conclude that a pension is not the right choice for them.

In our view, recognising a range of thoughtful responses to a nudge is better than letting people follow a default blindly—or worse, discovering years later that they were nudged into a decision they didn't fully understand. Failing to be transparent about long-term risks, such as those posed by extreme weather events, can undermine trust in policy-makers.

We therefore propose that even when nudges+ lead to different outcomes—or even 'fail' in a narrow policy sense—they can still contribute to a stronger, more trust-based relationship between citizens and the institutions that serve them. We will explore these ideas further as the book unfolds, but we hope this initial discussion of nudge+ shows how to combine reflection and nudging in ways that are ethical and empowering.

To summarise, this chapter has set the intellectual and policy context for our argument for nudge+. We have discussed the importance of the behavioural revolution that has transformed the social sciences, in particular economics, in ways that ensure that social science and by implication public policy are grounded in real human psychology (also see Banerjee and John 2025). This has created a more dynamic social science and also one that is more relevant to policy-makers, which nudge+ slipstreams into. But the result is not without limitations as nudge comes with a critique about how long lived and powerful are its effects. It is no surprise that several variants have emerged to build on and sometimes criticise nudge. Many wish to build in more autonomy and agency for the individual when being nudged by the state, partly as ethically better in itself, and that it builds a partnership between the citizen and the state, which could develop more significant and self-sustaining behaviour change.

These arguments present a broad outline of our ideas. The task of the rest of this book is to develop them in more detail, both in terms of the theory of human nature that nudge+ is based on and what empirical evidence exists about these claims. In the early part of the book, we elaborate what it means to be thinking and why we value self-conscious actions. Hence, the next chapter addresses the advantages of more conscious thinking and reflection.

References

Allais, Maurice. 1953. Le comportement de l'homme rationnel devant le risque: Critique des postulats et axiomes de l'école américaine. *Econometrica: Journal of the Econometric Society* 503–546. https://doi.org/10.2307/1907921.

Allcott, Hunt. 2011. Social norms and energy conservation. *Journal of Public Economics* 95 (9–10): 1082–1095. https://doi.org/10.1016/j.jpubeco.2011.03.003.

Allcott, Hunt, and Judd B. Kessler. 2019. The welfare effects of nudges: A case study of energy use social comparisons. *American Economic Journal: Applied Economics* 11 (1): 236–276. https://doi.org/10.1257/app.20170328.

Allison, Graham T., and Philip Zelikow. 1971. *Essence of decision: Explaining the Cuban missile crisis*. Vol. 327. Vol. 729.1: Little, Brown Boston.

Anderson, Joel. 2010. Review of Thaler & Sunstein 'Nudge: Improving decisions about health, wealth, and happiness'. *Economics & Philosophy* 26 (3): 369–376. https://doi.org/10.1017/S0266267110000301.

Andrieş, Alin Marius, and Sarah Walker. 2023. When the message hurts: The unintended impacts of nudges on saving. *Journal of Comparative Economics* 51 (2): 439–456. https://doi.org/10.1016/j.jce.2023.01.002.

Ashraf, Nava, Colin F. Camerer, and George Loewenstein. 2005. Adam Smith, behavioral economist. *Journal of Economic Perspectives* 19 (3): 131–145. https://doi.org/10.1257/089533005774357897.

Bächtiger, André, John S. Dryzek, Jane Mansbridge, and Mark E. Warren. 2018. *The Oxford handbook of deliberative democracy*. Oxford University Press.

Ball, Sarah, and Brian W. Head. 2021. Behavioural insights teams in practice: Nudge missions and methods on trial. *Policy & Politics* 49 (1): 105–120. https://doi.org/10.1332/030557320X15840777045205.

Banerjee, Sanchayan, and Peter John. 2023. Nudge+: Putting citizens at the heart of behavioural public policy. In *Research handbook on nudges and society*, 227–241. Edward Elgar Publishing.

Banerjee, Sanchayan, and Peter John. 2024. Nudge plus: Incorporating reflection into behavioral public policy. *Behavioural Public Policy* 8 (1): 69–84. https://doi.org/10.1017/bpp.2021.6.

Banerjee, Sanchayan, and Peter John. 2025. Behavioural public policy: Past, present, and future. Available at SSRN 5124029. https://doi.org/10.2139/ssrn.5124029.

Banerjee, Sanchayan, and Giuseppe A. Veltri. 2024. Harnessing pluralism in behavioral public policy requires insights from computational social science. *Frontiers in Behavioral Economics* 3:1503793. https://doi.org/10.3389/frbhe.2024.1503793.

Banerjee, Sanchayan, Matteo M. Galizzi, Peter John, and Susana Mourato. 2023. Sustainable dietary choices improved by reflection before a nudge in an online experiment. *Nature Sustainability* 6 (12): 1632–1642. https://doi.org/10.1038/s41893-023-01235-0.

Banerjee, Sanchayan, Till Grüne-Yanoff, Peter John, and Alice Moseley. 2024a. It's time we put agency into behavioural public policy. *Behavioural Public Policy* 8 (4): 789–806. https://doi.org/10.1017/bpp.2024.6.

Banerjee, Sanchayan, Laura Zimmermann, Alejandro Hortal, Malte Dold, Andriy Ivchenko, Leonhard Lades, Rebecca McDonald, and Manu M. Savani. 2024b. Recent developments in Behavioural Public Policy: IBPPC 2022. *Behavioural Public Policy* 8 (4): 633–638. https://doi.org/10.1017/bpp.2024.12.

Baumgartner, Frank, and Bryan Jones. 2010. *Agendas and instability in American politics*. University of Chicago Press.

Belardinelli, Paolo. 2024. *Mapping behavioral public policy*. Springer.

Benartzi, Shlomo, and Richard H. Thaler. 2013. Behavioral economics and the retirement savings crisis. *Science* 339 (6124): 1152–1153. https://doi.org/10.1126/science.1231320.

Benartzi, Shlomo, John Beshears, Katherine L. Milkman, Cass R. Sunstein, Richard H. Thaler, Maya Shankar, Will Tucker-Ray, William J. Congdon, and Steven Galing. 2017. Should governments invest more in nudging? *Psychological Science* 28 (8): 1041–1055. https://doi.org/10.1177/0956797617702501.

Beshears, John, and Harry Kosowsky. 2020. Nudging: Progress to date and future directions. *Organizational Behavior and Human Decision Processes* 161:3–19. https://doi.org/10.1016/j.obhdp.2020.09.001.

Blattman, Christopher, Julian C. Jamison, and Margaret Sheridan. 2017. Reducing crime and violence: Experimental evidence from cognitive behavioral therapy in Liberia. *American Economic Review* 107 (4): 1165–1206. https://doi.org/10.1257/aer.20150503.

Bovens, Luc. 2009. The ethics of nudge. In *Preference change: Approaches from philosophy, economics and psychology*, 207–219. Springer.

Bradt, Jacob. 2022. Comparing the effects of behaviorally informed interventions on flood insurance demand: An experimental analysis of 'boosts' and 'nudges'. *Behavioural Public Policy* 6 (3): 485–515. https://doi.org/10.1017/bpp.2019.31.

Brandon, Alec, Paul J. Ferraro, John A. List, Robert D. Metcalfe, Michael K. Price, and Florian Rundhammer. 2017. Do the effects of nudges persist? Theory and evidence from 38 natural field experiments. https://doi.org/10.3386/w23277.

Brehm, Sharon S., and Jack W. Brehm. 1981. *Psychological reactance: A theory of freedom and control*. Academic Press.

Bruns, Hendrik, Elena Kantorowicz-Reznichenko, Katharina Klement, Marijane Luistro Jonsson, and Bilel Rahali. 2018. Can nudges be transparent and yet effective? *Journal of Economic Psychology* 65:41–59. https://doi.org/10.1016/j.joep.2018.02.002.

Chater, Nick, and George Loewenstein. 2023. The i-frame and the s-frame: How focusing on individual-level solutions has led behavioral public policy astray. *Behavioral and Brain Sciences* 46:e147. https://doi.org/10.1017/S0140525X22002023.

Chetty, Raj, Adam Looney, and Kory Kroft. 2009. Salience and taxation: Theory and evidence. *American Economic Review* 99 (4): 1145–1177. https://doi.org/10.1257/aer.99.4.1145.

Chetty, Raj, John N. Friedman, Søren Leth-Petersen, Torben Heien Nielsen, and Tore Olsen. 2014. Active vs. passive decisions and crowd-out in retirement savings accounts: Evidence from Denmark. *The Quarterly Journal of Economics* 129 (3): 1141–1219. https://doi.org/10.1093/qje/qju013.

Cialdini, Robert B. 2003. Crafting normative messages to protect the environment. *Current Directions in Psychological Science* 12 (4): 105–109. https://doi.org/10.1111/1467-8721.01242.

Clarke, Nick, Jennings, Will, Moss, Jonathan and Stoker, Gerry. 2016. The rise of anti-politics in Britain Southampton, GB. University of Southampton 8pp.

Conly, Sarah. 2014. Against autonomy: Justifying coercive paternalism. *Journal of Medical Ethics* 40 (5): 349–349. https://doi.org/10.1136/medethics-2013-101444.

Curato, Nicole, Jensen Sass, Selen A. Ercan, and Simon Niemeyer. 2022. Deliberative democracy in the age of serial crisis. *International Political Science Review* 43 (1): 55–66. https://doi.org/10.1177/0192512120941882.

Cutts, David, Edward Fieldhouse, and Peter John. 2009. Is voting habit forming? The longitudinal impact of a GOTV campaign in the UK. *Journal of Elections, Public Opinion and Parties* 19 (3): 251–263. https://doi.org/10.1080/17457280903073914.

Dalton, Russell J. 2004. *Democratic challenges, democratic choices: The erosion of political support in advanced industrial democracies.* Oxford University Press.

Dawnay, Emma, and Hetan Shah. 2005. *Behavioural economics: Seven principles for policy makers.* Vol. 68. London: New Economics Foundation.

DellaVigna, Stefano, and Elizabeth Linos. 2022. RCTs to scale: Comprehensive evidence from two nudge units. *Econometrica* 90 (1): 81–116. https://doi.org/10.3982/ECTA18709.

Ding, Jianing, Ziqian Xia, Nathaniel Geiger, Jinquan Ye, Chao Zhang, Sara Constantino, and Kristian Nielsen. 2025. A meta-analysis of the real-world impact of sustainability labeling on consumer choices. https://doi.org/10.21203/rs.3.rs-6557928/v1.

Dolan, Paul, Michael Hallsworth, David Halpern, Dominic King, and Ivo Vlaev. 2010. MINDSPACE: Influencing behaviour for public policy.

Dolan, P., Hallsworth, M., Halpern, D., King, D., Metcalfe, R., & Vlaev, I. 2012. Influencing behaviour: The mindspace way. *Journal of economic psychology, 33* (1), 264–277.

Dold, Malte. 2025. The narrative that should guide applied behavioural science. *Behavioural Public Policy* 9 (2): 338–344. https://doi.org/10.1017/bpp.2024.21.

Durose, Catherine, and Liz Richardson. 2015. Designing public policy for co-production: Theory, practice and change. Bristol: Policy Press.

Dworkin, Gerald. 1972. Paternalism. *The Monist* 64–84. https://doi.org/10.5840/monist197256119.

Ewert, Benjamin, Kathrin Loer, and Eva Thomann. 2023. Beyond nudge: Advancing the state-of-the-art of Behavioural Public Policy and Administration. In *Beyond nudge*, 1–15. Policy Press.

Fishkin, James. 2009. *When the people speak: Deliberative democracy and public consultation.* Oxford University Press.

Fung, Archon. 2004. *Empowered participation: Reinventing urban democracy.* Princeton University Press.

Gerber, Alan S., Donald P. Green, and Ron Shachar. 2003. Voting may be habit-forming: Evidence from a randomized field experiment. *American Journal of*

Political Science 47 (3): 540–550. https://doi.org/10.1111/1540-5907.00038.
Gerver, Mollie, Sanchayan Banerjee, and Peter John. 2024. Nudging against consent is effective but lowers welfare. *Scientific Reports* 14 (1): 14864. https://doi.org/10.1038/s41598-024-65122-0.
Goodwin, Tom. 2012. Why we should reject 'nudge'. *Politics* 32 (2): 85–92. https://doi.org/10.1111/j.1467-9256.2012.01430.x.
Grüne-Yanoff, Till, and Ralph Hertwig. 2016. Nudge versus boost: How coherent are policy and theory? *Minds and Machines* 26 (1): 149–183. https://doi.org/10.1007/s11023-015-9367-9.
Grüne-Yanoff, T. 2025. Boosts are not educative or system-2 nudges. *Mind and Society,* 24 (2), 549–561.
Hagmann, David, Emily H. Ho, and George Loewenstein. 2019. Nudging out support for a carbon tax. *Nature Climate Change* 9 (6): 484–489. https://doi.org/10.1038/s41558-019-0474-0.
Hallsworth, Michael. 2023. A manifesto for applying behavioural science. *Nature Human Behaviour* 7 (3): 310–322. https://doi.org/10.1038/s41562-023-01555-3.
Halpern, David. 2015. The rise of psychology in policy: The UK's de facto Council of Psychological Science Advisers. *Perspectives on Psychological Science* 10 (6): 768–771. https://doi.org/10.1177/1745691615609917.
Halpern, David, Clive Bates, Greg Beales, and Adam Heathfield. 2004. *Personal responsibility and changing behaviour: The state of knowledge and its implications for public policy.* Cabinet Office London.
Hay, Colin. 2007. *Why we hate politics.* Vol. 5. Polity.
Heller, Sara B., Anuj K. Shah, Jonathan Guryan, Jens Ludwig, Sendhil Mullainathan, and Harold A. Pollack. 2017. Thinking, fast and slow? Some field experiments to reduce crime and dropout in Chicago. *The Quarterly Journal of Economics* 132 (1): 1–54. https://doi.org/10.1093/qje/qjw033.
Hertwig, Ralph. 2017. When to consider boosting: Some rules for policy-makers. *Behavioural Public Policy* 1 (2): 143–161. https://doi.org/10.1017/bpp.2016.14.
Hertwig, Ralph, and Till Grüne-Yanoff. 2017. Nudging and boosting: Steering or empowering good decisions. *Perspectives on Psychological Science* 12 (6): 973–986. https://doi.org/10.1177/1745691617702496.
Hirst, Paul. 2013. *Associative democracy: New forms of economic and social governance.* Wiley.
House of Lords. 2011. *Behaviour Change—Science and Technology Committee.* https://publications.parliament.uk/pa/ld201012/ldselect/ldsctech/179/17902.htm.
IJzerman, Hans, Neil A. Lewis Jr., Andrew K. Przybylski, Netta Weinstein, Lisa DeBruine, Stuart J. Ritchie, Simine Vazire, Patrick S. Forscher, Richard

D. Morey, and James D. Ivory. 2020. Use caution when applying behavioural science to policy. *Nature Human Behaviour* 4 (11): 1092–1094. https://doi.org/10.1038/s41562-020-00990-w.

Jachimowicz, Jon M., Shannon Duncan, Elke U. Weber, and Eric J. Johnson. 2019. When and why defaults influence decisions: A meta-analysis of default effects. *Behavioural Public Policy* 3 (2): 159–186. https://doi.org/10.1017/bpp.2018.43.

John, Peter. 2013. *Analyzing public policy*. Routledge.

John, Peter. 2014. Policy entrepreneurship in UK central government: The behavioural insights team and the use of randomized controlled trials. *Public Policy and Administration* 29 (3): 257–267. https://doi.org/10.1177/0952076713509297.

John, Peter. 2018. *How far to nudge?: Assessing behavioural public policy*. Edward Elgar Publishing.

John, Peter. 2019. The international appeal of behavioural public policy: Is nudge an Anglo-American phenomenon? *Journal of Chinese Governance* 4 (2): 144–162. https://doi.org/10.1080/23812346.2019.1576264.

John, Peter. 2025a. Hallsworth's manifesto through a cultural theory lens. *Behavioural Public Policy* 9 (2): 331–337. https://doi.org/10.1017/bpp.2024.20.

John, Peter. 2025b. *The political economy of public policy*. Unpublished Manuscript.

John, Peter, and Toby Blume. 2018. How best to nudge taxpayers?: The impact of message simplification and descriptive social norms on payment rates in a central London local authority. *Journal of Behavioral Public Administration* 1 (1): 1–11. https://doi.org/10.30636/jbpa.11.10.

John, Peter, and Gerry Stoker. 2019. Rethinking the role of experts and expertise in behavioural public policy. *Policy & Politics* 47 (2): 209–225. https://doi.org/10.1332/030557319X15526371698257.

John, Peter, Graham Smith, and Gerry Stoker. 2009. Nudge nudge, think think: Two strategies for changing civic behaviour. *The Political Quarterly* 80 (3): 361–370. https://doi.org/10.1111/j.1467-923X.2009.02001.x.

Johnson, Eric J., and Daniel Goldstein. 2003. *Do defaults save lives?* American Association for the Advancement of Science.

Jones, Rhys, Jessica Pykett, and Mark James Whitehead. 2013. *Changing behaviours: On the rise of the psychological state*. Edward Elgar Publishing.

Jung, Janice Y., and Barbara A. Mellers. 2016. American attitudes toward nudges. *Judgment and Decision Making* 11 (1): 62–74. https://doi.org/10.1017/S1930297500007592.

Just, David R., and Gnel Gabrielyan. 2025. On nudging and psychological reactance. *Applied Economic Perspectives and Policy*.

Kahneman, Daniel. 2011. *Thinking, fast and slow*. Macmillan.

Kahneman, Daniel, Paul Slovic, and Amos Tversky. 1982. *Judgement under uncertainty: Heuristics and biases*. Cambridge University Press.

Kettle, Stewart, Marco Hernandez, Simon Ruda, and Michael A. Sanders. 2016. Behavioral interventions in tax compliance: Evidence from Guatemala. *World Bank Policy Research Working Paper* (7690).

Kirchgässner, Gebhard. 2017. Soft paternalism, merit goods, and normative individualism. *European Journal of Law and Economics* 43 (1): 125–152. https://doi.org/10.2139/ssrn.2619711.

Leggett, Will. 2014. The politics of behaviour change: Nudge, neoliberalism and the state. *Policy & Politics* 42 (1): 3–19. https://doi.org/10.1332/030557312X655576.

Lenzi, Dominic. 2019. Deliberating about climate change: The case for 'thinking and nudging'. *Moral Philosophy and Politics* 6 (2): 313–336. https://doi.org/10.1515/mopp-2018-0034.

Levitt, Steven, and Stephen Dubner. 2014. *Freakonomics*. William Morrow Paperbacks.

Lewis, Michael. 2016. *The undoing project: A friendship that changed the world*. Penguin UK.

Lindblom, Charles. 1959. The science of "muddling through". *Public Administration Review* 19 (2): 79–88. https://doi.org/10.2307/973677.

Linde, Jona, and Barbara Vis. 2017. Do politicians take risks like the rest of us? An experimental test of prospect theory under MPs. *Political Psychology* 38 (1): 101–117. https://doi.org/10.1111/pops.12335.

Loewenstein, George, and Nick Chater. 2017. Putting nudges in perspective. *Behavioural Public Policy* 1 (1): 26–53. https://doi.org/10.1017/bpp.2016.7.

Loewenstein, George, Cindy Bryce, David Hagmann, and Sachin Rajpal. 2015. Warning: You are about to be nudged. *Behavioral Science & Policy* 1 (1): 35–42. https://doi.org/10.1177/237946151500100106.

Lohmann, Paul M., Elisabeth Gsottbauer, Christina Gravert, and Lucia A. Reisch. 2025. Nudging, fast and slow: Experimental evidence from food choices under time pressure. *Environmental and Resource Economics* 1–33. https://doi.org/10.1007/s10640-025-01012-x.

Maier, Maximilian, František Bartoš, T. D. Stanley, David R. Shanks, Adam J. L. Harris, and Eric-Jan Wagenmakers. 2022. No evidence for nudging after adjusting for publication bias. *Proceedings of the National Academy of Sciences* 119 (31): e2200300119. https://doi.org/10.1073/pnas.2200300119.

Marshall, Alfred. 1890. *Principles of economics: Unabridged eighth edition*. New York, NY: Cosimo, Inc.

Marteau, Theresa M., David Ogilvie, Martin Roland, Marc Suhrcke, and Michael P. Kelly. 2011. Judging nudging: Can nudging improve population health? *BMJ* 342. https://doi.org/10.1136/bmj.d228.

McKenzie, Craig R. M., and Michael J. Liersch. 2011. Misunderstanding savings growth: Implications for retirement savings behavior. *Journal of Marketing Research* 48 (SPL): S1–S13. https://doi.org/10.1509/jmkr.48.SPL.S1.

McKenzie, Craig R. M., Michael J. Liersch, and Stacey R. Finkelstein. 2006. Recommendations implicit in policy defaults. *Psychological Science* 17 (5): 414–420. https://doi.org/10.1111/j.1467-9280.2006.01721.x.

Michaelsen, Patrik. 2024. Transparency and nudging: An overview and methodological critique of empirical investigations. *Behavioural Public Policy* 8 (4): 807–817. https://doi.org/10.1017/bpp.2024.7.

Michaelsen, Patrik, Lina Nyström, Timothy J. Luke, and Martin Hedesström. 2021. Downstream consequences of disclosing defaults: Influences on perceptions of choice architects and subsequent behavior. *Comprehensive Results in Social Psychology* 5 (1–3): 25–48. https://doi.org/10.1080/23743603.2021.1983720.

Mills, Stuart, Richard Whittle, Rafi Ahmed, Tom Walsh, and Martin Wessel. 2023. Dark patterns and sludge audits: An integrated approach. *Behavioural Public Policy* 1–27. https://doi.org/10.1017/bpp.2023.24.

Mols, Frank, Alexander Haslam, Jolanda Jetten, and Niklas Steffens. 2015. Why a nudge is not enough: A social identity critique of governance by stealth. *European Journal of Political Research* 54 (1): 81–98. https://doi.org/10.1111/1475-6765.12073.

Mullainathan, Sendhil, and Eldar Shafir. 2013. *Scarcity: Why having too little means so much.* Macmillan.

Mutz, Diana C. 2006. *Hearing the other side: Deliberative versus participatory democracy.* Cambridge University Press.

Naru, Faisal. 2024. Behavioral public policy bodies: New developments & lessons. *Behavioral Science & Policy* 10 (1): 1–17. https://doi.org/10.1177/23794607241285614.

Neblo, Michael A. 2015. *Deliberative democracy between theory and practice.* Cambridge University Press.

OECD. 2017. *Behavioural insights and public policy: Lessons from around the world.* OECD Publishing.

Oliver, Adam. 2013. *Behavioural public policy.* Cambridge University Press.

Oliver, Adam. 2017. *The origins of behavioural public policy.* Cambridge University Press.

Oliver, Adam. 2023. *A political economy of Behavioural public policy.* Cambridge, UK: Cambridge University Press.

Oliver, Adam. 2025. *Clarifying by declassifying: removing the buzzwords from behavioral public policy.* Policy and Society, puaf010.

Osman, Magda. 2020. Backfiring, reactance, boomerang, spillovers, and rebound effects: Can we learn anything from examples where nudges do the opposite of what they intended. *PsyArXiv*. https://doi.org/10.31234/osf.io/ae756.

Ostrom, Elinor. 1986. An agenda for the study of institutions. *Public Choice* 48 (1): 3–25. https://doi.org/10.1007/BF00239556.

Paunov, Yavor, and Till Grüne-Yanoff. 2023. Boosting vs. nudging sustainable energy consumption: A long-term comparative field test in a residential context. *Behavioural Public Policy* 1–26. https://doi.org/10.1017/bpp.2023.30.

Pew Research Centre. 2023. *Public Trust in Government: 1958–2023*. https://www.pewresearch.org/politics/2023/09/19/public-trust-in-government-1958-2023/.

Rebonato, Riccardo. 2012. *Taking liberties: A critical examination of libertarian paternalism*.

Rebonato, Riccardo. 2014. A critical assessment of libertarian paternalism. *Journal of Consumer Policy* 37 (3): 357–396. https://doi.org/10.2139/ssrn.2346212.

Ruggeri, Kai, Friederike Stock, S. Alexander Haslam, Valerio Capraro, Paulo Boggio, Naomi Ellemers, Aleksandra Cichocka, Karen M. Douglas, David G. Rand, and Sander Van der Linden. 2023. A synthesis of evidence for policy from behavioural science during COVID-19. *Nature* 625 (7993): 134–147. https://doi.org/10.1038/s41586-023-06840-9.

Ryfe, David M. 2005. Does deliberative democracy work? *Annual Review of Political Science* 8 (1): 49–71. https://doi.org/10.1146/annurev.polisci.8.032904.154633.

Sallis, Anna, Hugo Harper, and Michael Sanders. 2018. Effect of persuasive messages on National Health Service Organ Donor Registrations: A pragmatic quasi-randomised controlled trial with one million UK road taxpayers. *Trials* 19 (1): 513. https://doi.org/10.1186/s13063-018-2855-5.

Saward, Michael. 2003. Enacting democracy. *Political Studies* 51 (1): 161–179. https://doi.org/10.1111/1467-9248.00418.

Sheffer, Lior, Peter John Loewen, Stuart Soroka, Stefaan Walgrave, and Tamir Sheafer. 2018. Nonrepresentative representatives: An experimental study of the decision making of elected politicians. *American Political Science Review* 112 (2): 302–321. https://doi.org/10.1017/S0003055417000569.

Shipman, Tim. 2016. *All out war: The full story of how Brexit sank Britain's political class*. HarperCollins UK.

Simon, Herbert A. 1955. A behavioral model of rational choice. *The Quarterly Journal of Economics* 99–118. https://doi.org/10.2307/1884852.

Smith, Adam. 1759. *The theory of moral sentiments*.

Smith, Graham. 2009. *Democratic innovations: Designing institutions for citizen participation*. Cambridge University Press.

Straßheim, Holger. 2020. The rise and spread of behavioral public policy: An opportunity for critical research and self-reflection. *International Review of Public Policy* 2 (2: 1): 115–128. https://doi.org/10.4000/irpp.897.

Sunstein, Cass R. 2016a. Do people like nudges. *Administrative Law Review* 68:177. https://doi.org/10.2139/ssrn.2604084.

Sunstein, Cass R. 2016b. People prefer system 2 nudges (kind of). *Duke Law Journal* 66:121. https://doi.org/10.2139/ssrn.2731868.

Sunstein, Cass R. 2017. Nudges that fail. *Behavioural Public Policy* 1 (1): 4–25. https://doi.org/10.1017/bpp.2016.3.

Sunstein, Cass R. 2019. Sludge and ordeals. *Duke Law Journal* 68 (8): 1843–1883.

Sunstein, Cass R., and Richard H. Thaler. 2003. Libertarian paternalism is not an oxymoron. *The University of Chicago Law Review* 1159–1202. https://doi.org/10.2307/1600573.

Sunstein, Cass R., Lucia A. Reisch, and Micha Kaiser. 2019. Trusting nudges? Lessons from an international survey. *Journal of European Public Policy* 26 (10): 1417–1443. https://doi.org/10.1080/13501763.2018.1531912.

Thaler, Richard H. 1992. *The winner's curse: Paradoxes and anomalies of economic life*. Simon and Schuster.

Thaler, Richard H. 2015. *Misbehaving: The making of behavioral economics*. WW Norton & Company.

Thaler, Richard H. 2018. *Nudge, not sludge*. American Association for the Advancement of Science.

Thaler, Richard H., and Shlomo Benartzi. 2004. Save more tomorrow™: Using behavioral economics to increase employee saving. *Journal of Political Economy* 112 (S1): S164–S187. https://doi.org/10.1086/380085.

Thaler, Richard H., and Hersh M. Shefrin. 1981. An economic theory of self-control. *Journal of Political Economy* 89 (2): 392–406. https://doi.org/10.1086/260971.

Thaler, Richard H., and Cass R. Sunstein. 2008. *Nudge: Improving decisions about health, wealth, and happiness*. Penguin.

Tiefenbeck, Verena, Thorsten Staake, Kurt Roth, and Olga Sachs. 2013. For better or for worse? Empirical evidence of moral licensing in a behavioral energy conservation campaign. *Energy Policy* 57:160–171. https://doi.org/10.1016/j.enpol.2013.01.021.

Tversky, Amos, and Daniel Kahneman. 1974. Judgment under Uncertainty: Heuristics and Biases: Biases in judgments reveal some heuristics of thinking under uncertainty. *Science* 185 (4157): 1124–1131. https://doi.org/10.1126/science.185.4157.1124.

Varazzani, Chiara, and Cale Hubble. 2025. Four SINS in behavioural public policy. *Behavioural Public Policy* 9 (2): 345–353. https://doi.org/10.1017/bpp.2024.22.

Venema, Tina A. G., Floor M. Kroese, and Denise T. D. De Ridder. 2018. I'm still standing: A longitudinal study on the effect of a default nudge. *Psychology & Health* 33 (5): 669–681. https://doi.org/10.1080/08870446.2017.1385786.

Whitehead, Mark, Rhys Jones, Rachel Lilley, Jessica Pykett, and Rachel Howell. 2017. *Neuroliberalism: Behavioural government in the twenty-first century*. Routledge.

Wittels, Annabelle S. 2023. Participatory governance and responsiveness: Do motivational interventions increase engagement with citizen input? *Political Research Quarterly* 76 (2): 741–756. https://doi.org/10.1177/10659129221100260.

World Bank. 2014. *World development report 2015: Mind, society, and behavior*. https://www.worldbank.org/en/publication/wdr2015.

CHAPTER 2

The Advantages of Thinking

Humans often think about their actions. In fact, this ability to be self-aware differentiates us from other animals. We are naturally thoughtful, especially when matters are important to us. When we are about to do something of significance, we try to understand what is happening around us and consider the situation we face: we like to make informed choices before we act, but sometimes we also like to delegate this decision-making to others, especially if we think we are unable to do it well ourselves or if we don't like to make such decisions. In all these cases, we think about how we choose to use our agency, whether it is first-order agency, where we exercise it ourselves, or second-order, when we delegate the choice to others (see Sunstein 2025).

People can embrace their actions as potentially important, both for themselves and others. The capacity to think is vital for a whole range of decisions, such as starting a new relationship, moving between jobs or across countries, making financial investments by choosing assets in a portfolio, and buying or renting a new house. The list goes on. Some of these decisions are personal. Others, such as the state of the environment or the persistence of high inequality, have greater ramifications for the collective welfare of broader society. Most things of significance, especially those that have important consequences, need weighing up and evaluating, ensuring that what we do is consistent with our long-term plans and comports with our core values. Without conscious choice, we simply

© The Author(s), under exclusive license to Springer Nature Switzerland AG 2026
S. Banerjee, P. John, *Nudge+*,
https://doi.org/10.1007/978-3-032-13261-1_2

become the product of our instincts, reactions, and automatic cues, which can make our life devoid of much of its substance, meaning, and significance. Thinking can encourage responsibility for actions taken; it builds in autonomy to take the right decisions; and it helps avoid regrets at making them later. Because if something is important, we probably want to give it due consideration and prefer to avoid making a mistake. Most of all, thinking is about a life lived so an individual experiences existence to the fullest.

Consider a few examples that drive home this point. Thinking is important for citizens in a democracy, such as when voting in an election. Even though someone might be habituated to vote for one party or a sitting incumbent, it is important to make a choice that leads to a change in public policy or a better quality of leadership and probity of public officials. It is essential for democratic politics that some debate takes place on the course a country or city has taken, and whether it needs to change or not. Certain elections can be crucial in removing an incumbent or rewarding a party for delivering on its promises. Such actions require individual voters to be aware of their own objectives, to be able to assess the candidates and government consciously, and to consider any special factors at work at a particular election. This is what democracy is all about. If people behave habitually or decide based on a coin toss, then no coherent signal is sent from citizens to government, and there is no electoral accountability for poor behaviour on the part of political elites. They can carry on behaving badly as there is no correction from the voters. It used to be said of British elections that some voters were so sure of voting for either Labour or Conservative in safe Westminster seats, which have large margins, that it was possible to put a donkey on the ticket and it would be elected so long as it had a party rosette pinned to it (e.g., as declared by Phillips 2021 Chapter 11). Even though just a humorous saying, it does show the need for reflection and debating to take place for democracy to work. People need to think about candidates, their qualities, and (proposed) policies, rather than unreflectively accept who are on the ballot paper. They can think whether their habitual choices are the right ones, and confront their natural prejudices and biases, even though these habits might be powerful in conditioning how they think and are the ultimate basis for their decisions. In recent work, Neblo et al. (2010, 566) have argued for the United States that: 'willingness to deliberate is much more widespread than expected, and it is precisely those people less likely to participate in traditional partisan politics who are most interested in deliberative participation.'

This idea of deliberation is key to politics, for example, whether people like to deliberate or not, especially when they engage to vote has received a lot of consideration by political scientists. Contrary to our main thesis that reflection is key for voters, in their influential book *Stealth Democracy*, Hibbing and Theiss-Morse (2002) argue that most citizens do not genuinely desire more political participation or deliberation but rather engage reluctantly—mainly when they perceive political corruption—preferring that politics operate quietly in the background. They interpret public calls for engagement as 'nonseparable preferences', driven not by enthusiasm for deliberation but by fear of unchecked elites (Lacy 2001; Hibbing and Theiss-Morse 2002). This view challenges a central claim of deliberative theory: that apathy stems from disempowerment and would diminish if the system became more rational and inclusive. Other sceptics, such as Bartels (1996), Eliasoph (1998), and Posner (2009), argue that participation is burdensome and generally unwanted, with Posner famously dismissing 'deliberation day' by suggesting that if people truly valued such engagement, they wouldn't need to be paid. However, in response, Thompson (2008) emphasises that deliberative democracy is a normative ideal aimed at transforming, not reflecting, the status quo; Muhlberger (2018) links deliberative attitudes to broader antidemocratic dispositions; and Dryzek (2005) critiques standard surveys for failing to capture the inherently social and dynamic nature of deliberative opinion formation. While voters might act instinctively, to think that the whole pool of voters vote without thinking would reduce most democratic society to tatters.

Thinking is also important for citizens when they think about their families and what they would like to make of them as they build on generations. Evidence from positive psychology suggests that people rely on various deliberative mechanisms to craft the lives that they ultimately would like to build. Sometimes they fail in delivering on the ends of such life crafting exercises, but nonetheless, thinking is often at the forefront of these interventions. For example, new evidence suggests that enabling people to think about the future could make them more resilient to what comes ahead. This idea is core to a new deliberative toolkit, commonly referred to as the 'Letters to the Future' (LtF) (Schippers et al. 2025). LtF comes in many forms, for example, where individuals are encouraged to write a letter to their future self, or to a member of their family in the next generation, or even reflect on the future state of the world and compare and contrast it with the status quo today, thereafter making goal plans to get them to where they would like to be in the future. Such thinking interventions have been shown to improve people's resilience and autonomy (see Schippers et al. 2025 for a discussion).

Overall, thinking is key to the survival of humanity and humans. People must also think when they confront crises, be it climate change, the outbreak of a deadly disease, war, or massive financial setbacks. What facilitates the chances of getting through these crises is our ability to think about their urgency, so we can act and assume responsibility for change (Mann 2021). In this way, thinking is the precursor to long-lasting behaviour change. We don't always need a crisis to think. Sometimes, we simply feel the need to be part of a bigger collective, such as our desire for a healthier society or to address crime or reduce inequality or even promote our well-being. When called to think about these decisions, citizens have willingly stepped up and agreed to help achieve better outcomes with their collective thinking efforts. This new inclination to think has been evidenced by the recent popularity of citizen juries and other deliberative innovations (often called mini publics) at many different levels of government (Smith 2009), as discussed in the last chapter. Governments around Europe commission citizen assembles, which can be good ways to engage in thinking (see Perlaviciute et al. 2024).

So, what might be the benefits of reflection? Deliberate reflection helps people override error-prone intuitive responses, align judgements with normative standards, and improve decision quality across domains of risk, probability, and reasoning. Dual-process theories distinguish fast, intuitive type 1 processes from slower, effortful type 2 processes; engaging the latter allows people to inhibit initial responses and simulate alternatives (Stanovich et al. 2000; Kahneman 2011; Evans and Stanovich 2013). Individual differences in cognitive reflection—the tendency to engage analytic reasoning—predict resistance to common reasoning errors and susceptibility to misinformation, as well as better calibration in probabilistic and intertemporal decisions (Frederick 2005; Pennycook and Rand 2019). Interventions that prompt reflective engagement, such as structured decision-making aids, have been shown to reduce bias and improve choice quality in policy and organisational settings (Milkman et al. 2009).

Reflection also plays a foundational role in self-regulation—the ability to align impulses with long-term goals. Studies on delay of gratification reveal that individuals who can shift attention and mentally reframe temptations exhibit better outcomes across life domains (Mischel et al. 1989; Metcalfe and Mischel 1999). Neurocognitive follow-ups indicate that effective self-control involves reflective processes mediated by the prefrontal cortex (Casey et al. 2011). Still, reflective thinking has cognitive costs, and can be depleted under pressure (Baumeister et al. 2007). Motivational factors such as accountability can offset these costs and promote reflective reasoning, particularly when evaluative contexts reward accuracy and openness (Lerner and Tetlock 1999).

At the learning level, metacognitive reflection supports accurate self-monitoring, adaptive strategy use, and transfer of knowledge. Foundationally defined as the ability to think about one's own thinking (Flavell 1979), metacognitive processes enable learners to plan, monitor, and evaluate their performance. While learners' metacognitive judgements are often biased, they can be improved with feedback and cue-based strategies (Dunlosky and Lipko 2007; Dunlosky and Metcalfe 2008). In professional and expert domains, metacognition is central to reflective practice and supports continual learning through structured cycles of assessment and adaptation (Schon 1986).

Finally, as we discussed for democratic contexts, reflection can produce more informed, considered, and public-regarding political judgements. Deliberative forums that allow citizens time, balanced information, and respectful dialogue consistently show increases in knowledge, opinion quality, and perceived legitimacy (Mendelberg 2002; Ackerman and Fishkin 2005; Fishkin 2009). Still, some research suggests that many citizens avoid political engagement unless corruption threatens the public good, casting doubt on the universal appeal of deliberative participation (Hibbing and Theiss-Morse 2002; Posner 2009). The challenge, then, is designing reflective spaces that are inclusive, well-facilitated, and meaningfully connected to decision-making processes (Dryzek 2005; Thompson 2008).

Our thoughts for change therefore can go a long way to making a difference in the world. What we think will manifest via our actions into what we eventually see around us. For instance, if voters start thinking about the performance of their political candidates, such as whether they have delivered on the promises they made earlier or implemented their proposed policies for development and change, they can avoid casting a vote as if for a donkey, effectively instituting a government that potentially delivers newer and effective public policies. Similarly, if citizens were to think seriously about the dismal future that awaits future generations, arising from their inattentive actions today, they could adopt better behaviours that build a better planet to come.

How Much Thinking Is Too Much Thinking?

Imagine, however, having to think all the time. How would that be? Could sleep take place? It would be a form of hyperactivity. Often people do not want to give up on the time that entails. As much thinking goes on in meetings and activities, most people would prefer doing sports, going to the opera, or spending time with friends and family, where the cognitive burdens reduce over routine actions (some thinking of course still happens when doing these activities). People are right. Most of the daily activities rely on habits and on being able to switch off for a bit. We acquire and process the information we need for a given task at some point of time in our lives (Stern 2017), and we certainly benefit from these reflexes. Thinking at all times is quite a strain, as overthinking can easily distract us from many other things. Sometimes, individuals might not be able to get to the right solution as issues start becoming complex, so they can feel frustrated and just plump for any choice out of desperation (Schwartz 2002). Thinking, if overdone, can also be welfare-reducing. If this happens, it is more likely that people lose perspective rather than gain new insights. Maybe here, unlike as in the voting example, gut feelings are right as they reflect underlying values. For example, it is preferable to run immediately to save the child before a hurtling bus. Thinking or having to think about this moral decision would delay our response, and one might choose not to act simply because of an overemphasis on one's own safety. How would we look as human beings when weighing up the choices while the bus collides with the child? That would be inhumane! It is also true that repeated habitual actions generally result from some fruitful thinking in the past. To throw that all away, just to think once again, might not be the best use of our time. If people have made a conscious choice of a certain type of a public transport or a particular coffee every morning, it is safer to assume their habits are generally welfare-preserving. Except on certain days, such as when there is a rail strike or our favourite oat milk is out of stock, where thinking could have made us happier. But is there a middle course between full-on reflective thinking and more habit driven unconscious choices, or a way of efficiently moving between these two kinds of activities?

Some kinds of behaviours are the result of instincts and automatic responses and are probably best left that way. Some others need us going another extra mile. Consider driving a car, which mostly relies on the automatic reflexes of drivers. When people drive, they develop a mental model of shortcuts that enables them to react to road situations as we recognise a necessary stimulus. Educating people or trying to signal them transparently towards a better driving choice can be potentially welfare-reducing. For example, a recent study showed when people were informed about the number of statewide roadside fatalities on previously installed highway dynamic message signs in 28 states in the USA, the signage inadvertently led to more accidents (Hall and Madsen 2022). While there can be many different explanations for this unexpected finding, one that comes to mind rather quickly is that showing additional information distracted the driver's attention and focus, increasing the chances of running into an accident as the authors write: 'our proposed explanation for this surprising finding is that these "in-your-face," "sobering," negatively framed messages seize too much attention (i.e., are too salient), interfering with drivers' ability to respond to changes in traffic conditions'.

On the other hand, consider climate change and our actions that cause it. What can we do to mitigate it? Here, evidence shows that globally people want to change their behaviours to reduce their impact on the climate, but they are unsure whether their actions will have any positive impact in bringing forth such a change (Pew Research Centre 2023). In this case, when people are encouraged to think about the different ways in which they can engage in decisions to reduce their climate footprint, they tend to outperform others who are mindlessly prompted towards the right choice. Thinking can empower people and strengthen the effectiveness of their decisions.

For the first type of decision, those that are mostly automatically driven, based on heuristics (shortcuts), policy-makers are better off providing incentives as a signal to citizens to get them to where they want them to be. These are easy to pick and often rely on people's unconscious choices. For the other decisions, those that need us to act constantly in a good way and go the distant mile, like to solve climate change, it is legitimate and effective if citizens can actively think about these choices and then make final decisions. For the latter, these are usually also the bigger issues in our society where simple reflexes fail to get to a welfare-improving point. Even if the aim eventually is to sit back and let habits do all the hard work, without necessarily exerting too much effort all the time, people need to think about how we can get to this stage. It is like getting to the autopilot phase: we must get started first and then it gets much easier. If we can successfully engage in doing this task, we can still let our habits and reactions in play to get through the day. To overcome the initial inertia of current actions or status-quo bias, there is a need to find a way to move quickly between thinking fast for all those habitual actions we mentioned earlier and thinking slow for the big issues that deserve more deliberation. Can we do this? Finding out if we can and how it is done are key tasks of this book.

Fast and slow thinking has long been understood by psychologists, notably Kahneman (2011), as dual types of cognitive reasoning. It is represented by a system 1 of automatic responses, resembling the fast activities in our brain, and a system 2 of reflection, corresponding to the slower and more thoughtful activities in the brain. While such a psychological conceptualisation lacks a robust neural correlate in our brain, fast and slow thinking enables people to theorise how they perceive the brain to work in response to different situations. We will elaborate on this in much more detail later in Chap. 5, when we discuss how these different types of cognitive reasoning have been traditionally thought to interact with each other. It is important to understand how the proposition of a new transitory cognitive system works, one where individuals can effectively switch between fast and slow thinking. However, for now, it suffices to say that such hybrid possibilities may exist where people can actively engage their slow thinking when needed, and juggle between fast and slow thinking.

It is important to be both reflective citizens, those who know how to think, yet can also live their lives confidently, using shortcuts to make decisions day-to-day, because they have made effortful yet right decisions to start with. With both thinking and nudging tools to help, they get a chance to reflect about their choices and see if they agree on whether they are biased or not, and then think about how to change them, if needed. Then they can return to more routine and habit-informed decision-making. Just like voting or acting in a crisis, it involves a collaboration that is implied as like someone who pays taxes, looks after their health, cares for others, and so on. It is a partnership between citizens and government; it is also a bond between fellow citizens. Thinking and improving decisions are integral to who we are. These people will realise that it is desirable to think or at least have the scope to think about something rather than just doing it automatically based on their instincts, as it might lead to better outcomes. One might ask, why is that so? It is because we get committed to doing things as they think about them, rather than being tricked into doing them just because others want or do. This is a key claim of this book. It is designed to revive our ability to reflect on our personal lives and then on public policy. We can correct the move by policy-makers to rely simply on automatic processes: this is the nudge revolution, which has been so valuable in recent years, but has stayed on the same course in the same way as can be seen in the revised edition of the eponymous book (Thaler and Sunstein 2021) in which there is no basic change in the message that making things easy and automatic is for the best. The nudge programme is, of course, a long way from thinking. And increasingly with more nudging, we also come to realise that such a way to automatising decisions has natural limitations where people fail to take ownership of any behaviour change.

For example, we can either live an intense life where we constantly try to manage our expenses and revisit savings every day, caring not to spend too much now just to not have too little when we grow old. Or we evaluate the means (actions) that will deliver these ends (goals and objectives). In this slow thinking about what works best for us, we can devise rules or choose defaults, as we try to work out the right pension contribution. It is important to note that slow thinking does not rule out relying on automatic reflexes, it only makes them safer and more effective for us. Once done, we get to spend years, not worrying about the pension, just to enjoy it when retirement comes. Of course, most people would need to revisit this, at different points in their lives, but hopefully less frequently than the daily hassle of budgeting. Relying pointlessly on an automatic decision cue such as the nudge takes away this opportunity, as there is no scope to understand or revisit the nudge, unless one really wants to or as they say if one is watchful enough to do it (some defaults are hard to opt out from even when stakes are very high, see Berger et al. 2022).

What we propose in this book, therefore, is a modified nudge—the nudge+—where reflection on the part of citizens, delivered alongside the nudge, helps them reclaim their autonomy, the ability to have control over one's decisions and agency, the ability to act and make choices freely, while taking advantage of the ease of automaticity that comes with the nudge. Doing so also gives us the scope to reassess the important role of citizens in a state. Every time someone chooses the nudge after a thoughtful evaluation, it manifests confidence in public policies. If they reject it, citizens send signals to governments that help them improve these public policies. With nudge+, we suggest ways to empower people to become more reflective in their everyday lives.

Beyond Nudges with Nudge+

So what exactly is a nudge+? Simply put, a nudge+ is a nudge *plus* reflection. It is a hybrid between top-down and bottom-up governance, which engages people's deliberative capacities alongside nudging—a participatory, citizen-oriented behavioural public policy.

Nudge+ is best understood by working through an example. There are many people around us who are trying to change their diets to make it better for the environment or their personal health or for animal welfare. However, as it is, there is no magic solution to get this done right for everyone with a single policy. Why? Consider two different people—Sam and Manuela. Say that both want to switch to meat-free diets. While Sam and Manuela are alike in their goals (ends), they are not quite the same in what prevents them from realising their goals (means). It could be that Sam eats meat because he is tempted by the numerous options on the menu. Whereas Manuela eats meat because she is unaware of the harms of the food on her plate. To get both to switch away from meat permanently, we need a policy that overcomes their own barriers, rather than suggesting ways to alter the ends for them.

The latter, which is a nudge, is a quick fix for any given setting. So, what happens if we were to nudge Sam and Manuela towards a meat-free diet? Well, let's say, we choose to do it with a default nudge that changes the offer made to people. A meaningful default, in this case, can be a set menu of meatless items which is provided as the standard option for all customers. Of course, people can opt out of this standard nudge and ask to see the whole menu. For Sam, and many others like him, this default menu will work very well. Sam is no longer tempted by the meat options on the menu, the ones he was always looking to avoid. But does this nudge work equally well for Manuela too?

Maybe the default menu works for Manuela whenever she is at the restaurant, but it is not a permanent cure for her certainly; for whenever Manuela finds herself in different settings that do not provide her with the default, she will struggle to navigate between items and choose the meat-free ones. This lack of knowledge of the behaviour change process emerges because she still needs to understand which food is better than the others to make an effective choice sans the nudge, particularly as these situations unfold in the future.

Similarly, if Sam is not reflective of the nudge, take the nudge away, and Sam would be tempted by bigger menus again. It is only when Sam understands the role of the default nudge on his behaviour and actively chooses it, he can move to a permanent behaviour change. A typical climate label, which informs Manuela of the environmental impact of food items, or nutrition calorie label, or protein source label, is more appropriate given her biases. With these labels at her disposal, Manuela can overcome her inner barriers and engage in long-term meat-free consumption. The society can, therefore, be better off with a nudge that can signal to people hidden information that then helps them choose the right food item with the right nudge. This style of tailoring nudges where people are first encouraged to reflect on their true preferences is an example of a nudge+, where reflection precedes the delivery of the nudge, allowing policy-makers to identify and tailor nudge applications. In the later chapters of this book, we will elaborate on more such examples of nudge+ interventions, like pledges, cool-offs, and instant pop-ups. These nudge+ interventions work on the same principle that they are designed to give people a split second to think when they are faced with a nudge.

But in the example above, there is another problem with nudging that has not been addressed in the previous chapter: the issue of offering one-size-fits-all solutions. A nudge tends to be effective only when it benefits the majority—what one might call a 'majoritarian rule'. However, soft paternalism of this kind often leads to asymmetric benefits (Camerer et al. 2003). As the example above suggests, this can be remedied when individuals are prompted to reflect before being nudged—hence the title of this book: Think, Before You Nudge. The problem with recommending any single nudge is that it fails to reach the root of the issue without first acknowledging people's real needs and preferences. A nudge works by co-opting individuals' biases, effectively engineering their behaviour. In doing so, it can dilute human capacity to determine what is best for themselves.

This is where nudge+ offers a simple but powerful fix. By allowing individuals like Sam and Manuela to first reflect on their own barriers to achieving successful behaviour change, nudge+ encourages them to exercise control—autonomy—over the public policies available to them. They may end up customising a policy into a personalised nudge, as some have described it (see Mills 2022), to better align with their goals and intentions. This process—thinking first, nudging second—is a defining feature of nudge+.

Another example is when Sam and Manuela are invited to understand the design of a given nudge before it is applied to them. In this case, nudge+ enables them to choose whether to respond to the intervention, and only when it aligns with their own, and society's, genuine needs. Going further, Sam and Manuela can be prompted to reflect on who is delivering the nudge+. This helps them evaluate the trustworthiness of the communicator—such as identifying whether they are being subjected to (commercial) micro-targeting.

Nudge+ varies in the way it engages people to think openly. This reflection is what distinguishes a standard nudge from this modified policy. With this thinking element, citizens can step up and take charge of the problem, rather than feeling it is the responsibility of others. In some ways, they are forced to act (there are pitfalls of this, as we discuss later). However, set up in this way, a nudge+ is transparent by design, as people can assess a nudge on its true merits themselves as there are no hidden tricks, no small print to be watchful of. These benefits of nudge+ that come from the enhanced transparency and autonomy that the individual enjoys also map on to the effectiveness of the nudge, mostly. Putting citizens into the heart of public policy in this way means they are better situated to use the nudge that was designed to get them to where they wanted to be. But sometimes, the nudge+ can also backfire—when this happens, the nudge does not work as intended, but as we will argue this is not necessarily a bad signal to the policy-maker who can then adapt the means with which they choose to engage with the citizen. This possibility of backlash: when people do not agree with the nudge and behave opposite to the intended direction of the nudge, allows people to express their genuine concern about nudge. In all other cases, the nudge+ is more effective, especially as they are deemed appropriate by citizens. We will unpack these nuances of the effectiveness of nudge+ and trade-offs with autonomy and agency, as we go along in this book.

One might ask at this stage, so what is it about nudge+ that works better? Well, for starters, it enables us to update our beliefs, our thoughts, and our facts from time to time. For if we do not, we stand still with beliefs and habits that worked for us in a previous time but no longer are appropriate for cases where we need new tools and ideas to help us through. Think of the case when you had to first choose your pension at the time of your first job, but as you grow in life, maybe you would like to revisit your pension contributions time to time to reflect what suits your current financial self. It is quite natural to assume that as people go through different life-course transitions, their financial standing changes, and therefore they need to have the ability to revisit important financial decisions at different points in their lifetime. This process of updating and reconsidering ideas is what we call 'perspective transformation', the main facilitator of fast- and slow-thinking processes. We will outline this mechanism in more detail in the next chapter. It will become clearer that perspective transformation is key to behaviour change with a nudge+ as our biases in many cases arise, not from our laziness to rely on pre-set reflexes and shortcuts—that's a necessary evil—but from these reflexes being outdated over time, just like the default pension contribution which was set for someone in the first job does not work any longer when they are about to start a family. This point also becomes easy to conceive when comparing social norms and habits over time as thirty years back it was normal to use a manual phone book to store contact details. It is no longer today! Not long ago, it was not normal to use a large language model like ChatGPT but is very much the case today. As things evolve, people need to update how they deal with day-to-day situations. This is where nudge+ helps. While, a nudge is stationary, the nudge+ allows for adaption. The extra touch of reflection allows someone to choose the new nudge that is right for them. Only if people were allowed to think in brief life-course transitions about their new pension contribution rates, they could once again set the default and live hassle-free until they are needed to rethink about it at their next life-transition.

Recall our example where people choose the same political candidate for every term. We argued initially that reflection can be welfare-preserving and can also lead to effective public policies. However, it might not be quite so prominent in the very immediate future. A future where we are required to evaluate our political candidates intermittently is very costly for citizens in terms of time needed to collect information about the candidates. Nonetheless, someone who is thinking they will be able to hold a candidate accountable for their actions over time will not be swayed by the recent triumphs or communication gimmicks, unlike a non-thinking person, close to the poll. Further as time passes by, there can be also changes in preferences that make prior choices welfare-reducing. For example, if people grow critical of some political candidates, the hope is that such an empowered and educated citizenry will be capable of holding such incumbents accountable for their weak performance at the end of their candidature (unless they turn off politics completely). As different events take place, people will constantly revise their prior beliefs for whom to vote in the next poll, so when it is time, they cast an informed vote. This is what the reflective element of nudge+ does, it kickstarts analytical thinking which ultimately enables us to switch from the fast cognition to the slow one. We will discuss this further in Chap. 5.

One criticism here is that these events can often throw a lot of information towards us, some requiring active filtering more than others. When thinking, how do we know which information to rely on? Sunstein (2020) argues that too much information provision means that people cannot work out what is good for them. People need information that makes sense to them and their well-being. Currently there is too much information which makes automatic reactions more understandable. Nonetheless if people were to acknowledge the premise of this hybrid cognition, where we think about the shortcuts we take, how do they know when they must re-think and update their heuristics? Life might have been easier if everyone had a troubleshooting button available to them in their brain which could turn on anytime to check for new available updates; and get up and running with all the latest facts that need to be considered. It would be just like an iPhone or other device that updates itself when people sleep at night. Sadly, or perhaps happily, automatic updates cannot be implanted into brains. People must find a way to feed back into the reflective shortcuts enabling them to update their beliefs constantly. Understanding how to achieve efficient updating is another task of this book.

At this point, it might be useful to consider another example of how individuals make decisions in everyday life. Take the decision to settle down and secure housing—whether by purchasing a home or signing a long-term lease. One approach involves extensive research into school catchment areas, property values, rental markets, and local amenities. Alternatively, individuals may rely on digital tools that simplify this process, using algorithms and labels to streamline decision-making. This latter approach is often more convenient—and it is precisely this convenience that nudges aim to provide. They simplify life by offering easily digestible cues that guide behaviour.

However, exclusive reliance on such signals places individuals at the mercy of those who design them. The system may function well, assuming the benevolence and competence of the signal designers. But this assumption is risky. If the signals are poorly designed or manipulated, individuals may end up making decisions that do not serve their interests—such as choosing a property ill-suited to their needs. This creates a troubling dynamic: it implicitly suggests that others know better than we do what is best for us. Such thinking undermines individual agency.

Instead, individuals should have the opportunity to design or at least co-determine the signals that shape their choices, so they are empowered to act autonomously—without requiring constant vigilance. This is the central proposition of nudge+, a nudge that incorporates deliberation. It removes the need to rely on the goodwill of policy-makers or the attentiveness of citizens by embedding reflection into the choice architecture. Nudge+ enables individuals to pursue their own goals—divergent though they may be—at their own pace. It champions equal agency, offering space for reflection without negating the utility of nudges themselves. Indeed, we suggest that when people are invited to think, they are more likely to engage with nudges willingly and constructively. They can evaluate the cues designed to assist them, make decisions accordingly, and prepare themselves for the next step in the behavioural journey—one that involves planning, re-evaluating, and thinking again.

Designing a nudge+ is, however, non-trivial. While individuals possess the capacity for reflection, current approaches often fail to strike the right balance between automaticity and deliberation. The challenge lies in determining not only when to think but also how much. This is not a matter of indulging in over-reflection or rejecting heuristics altogether. It is, rather, akin to knowing how and when to engage with complex decisions—selectively and purposefully, as one might enjoy parts of a cake now and leave the rest for later. The key lies in learning to switch reflective modes on and off effectively—putting on the 'thinking hat' just enough to navigate life's challenges with clarity and without regret.

This is the direction in which public policy must evolve: towards fostering more reflective individuals and cultivating policy-makers capable of engaging citizens through empowerment by design. In a world saturated with nudges, what is needed are signals that embed just a small degree of reflection. This is the world that could emerge if the principles of nudge+ were taken seriously.

We remain some distance from this vision of thoughtfully designed public policy. At present, many interventions rely heavily on automatic behavioural triggers and habitual responses—such as for tax compliance or waste recycling—mirroring the routines of private life. These features are valuable and should not be discarded. Yet it is not contradictory to argue that people can act automatically while also retaining a degree of awareness. There are frequent, underutilised opportunities to pause and reflect, even briefly, within the flow of behaviour. Over time, these micro-moments can accumulate and enable individuals to better achieve their desired outcomes. Viewed over a lifetime, the effects of nudge+ are not simply the result of large deliberative moments that fade with time. Rather, they emerge from consistent, small reflections that support sustained, autonomous, and legitimate behaviour change.

References

Ackerman, Bruce, and James Fishkin. 2005. Deliberation day. New Haven: Yale University Press.

Bartels, Larry M. 1996. Uninformed votes: Information effects in presidential elections. *American Journal of Political Science* 194–230. https://doi.org/10.2307/2111700.

Baumeister, Roy F., Kathleen D. Vohs, and Dianne M. Tice. 2007. The strength model of self-control. *Current Directions in Psychological Science* 16 (6): 351–355. https://doi.org/10.1111/j.1467-8721.2007.00534.x.

Berger, Sebastian, Andreas Kilchenmann, Oliver Lenz, Axel Ockenfels, Francisco Schlöder, and Annika M. Wyss. 2022. Large but diminishing effects of climate action nudges under rising costs. *Nature Human Behaviour* 6 (10): 1381–1385. https://doi.org/10.1038/s41562-022-01379-7.

Camerer, Colin, Samuel Issacharoff, George Loewenstein, Ted O'donoghue, and Matthew Rabin. 2003. Regulation for conservatives: Behavioral economics and the case for "asymmetric paternalism". *University of Pennsylvania Law Review* 151 (3): 1211–1254. https://doi.org/10.2307/3312889.

Casey, Betty Joe, Leah H. Somerville, Ian H. Gotlib, Ozlem Ayduk, Nicholas T. Franklin, Mary K. Askren, John Jonides, Marc G. Berman, Nicole L. Wilson, and Theresa Teslovich. 2011. Behavioral and neural correlates of delay of gratification 40 years later. *Proceedings of the National Academy of Sciences* 108 (36): 14998–15003. https://doi.org/10.1073/pnas.1108561108.

Dryzek, John S. 2005. Deliberative democracy in divided societies: Alternatives to agonism and analgesia. *Political Theory* 33 (2): 218–242. https://doi.org/10.1177/0090591704268372.

Dunlosky, John, and Amanda R. Lipko. 2007. Metacomprehension: A brief history and how to improve its accuracy. *Current Directions in Psychological Science* 16 (4): 228–232. https://doi.org/10.1111/j.1467-8721.2007.00509.x.

Dunlosky, John, and Janet Metcalfe. 2008. *Metacognition*. Sage Publications.

Eliasoph, Nina. 1998. *Avoiding politics: How Americans produce apathy in everyday life*. Cambridge University Press.

Evans, Jonathan, and Keith E. Stanovich. 2013. Dual-process theories of higher cognition: Advancing the debate. *Perspectives on Psychological Science* 8 (3): 223–241. https://doi.org/10.1177/1745691612460685.

Fishkin, James. 2009. *When the people speak: Deliberative democracy and public consultation*. Oxford University Press.
Flavell, John H. 1979. Metacognition and cognitive monitoring: A new area of cognitive–developmental inquiry. *American Psychologist* 34 (10): 906. https://doi.org/10.1037/0003-066X.34.10.906.
Frederick, Shane. 2005. Cognitive reflection and decision making. *Journal of Economic Perspectives* 19 (4): 25–42. https://doi.org/10.1257/089533005775196732.
Hall, Jonathan D., and Joshua M. Madsen. 2022. Can behavioral interventions be too salient? Evidence from traffic safety messages. *Science* 376 (6591): eabm3427.
Hibbing, John R., and Elizabeth Theiss-Morse. 2002. *Stealth democracy: Americans' beliefs about how government should work*. Cambridge University Press.
Kahneman, Daniel. 2011. *Thinking, fast and slow*. Macmillan.
Lacy, Dean. 2001. A theory of nonseparable preferences in survey responses. *American Journal of Political Science* 239–258. https://doi.org/10.2307/2669339.
Lerner, Jennifer S., and Philip E. Tetlock. 1999. Accounting for the effects of accountability. *Psychological Bulletin* 125 (2): 255. https://doi.org/10.1037/0033-2909.125.2.255.
Mann, Michael E. 2021. *The new climate war: The fight to take back our planet*. PublicAffairs.
Mendelberg, Tali. 2002. The deliberative citizen: Theory and evidence. In *Political decision making, deliberation and participation*, vol. 6 (1), 151–193.
Metcalfe, Janet, and Walter Mischel. 1999. A hot/cool-system analysis of delay of gratification: Dynamics of willpower. *Psychological Review* 106 (1): 3. https://doi.org/10.1037/0033-295X.106.1.3.
Milkman, Katherine L., Dolly Chugh, and Max H. Bazerman. 2009. How can decision making be improved? *Perspectives on Psychological Science* 4 (4): 379–383. https://doi.org/10.1111/j.1745-6924.2009.01142.x.
Mills, Stuart. 2022. Personalized nudging. *Behavioural Public Policy* 6 (1): 150–159. https://doi.org/10.1017/bpp.2020.7.
Mischel, Walter, Yuichi Shoda, and Monica L. Rodriguez. 1989. Delay of gratification in children. *Science* 244 (4907): 933–938. https://doi.org/10.1126/science.2658056.
Muhlberger, Peter. 2018. Stealth democracy: Authoritarianism and democratic deliberation. *Journal of Deliberative Democracy* 14 (2). https://doi.org/10.16997/jdd.309.
Neblo, Michael A., Kevin M. Esterling, Ryan P. Kennedy, David M. J. Lazer, and Anand E. Sokhey. 2010. Who wants to deliberate—And why? *American Political Science Review* 104 (3): 566–583. https://doi.org/10.1017/S0003055410000298.

Pennycook, Gordon, and David G. Rand. 2019. Fighting misinformation on social media using crowdsourced judgments of news source quality. *Proceedings of the National Academy of Sciences* 116 (7): 2521–2526. https://doi.org/10.1073/pnas.1806781116.

Perlaviciute, G., W. A. Gorter, and G. Muinos. 2024. Unveiling citizens' perspective on citizen assemblies among participants and non-participants of a citizen assembly on energy. *Environmental Research Communications* 6 (11): 115001. https://doi.org/10.1088/2515-7620/ad8868.

Pew Research Centre. 2023. *Public Trust in Government: 1958–2023*. https://www.pewresearch.org/politics/2023/09/19/public-trust-in-government-1958-2023/.

Phillips, Jess. 2021. *The life of an MP: Everything you really need to know about politics*. Simon and Schuster.

Posner, Richard A. 2009. *Law, pragmatism, and democracy*. Harvard University Press.

Schippers, Michaéla C., Elisabeth M. de Jong, Diana C. Rus, Huib Rommers, and Sanchayan Banerjee. 2025. Letters to the future challenge: A scalable online tool to engage management students with the SDGs. *The International Journal of Management Education* 23 (3): 101233. https://doi.org/10.1016/j.ijme.2025.101233.

Schon, Donald A. 1986. *The reflective practitioner: How professionals think in action*. Taylor & Francis.

Schwartz, Barry. 2002. *The paradox of choice. Why more is less*. Harper Perennial.

Smith, Graham. 2009. *Democratic innovations: Designing institutions for citizen participation*. Cambridge University Press.

Stanovich, Keith E., and Richard F. West. 2000. Individual differences in reasoning: Implications for the rationality debate? *Behavioral and Brain Sciences* 23 (5): 645–665. https://doi.org/10.1017/S0140525X00003435.

Stern, Elsbeth. 2017. Individual differences in the learning potential of human beings. *npj Science of Learning* 2 (1): 2. https://doi.org/10.1038/s41539-016-0003-0.

Sunstein, Cass R. 2020. *Too much information: Understanding what you don't want to know*. MIT Press.

Sunstein, Cass R. 2025. Second-order agency. *Mind & Society* 1–15. https://doi.org/10.1007/s11299-025-00321-4.

Thaler, Richard H., and Cass R. Sunstein. 2021. *Nudge: The final edition*. Penguin.

Thompson, Dennis F. 2008. Deliberative democratic theory and empirical political science. *Annual Review of Political Science* 11 (1): 497–520. https://doi.org/10.1146/annurev.polisci.11.081306.070555.

CHAPTER 3

What Is Reflection?

We are endowed with an ability to think. It is this reflective capacity in us that empowers us to choose wisely. Reflection allows us to weigh up the true benefits and costs of our decisions. In the previous two chapters, we discussed why reflection is important for us and the advantages it can have, especially when we are faced with nudges. But what does this reflection entail? What is it that we should think about?

Is it mindless thinking, where the mind wavers unnecessarily over all actions we take, or is it goal directed, at the behest of the individual or someone else? Is it conscious, where we are aware of what triggers our thoughts, or not? If so, we must engage thoroughly with the process of thinking. Or if it is merely unconscious and outside our control, we are prompted to think without any knowledge of deliberation happening. And is it at the level of the individual, or rather some kind of group thinking? Further, is it costly for us to think? Do reflective capacities exist within us, so we can harness them when we need to? Maybe then we can dial up our reflective capacities as required—not all actions might warrant the same degree of deliberation. But this creates a second-order problem of what thought is needed to make one capable of thinking, which in the end might create an infinite regress of capacities, where one level is needed to unlock the other. For most people, choosing our next political leader, for instance, might be a more thoughtful process than choosing what to cook for our next meal.

© The Author(s), under exclusive license to Springer Nature Switzerland AG 2026
S. Banerjee, P. John, *Nudge+*,
https://doi.org/10.1007/978-3-032-13261-1_3

Contrarily, if our reflective capacities are a product of our cognitive development, which in turn depends on many factors, such as our level of education, exposure to worldly knowledge, socio-economic statuses, and other ecological factors, then it is natural to expect some differences among humans and their reflective potential. Then, can the disparate be aligned in their thinking abilities, so that those with lower reflective potential may eventually improve with some guidance and signals from policy-makers? If a deliberate policy requires us to weigh up the costs and benefits of a public policy programme, and we happen to lack formal understanding of how such processes work, it is very unlikely that we will be able to assess the potential of this programme. Consequently, there are clear advantages for thinkers who possess basic intellectual capacities to think critically and analyse, hence the worry that reflection could risk widening existing inequalities and gaps in the delivery and use of public policies that rely on reflection. All of this is to say that reflective potential can vary widely across people, our thinking humans, mostly as it is an artefact of socio-economic and ecological conditions that shape them, including the environment in which people make their choices. This observation, in turn, leads to the argument that nudge, which is conceived as mostly automatic cues, can become disadvantageous to those who lack the potential to be watchful[1] of a nudge. Our thinking selves, nonetheless, can dial up their reflective potential, either with their inherent capacities, or might be boosted to develop better capabilities (see Hertwig and Grüne-Yanoff 2017), and can be brought at par with those who have been already watchful. Such a reflective process will enable our thinking humans to engage fully with a policy signal and undertake long-term behaviour change. We will continue this discussion later in Chap. 4 as well.

So, there arise many questions that we must answer to convince you of the strengths of more thoughtful humans. This is what we set out to do in this chapter. By the end of it, we will come up with a comprehensive understanding of reflection and a taxonomy of reflective prompts that policy-makers can deliver alongside standard behavioural public policies, notably the nudge, in enabling to engage with long-term behaviour change with more autonomy and agency. Later in the book, we will discuss, how these reflective prompts can be combined together in the nudge. But before we get there, we will unpack the idea of perspective

[1] Watchfulness is a criterion that allows those receiving a nudge to opt out of it, if they do not align with the ends of the nudge. Watchfulness makes a nudge libertarian in its design.

transformation. This is at the core of what reflection entails. We will argue that unless deliberation transforms one's current perspectives, either by changing them, or by building on them further, reflection will eventually fail to effectuate behaviour change successfully. This leads us to the next point that reflection must, therefore, be an active process, albeit as we discuss, many tools and applications of contemporary behavioural public policies, such as nudge, in the past have had an element of passive thinking embedded in them. Our main task with nudge+ would be to dial up these reflection possibilities alongside the nudge. To realise the benefits of reflection fully, this process of reflection must happen actively as we assert throughout in this chapter.

By the end of this chapter, we will have discussed ways in which thinking citizens can be encouraged to think with a nudge, using the nudge+. One of our main propositions is that repeated reflection will end up in unconscious, automatic actions, thereby making reflection less effortful as thinkers keep deliberating, unless there is a need to update beliefs once again. Any reflection of this kind will be always goal directed. However, it might also happen consciously in individually targeted people, for example, where citizens meet to discuss new pathways for societies to develop and change, as in citizen forums or juries, or as part of such individual policies, through reflective prompts. This point will become important as we go along, particularly in the next chapters when we discuss ways to combine reflection with such tools like nudge. There, we will outline two different schools of thought on adding reflection to a nudge: the traditional wisdom that reflection is group-led and happens outside the nudge at the level of a wider population in the form of a collective, or the contemporary idea that deliberation occurs as a mini-think embedded within a nudge tailored to particular individuals or with the help of a digital assistants such as a prompt or a bot.

This chapter will generally pave the path for a discussion on the many purposes that reflection has. Where possible, we will deduce testable predictions on the effectiveness of behavioural public policies when targeted by different reflective prompts later in the book.

What Does It Mean to Reflect?

Before we can start, we must ask: what do we mean by reflection? Reflection is what we see of ourselves, for example, in the mirror. Every time we put on a nice dress, and we stand before the mirror, we see our reflection—a sense of how we and others might see us. This reflection is key to our identity at that moment because it helps us make peace with reality and our vision of how we should look. If we do not like how we look, we make efforts to change our appearance straight away. If we like it, then we continue with our dress choice! It becomes our look for the day. Anything we do that day we have chosen to let people remember us that way. Of course, it is never so simple as this as we sometimes regret our choices or not look in the mirror carefully enough but for the purposes of this book, the meaning of reflection is not very far away from this image that we make of ourselves when we look in the mirror.

Reflection, as we will use it, implies a cue to our thoughts. This cue enables us to understand how things appear when they are happening and then helps us act according to what we see. In some sense, this reflection builds up our perspective of reality. Just like it happens when we see ourselves in the mirror with our dress, it also gives us the chance to transform our perspective, like we would change our dress if we did not feel highly of it. For example, when we see something that we had not believed to have happened or had not expected to have seen. Have you ever woken up one morning, walked up to the mirror, and having spotted dark circles underneath your eyes, thought to yourself, 'I must be burning myself out, I need to take a break'? Introspective thoughts of this type that cross our mind when we analyse an event of the past or that is to happen in future, is an inevitable outcome of reflection. Reflection, thus, often marks the beginning of a long process of behaviour change which we are part of.

A Brief History of Reflection

Nonetheless, despite its widespread use in educational, professional, and psychological contexts, the concept of reflection lacks a single, universally accepted definition. Reflection is widely understood as a systematic and intentional form of thinking that enables individuals to examine critically their beliefs, experiences, and actions. Systematic reviews of what reflection entails suggest it is typically conceptualised as cognitive, integrative, iterative, and active. These characteristics cut across disciplinary boundaries, allowing reflection to be recognised as a disciplined form of sense-making and knowledge transformation.

For example, John Dewey (1933), a foundational figure in this domain, defined reflective thinking as an 'active, persistent, and careful consideration of any belief or supposed form of knowledge in light of the grounds that support it and the further conclusions to which it tends'. Donald Schon (1986) later extended this view to professional learning, introducing the notions of reflection-in-action (which occurs during a task) and reflection-on-action (which happens afterward). Both perspectives emphasise the developmental and adaptive functions of reflection.

Similarly, modern learning and development frameworks have integrated reflection as a core mechanism of experiential learning. David Kolb's (2014) experiential learning theory identifies reflection (as 'reflective observation') as a necessary stage in the transformation of experience into learning. The ALACT model, developed by Korthagen and Vasalos (2005), expands on this by identifying levels of reflection, from surface-level behaviour to deep-rooted aspects such as identity and mission, suggesting that effective reflection involves not only technical problem-solving but also personal meaning-making. These models emphasise that reflection is not merely a cognitive tool but also a means of self-exploration and professional growth.

Decades of research has also shown that reflection serves multiple cognitive functions, including self-assessment, metacognitive regulation, and performance improvement (Flavell, 1979; Zimmerman, 2002). This relates to the foundational theoretical work mentioned before which conceptualises reflection as a process that transforms experience into learning and supports the integration of theory and practice (Dewey, 1933; Schön, 1986; Kolb, 2014). Empirical findings suggest that structured reflective activities—such as journaling, feedback analysis, and guided questioning—can enhance academic learning and professional competence (Hattie, 2008; MacLeod et al., 2009). For instance, meta-analytic and longitudinal studies have found that reflective thinking contributes to better integration of theory and practice in domains, such as medicine (Mamede et al., 2007) and teaching (MacLeod et al., 2009). Reflection has also been shown to improve ethical reasoning, interpersonal sensitivity, and the ability to revise initial judgements when confronted with new information (Mezirow, 1991; King & Kitchener, 1994). Thus reflection also has a home in cognition where it can be thought of as an exercise to improve one's critical thinking skills.

Reflection is a key concern in therapeutic settings, where it intersects with constructs like mentalisation, metacognition, and insight (Fonagy, 2018). In psychotherapy, reflective functioning—the ability to think about one's own and others' mental states—has been linked to better outcomes, but also poses challenges in terms of how it is conceptualised and measured (Luyten et al., 2020). Reflection in therapy is often more relational and co-constructed than traditionally assumed. This shift mirrors a broader move across disciplines to view reflection not as a solitary act of cognition, but as a dialogical and socially embedded process (Vygotsky, 1978; Boud & Walker, 1998). This is also what was transpired into the more traditional view of a group think, where people could come together to discuss an issue, and develop a common solution to counter that problem. But we will come onto this later in the chapter.

In other domains, such as in education, reflection is increasingly seen as a developmental skill (see Mezirow, 1991). Studies in higher education suggest that students benefit most from structured forms of reflection early in their learning, while more open-ended or creative methods become useful as learners develop expertise and self-direction. Pedagogical frameworks that scaffold reflective thinking—from structured templates to open-ended diaries and arts-based media—help learners internalise reflective habits. Overall, reflection is now considered foundational to learning, professional identity formation, and adaptive expertise. However, its benefits are contingent upon intentional design, appropriate scaffolding, and awareness of the cognitive and emotional demands it imposes.

In this chapter, and based on this literature, we take reflection to refer to the mind's capacity to review its actions, and generate a signal to enable people to see how actions have led to consequences in the past, which then informs future decisions if something similar were to happen. In this setup, reflection is very much like looking at the past, where some form of evaluation is happening either when we are in action or afterward, much like Schön's take. But unlike Schön, reflection can be prospective, that is, imply that humans are also able to anticipate a range of scenarios that are linked to their actions in the future, especially when they have faced something similar in the past. Then, after this signal is generated, by some complex rules of the brain, people choose an action that is best for them. The rational actor model in economic theory often simplifies this exercise by associating costs and benefits arising from so many actions, and ranking alternatives based on the net benefits they generate. Reflection then becomes a precursor for the brain to execute the preliminaries of these cost-benefit analyses. For all these kinds of events, those in the past or in future, it is not wrong to say, reflection enables people to become critical of their actions and to choose wisely.

Perspective Transformation

How, then, does the process of reflection unfold in practice? Building on these theoretical and empirical foundations discussed earlier, reflection is best understood as an iterative cognitive and emotional sequence that begins with the recognition of a cue or a stimulus—typically a problematic or incongruent experience—that culminates in some form of belief revision or behavioural adjustment. This dynamic is especially well captured by Mezirow (1991, 1997) in his theory of transformative learning, where reflection is not merely about reviewing the past but about interrogating one's underlying assumptions and perspectives. According to Mezirow, reflection often begins with a disorienting dilemma—an experience that challenges our taken-for-granted frames of reference—and progresses through stages of critical self-examination, recognition of shared experiences, and exploration of new roles or actions.

To illustrate this, consider a concrete example. Imagine you have recently visited a car showroom. A salesperson enthusiastically presents several models and successfully persuades you to commit to purchasing one. Overwhelmed by the sensory appeal and immediacy of the interaction, you make a hasty decision. However, as you exit the showroom, doubt creeps in: was this the right choice? This moment of doubt exemplifies what Mezirow (1991) would call a disorienting dilemma—a catalyst for reflection. More specifically, this is the stimulus that triggers the first phase of reflective processing, as outlined in both experiential learning models (Kolb 1984) and cognitive theories of self-regulation (Flavell 1979; Schraw and Dennison 1994).

Such a stimulus often invokes an affect response—frequently in the form of discomfort, confusion, or regret—which in turn activates deeper levels of cognitive engagement. In this case, the experience of buyer's remorse constitutes an affectively charged cue that prompts reflection. If this stimulus produces no dissonance with one's existing beliefs or values, it may be dismissed as trivial. However, when it creates a tension between prior expectations and current understanding, it produces what Festinger (1957) and others after him have called cognitive dissonance, thereby inviting the second phase of reflection. At this stage, individuals begin to compare the implications of the stimulus against their existing beliefs and commitments. In our example, this involves reassessing the decision to buy the car: was it driven by need or impulse? Does it align with one's financial goals, values, or social identity?

This stage is marked by deliberative weighing of benefits and costs, which may include both instrumental and psychological considerations. Research in consumer psychology and behavioural economics confirms that such post-decisional evaluations are central to how individuals process regret and make future-oriented judgements (Gilovich and Medvec 1995; Zeelenberg and Pieters 2007). These evaluations are not purely rational. Emotional and identity-related considerations—such as the discomfort of going back on one's word or the desire to signal status—play a key role in shaping the reflective process.

Once this evaluative process has been undertaken, individuals typically reach a point where they must act upon their revised understanding. This is the final phase of reflection: the point at which one either reaffirms the original decision or alters one's course of action. Returning to the example, this might mean following through with the car purchase, thus resolving the dissonance through rationalisation, or contacting the dealer to withdraw from the agreement, thereby aligning future behaviour with revised beliefs. This outcome—whether it involves change or confirmation—is what Mezirow (1991) referred to as perspective transformation: a restructuring of a person's frames of reference in response to critical reflection.

Perspective transformation is thus a hallmark of deep, constructive reflection. Unlike surface-level adjustments or post-hoc justifications, it involves a fundamental re-examination of meaning structures—those ingrained assumptions, norms, and expectations that shape how individuals interpret their experiences. Empirical studies on adult learning (Cranton 2006; Taylor 2007) have shown that perspective transformation can lead to lasting behavioural change, greater self-awareness, and improved alignment between values and actions. In this sense, the process of reflection described above is not just a cognitive exercise, but a potentially transformative encounter with one's self-concept, intentions, and place in the world.

So how does this process of perspective transformation kick in? It can be prompted by others for us. Consider the example above, once again. Here, it could have been the case, that the buyer's remorse was triggered not by the buyer, but by someone they knew. For instance, someone they had discussed this purchase decision with, such as a friend, their partner, a colleague, or a financial consultant. The source of the stimulus is immaterial to the initiation of perspective transformation, but the way it might unfold can be quite different therein. We will revisit this point in the next chapter, when we discuss the different aspects one can reflect upon. But for now, we acknowledge that reflection and the perspective transformation there in can be delivered as a public policy signal externally by many different actors in the society.

It can also happen when we become self-aware of our own behaviours and want to reflect on them, changing them to a certain course along the way. In recent literature, this has been called a type of self-induced introspection, what is popularly known as self-nudging[2] (Reijula and Hertwig 2022). When people nudge themselves in this way, they must have devised some reflective mechanisms that transformed their perspectives, which has caused them to try and change how they are or would like to be. For instance, take the example of Samuela, once again, who is trying to cut meat from her diet. Samuela is also trying to tackle obesity. It has since then proved hard for Samuela to choose the right (veg*n) meal without the nudge, so Samuela has decided to phase in measures that help her become healthier. As a result, she weighs herself monthly and comes up with new lifestyle changes after every evaluation. When Samuela weighs herself, she generates some a cue that allows her to evaluate her perspectives critically. For example, every month, Samuela has some expectations of her target weight. Now based on her expectations of weight loss, and what she sees is happening monthly, Samuela revaluates her prior lifestyle choices (e.g., a certain form of diet that she might be on) and institutes new lifestyle changes (maybe a different form of diet or a new pattern of exercise). This is the result of the perspective transformation that Samuela has begun herself, and is a precursor to the process of self-nudging she subjects herself too, which does require some thinking to begin with, as this case exemplifies.

How would it look here if this process of perspective transformation were prompted externally instead, like in the previous example of the buyer's remorse? In this case, Samuela can receive this stimulus to think from other parties. For example, say the government launches a national fitness campaign which increases the availability of fitness centres in her neighbourhood, provides free health plans for those who are planning to tackle obesity, and delivers free online workout regimes and diet plans if people sign up for it. The provider informs Samuela of such plans via text

[2] Often thought to include interventions that can 'enable people to design and structure their own decision environments – that is, to act as citizen choice architects' (Reijula and Hertwig 2022, 119).

messages. Receiving this text message in this case is like receiving a new stimulus for change, which prompts Samuela to think and thereby the process of perspective transformation unfolds. It is true that not all who receive this reflective prompt will engage with it, a point we address later in this chapter when we discuss conditions that are necessary and sufficient to act on one's perspective transformation. Yet the point is simply to recognise that there can be many alternative sources, in this case—the government or the provider—which are external to one's own self and can deliver such prompts for engaging people in perspective transformation.

Beyond the individual and the state, there are also commercial actors in our society, those who invest heavily to design and alter the choice environment to influence our behaviours. We call them the commercial choice architects. They include firms and companies who use insights from behavioural sciences to change our behaviour, for good or bad. In our example above, now consider a fitness club where Samuela is a member. The club has recently, for interests unknown, launched a new programme to help their members reduce obesity. From its database, it has identified Samuela as someone who could benefit from this scheme. They then have reached out to her to partake in the new fitness programme. This prompt can also initiate the process of perspective transformation in Samuela as was shown in the last chapter.

To sum up, reflection of all kinds must involve perspective transformation, and this process can be initiated by different kinds of choice architects, such as the citizens themselves, the state, or commercial parties. Now while the credibility of all such reflective prompts must be assessed properly, if they are delivered by third parties such as agents of the government or commercial choice architects, this is less concerning if these actors deliver purely reflective prompts. Purely reflective prompts, as we will discuss in the next chapter, will include cues and stimuli that enable people to think clearly and articulate their genuine preferences,[3] without necessarily biasing them towards one alternative or the other. If so, then chances of manipulation, as has been recently seen with dark nudge or sludge (a

[3] There is considerable debate in economics versus psychology around whether one's preferences can be genuine. While neoclassical economics often assumes and labels preferences to be consistent and stable, critics suggest that preferences are context-dependent and hard to elicit (or know for individuals). This is also the argument of the nudge where the state or the nudger can get people to where they would like to be with the nudge.

behavioural device designed to make choices, even prosocial ones, more difficult), those that increase frictions to make better choices, are limited.

This, in turn, leads us to another key feature of reflection. It must enable people to assess freely all options and evaluate them, despite anchors and biases of commercial choice architects or biased policy-makers. In the example above, if Samuela is contacted by her fitness gym and prompted to think about joining the new fitness programme that helps her tackle obesity and reach her goals, she is truly empowered to weigh up the true costs and benefits of joining the scheme. If Samuela decides that the cost of this programme outweighs the benefits that are promised to her, she is free to reject this proposal. This is where reflection is different from the nudge, which could have been very difficult to avoid once it has been administered. If her fitness club decided to sign Samuela up automatically into their new fitness programme by default, with the possibility to opt out if she wanted to, Samuela would have been denied the opportunity to evaluate fully if this programme was truly beneficial for her. If Samuela suffered from over-optimism at the moment or status-quo bias, this would make it even harder for Samuela to opt out. Taking away this opportunity from Samuela to gauge her own preferences is limiting her agency to choose what is best for herself and develop her opinions and judgements freely.

For a long time, critics have argued that nudge does help citizens, like Samuela, to reach their end goals whereas a free-choice alternative might in fact be welfare-reducing. There is some truth to this, as reflection has its limitations. To engage with the programme is cognitively burdensome for Samuela. She has to make an active effort to decide for herself. But nudging Samuela into a certain direction can also be welfare-reducing, as paternalism of this kind often generates unequal benefits in the society, while some win, others lose, as we have discussed in the previous chapters (see also Camerer et al. 2003). So, how to reduce this trade-off between increasing agency and reaching effective (optimal) solutions?

This is where we believe nudge+ can make a lot of difference. If this reflection is combined with the nudge, it is possible to overcome the shortcomings of both these policies: nudge and pure reflection, at the same time. That is the role of the reflective prompt in a nudge+, as we will elaborate next. The reflective prompt empowers Samuela and informs her transparently about her choices. Then the nudge makes it easier for her to take decisions which are fully compliant with her own thoughts. How would this look like? An example could be that Samuela is given a chance to think about this new scheme, via a text message, before her fitness gym opts her into it. The ramifications of the nudge in this situation change drastically to when the standard is enforced without her active consideration. Note this is not the same as active choice—where Samuela would have had to make a choice to opt-in, a nudge+ simply requires consideration, where Samuela is given a chance to assess if the nudge is meant for her, given what she knows (or makes) of her own preferences. In many ways, this reflection before the nudge actually unlocks the potential of the nudge, as Samuela is not anchored by it, yet she gets to make the best of it, only if she thinks it is best for her. This is what libertarian paternalism is all about. We will revisit this point several times in the book, but for now, it suffices to say reflection can be initiated by different choice architects in the society, and in all cases, it must transform our perspectives freely, that is, without constraining any of our choices or anchoring our beliefs.

Is Reflection Active or Passive?

Most applications of behavioural public policies include an element of reflection in them, albeit passive. Even when subjected to a nudge, type two processes of our brain, the slower type, are cued to a certain extent, like a fly in the urinal helping a man pee straight or narrowing car lanes from afar before a sharp turn to warn the driver that they need to pay attention to what is going to happen. This is core to the capability of human beings that some kind of cognitive understanding is brought to task at hand falling short of full-scale reflection. For if it were not so, we would have been reduced to bots that lack any social or emotional intelligence. Every nudge or psychological intervention that we face produces a stimulus of kinds. Maybe some are not strong enough for us to engage fully in the process of perspective transformation, they are passive, and we are unable to rationalise the costs and benefits of engaging with the said action. This idea of passive deliberation has been reflected in how policy tools like nudge have evolved over the last decade or so. Cass Sunstein (2016), for example, introduced the idea of the system 2 nudge (also see type 2 nudge by Hansen and Jespersen (2013)), where the focus has been on a nudge that is educative and inspires broad thinking on the part of individuals. A starting point therefore is to dial up these reflective elements in nudge to make it stronger to facilitate perspective transformation. Next are a few examples to make this point more precisely.

Consider a norms nudge. This nudge works by facilitating peer comparison and directing individual behaviours towards what is generally acceptable as a socially good behaviour. When people receive home energy reports that tell them they have underperformed, that is, on average, their energy consumption is more than their neighbours or their previous selves in the last billing period, these low-performing individuals are prompted to conform with what is socially acceptable by trying to reduce their energy demand in the following period. However, to think this nudge is fully automatic[4] on our decision process is misleading. There is some level of passive thinking implicit in the behaviour change that follows this nudge. First, receiving a home energy report might trigger an emotional response, such as guilt or anger, which acts as a stimulus to change behaviours by thinking about these actions. Second, any willingness to conform with the socially acceptable behaviour embodies some thinking on the part of the individual about their own preferences and how they can alter those to match newer, better preferences. Not all people, however, internalise these norms when this process is passive, and therefore this nudge can be seen to fail where norm internalisation is inadequate. Passive reflection in nudge fails to emulate enough stimulus for people to engage in perspective transformation.

Only if the process of reflection is actively strengthened, where the objective of the nudge is clear to citizens who receive it, the nudge will engage citizens who otherwise might be outside its remit. We investigated this by adding different layers of reflection to a social norms nudge directed at promoting climatarian diets (Banerjee and Picard 2023). In this experiment, 5,555 British individuals were randomly assigned to four different experimental vignettes. In the first control condition, people were asked to order a food item from a set of menus. In the second nudge condition, individuals were additionally exposed to a social norm message that emphasised increasing vegetarianism in the United Kingdom. In the last two conditions, this nudge was preceded by two active prompts of reflection: first some were asked to reveal their personal intentions towards climatarian diets randomly, and second, they were asked to think, given their personal intentions, if they would be willing to align them with the said social norms. Their experimental results indicated that when an active

[4] Some authors have recently claimed that if the nudge happens far distant from the point of decision-making, such as the feedback letters, it does not qualify to be a nudge as it fails to change the immediate choice environment (see Carrel et al. 2023).

reflection was embedded along with the nudge, individuals almost doubled their intentions for climate-friendly diets, on average, versus the standalone social norms nudge.

However, this element of passive reflection is not just limited to norms nudges, but is also visible in other kinds of nudge. Consider the commitment device. A commitment contract prompts people to commit to a certain behaviour and works by reinforcing this commitment towards some welfare-improving actions (Bryan et al. 2010). However, all commitments by design must involve some form of thinking which precedes the signature of the contract (Banerjee and John 2024). People need to think before they sign up. Drawing on this passive reflection can facilitate a greater uptake of the contract by those who understand and conform with its goals. In another experiment, we tested this experimentally by designing a commitment contract explicitly as an active mechanism design. Here, British individuals were first asked to think about a pledge for consuming a climate-friendly diet, and they were given the option to either pledge in favour of it, reject it, or be indifferent. We then tested two different versions of this pledge—one where the respondents were further asked to choose a nudge to their liking, based on what they thought could be a barrier to their goals (of consuming a climate-friendly diet), or we automatically assigned them the green menu if they made a pledge. The first option resembled a full-on think, where the participants think all the way through, whereas the second was a nudge+, where first respondents are encouraged to think of their own goals, following which the nudge kicks in to make it more convenient for them to achieve these goals. Our findings indicated that introducing this active mechanism in the commitment contracts, in the form of the nudge+, reduced orders over carbon-intensive food items compared to both the full-on think or the standalone default nudge. This also was better compared to a no-manipulation condition (Banerjee et al. 2023).

Just like the norms nudge study, this example suggests that in order to harness the benefits of reflection, it is necessary that we must fully and actively engage with the process of perspective transformation. Passive thinking, while effective at times, can be weak and might not fully translate the goals and objectives of the public policy at hand. In such cases, we can dial up reflection by actively engaging them in a process of behaviour change. Nonetheless, active reflection brings forward the caveat, that it can also backfire on people, who now fully realise their own preferences and have no intentions to change their current behaviours. We defer a discussion on this case until the next part of this book, when we discuss the ethics of such behaviour change in greater detail.

Is Reflection Conscious or Not?

We now turn to another key feature of reflection—its relationship with cognitive effort and the development of experiential learning. As discussed earlier, engaging in reflection requires conscious mental engagement and exerts a measurable cognitive load. Reflection, particularly in its active form, demands deliberate attentional resources and metacognitive control (Schraw and Dennison 1994; Dunlosky and Metcalfe 2008). Repeated engagement in such effortful reflective processes, however, can yield long-term benefits by facilitating experiential learning—learning derived from direct experience that becomes internalised over time (Kolb 1984; Moon 2004). In Kolb's experiential learning cycle, reflection plays a critical role in converting lived experience into abstract conceptualisation, which is then tested in future behaviour. When reflection is repeated over time, it enables the consolidation of insights, which in turn reduces the cognitive burden of future decision-making. This iterative cycle contributes to what is often described as learning to learn—the development of self-regulated, adaptive cognition.

Crucially, this process can, with repetition, become increasingly automatic. Evidence from cognitive psychology supports the idea that repeated exposure to similar decision environments, coupled with reflective learning, can produce heuristic responses that feel intuitive or reflexive, yet are grounded in prior deliberation (Kahneman and Klein 2009; Ericsson and Lehmann 1996). This is not to say that the underlying learning is unconscious; rather, it reflects a transition from conscious reflective engagement to routinised competence—a hallmark of expertise development (Chi et al. 1988). In this way, reflection can reduce its own burden over time, enabling individuals to respond to familiar stimuli with efficient, contextually appropriate judgements shaped by prior perspective transformations.

However, the benefits of such internalised learning depend critically on the quality of the reflection that preceded it. As Mezirow (1997) and Cranton (2006) argue, transformative learning arises not simply from experience but from critical reflection upon that experience—particularly in relation to core values, assumptions, and meaning structures. When active reflection is missing, and individuals instead form habits or conditioned responses without adequate critical engagement, their reactions to stimuli become prone to error, bias, and rigidity. This aligns with findings in behavioural decision-making, where over-reliance on intuitive judgements in the absence of reflective calibration can lead to systematic errors (Frederick 2005; Kahneman 2011). While reflection can lay the foundation for experiential learning and adaptive expertise, it must be periodically renewed—especially when situational changes render past experience less relevant or obsolete. This is also where an instrument like the nudge+ can really deliver gains, especially when people are encouraged to think time-to-time with the nudge+, to revisit their goals and preferences.

Consider the following example of using a Global Positioning System (GPS) as a navigational guide when we are driving. The GPS is a classic case of a navigability nudge (Sunstein 2015) that 'does not impose sanctions or costs' (p. 208) but gets people to where they need to be. We have argued in the past that such a nudge often relies on some accumulated wisdom, the experiential learning, so to say, of using this tool, that when combined with the nudge, it improves the user's experience of a GPS device (Banerjee and John 2024). But GPS devices sometimes fail to update in real time. Often a GPS device works with a mapping signal, the accuracy of which could deteriorate for several reasons, such as loss of internet connection or an error in the map. In these circumstances, when fearing being misguided by a GPS device, people often resort to our own cognitive resources in finding the right direction, such as asking a passer-by, using a compass, or finding a physical map, often using a sense of direction or intuition until the GPS resumes functionality again. This suggests that experiential learning helps create an active user and makes for a more efficient and less risky use of the device. If such encounters happen repeatedly, people can become very skilful at handling such odd situations,[5] which can help them avoid accidents but still benefit from the support these devices can provide the intelligent user. This process of active reflection can seem to end in an automatic experiential learning experience for users.

Another example shows how this process of habituation through reflection works. The onset of the pandemic, five years ago, necessitated a

[5] Sanchayan had his own experience once when he was driving in India. While driving to a completely new place, totally reliant on the maps, he ended up at a pond, where the maps constantly suggested there was a road. Thanks to this experience, he now periodically seeks local guidance at different milestones when he is enroute to a new place by car in a new country.

complete change in personal daily routines. Things we were habituated with, were suddenly made void. One such habit was travelling to work and interacting with people physically. The spread of the virus meant most countries curtailed commuting and imposed standards for remote working (Banerjee et al. 2021). A change of this size wiped away our current reflexes and habits. We could no longer use our existing shortcuts to get work done. For example, we stopped taking the same mode of transport, we did not visit our favourite coffee shop, and we did not have face-to-face meetings to attend. We were suddenly required to adapt, mostly without any previous experience about how to do these new forms of working. We had to learn to respond to this new stimulus. All of us needed to think afresh of the best ways to work remotely and regain our comfort levels. There was clearly a psychological cost, so much so, that our social interlinkages were compromised. For example, a Harvard Business Review survey, carried out in the early days of the pandemic, revealed challenges for managers who felt they could not trust their team members. Sharon Parker and colleagues (2020) in this study, examined how the abrupt shift to remote work during the COVID-19 pandemic exposed gaps in managerial preparedness and eroded trust in remote workplace contexts. Based on survey responses from roughly 215 supervisors and managers, nearly 40 per cent reported low self-confidence in their ability to lead remote teams effectively. This lack of managerial self-efficacy contributed to negative attitudes towards remote work and scepticism about employees' motivation and competence. In reaction to this uncertainty, many managers resorted to micromanagement—high-frequency check-ins, spontaneous monitoring, and heightened scrutiny through communication tools such as Slack or Teams. While respondents noted that regular, predictable check-ins can be helpful, the unpredictability and perception of surveillance often increased worker stress and undermined productivity and engagement. The cumulative picture painted by the study was troubling: many managers lacked confidence in their remote leadership capabilities, expressed distrust in their employees, and relied on intrusive oversight methods that paradoxically reduce performance and well-being. The authors recommended that organisations address this by enhancing managerial training in remote work practices, shifting towards autonomy-supportive approaches, and promoting management that emphasises outcomes rather than visible activity. So did we do away with remote working?

The answer is no as things changed drastically over time. With more time and training to adapt to remote working, and more thoughtful learning on how to function in this new situation which now appears normal, we have reached a stage where we have become comfortable again with how things become, with strong preferences to stay in the current status quo rather than return to old patterns of working. Recent research suggests that such remote working-from-home have now become normalised globally, with a large number of countries gravitating towards a one-day remote working rule, albeit with variations such as in Asia (Aksoy et al. 2025). While this example makes a strong case for our preference for the status quo, it also shows that repeated thoughtful actions help us develop an unconscious and conditioned reflex to a stimulus which then benefits from this bias. We end with an unconscious experiential learning experience that ties us to such biases. Does this mean a pitfall of thinking is unconscious actions? The answer is not really, as we argue next.

The preceding examples support the notion that repeated thoughtful actions can, over time, give rise to routinised or automatic responses—what might be described as conditioned cognitive reflexes. However, this beneficial form of experiential learning depends critically on the quality and depth of prior engagement. If reflection is passive, fragmentary, or repeated too infrequently—such that it fades into the background of conscious awareness—it may fail to produce durable or accessible learning. In such cases, individuals may not consciously associate a later stimulus with the reflective process that initially accompanied it. This marks a fundamental pitfall of shallow or unconscious thinking: the absence of an accessible cognitive trace linking stimulus to learning outcome.

When faced with a future stimulus that is similar but not identical to one encountered before, people may default to heuristics formed during the earlier episode. Yet if the original reflection was superficial or inattentive, these heuristic responses risk being misaligned with current context. As Kahneman (2011) notes, while heuristics can be efficient, they often substitute questions and misapply prior reasoning when similarity is only superficial. In such situations, individuals act from what might be described as 'cognitive residue'—residual knowledge retained from a poorly consolidated reflective experience, often inaccessible to introspection or deliberate control. These phenomena resemble what some describe as a sense of déjà vu: a vague feeling of familiarity accompanied by an inability to recall the specific context in which the original experience occurred (Brown 2004). From a cognitive standpoint, this reflects the distinction between implicit and explicit memory systems. While implicit memory may prompt action through familiarity, it does not support the conscious appraisal or adaptation needed for perspective transformation (Squire and Dede 2015).

Thus, without conscious awareness during the initial reflection, future judgements and actions may be driven by partial or decontextualised experiential knowledge, applied indiscriminately to novel situations. As we argued in our earlier work (Banerjee and John 2024, 9–10), reflective prompts that fail to engage individuals in deep processing are unlikely to produce lasting learning. This has direct implications for the design of public policy interventions. Policy tools that rely on passive or automatic elements—such as many system 1 nudges—may trigger behavioural responses anchored in prior habits or associations, but without stimulating the active cognitive engagement necessary for transformative learning. Although such tools may appear effective in the short term, they risk bypassing the reflective mechanisms required for generalisation, adaptation, or normative reasoning.

To benefit fully from unconscious or automatic experiential learning—particularly in ways that reduce cognitive costs over time—it is essential that individuals first engage in active, deliberate reflection. The transition from conscious reasoning to unconscious competence, as described in skill acquisition theory (Fitts and Posner 1967; Anderson 1982), depends on the integrity of early-stage learning processes. Without these, subsequent behaviours may reflect familiarity rather than understanding, and rigidity rather than adaptability. Ultimately, it is the quality of conscious engagement at the outset that determines whether experiential learning can support future reflection, adaptation, and perspective transformation.

A Taxonomy of Reflection

Our classification of reflection—as either an active or passive process that results in either conscious or unconscious experiential learning—allows us to propose a taxonomy situating different types of reflection tools according to these dimensions. Table 3.1 presents this framework. Different behavioural public policy instruments can be located within this typology, depending on the nature of reflection they require and the form of experiential learning they enable.

Consider first the top-left quadrant: tools that foster active reflection and culminate in conscious, thoughtful learning. These interventions demand that individuals fully engage with a process of perspective

Table 3.1 Classification of behavioural public policies by type of reflection

Activity level ➔/ consciousness ↓	*Active*	*Passive*
Conscious	**Pure reflection** (e.g., citizen jury, forum, active mechanism design)	**Quasi reflection** (e.g., commitment contract, norms nudge)
Unconscious	**Quasi reflection** (e.g., GPS device, status quo default)	**Pure Reflexion** (e.g., fly in the urinal, priming cue)

transformation in response to a stimulus. Reflection here is deliberate and sustained. Tools such as citizen juries, deliberative forums, or active mechanism design approaches (e.g., participatory budgeting) exemplify this category. These tools aim not just to shape behaviour, but to cultivate new ways of thinking. In doing so, they reflect the fullest form of reflection envisioned in this framework.

Now consider the bottom-right quadrant: tools that involve passive reflection and produce an unconscious form of experiential learning. In these cases, individuals are typically unaware that any reflection has occurred. They retain the effects of a past experience—often through familiarity or learned response—but cannot trace these effects back to a specific stimulus. This category includes cue-based system 1 nudges, such as placing a fly in a urinal, using subliminal messages, or employing environmental priming. These tools can effectively alter simple, habitual behaviours but are limited in their generalisability. They struggle to influence domains requiring deeper deliberation or abstract thinking, such as civic participation or climate action. Their effectiveness, while contextually powerful, tends to be narrow in scope and short-lived in cognitive imprint.

Between these poles lie tools that we classify as quasi-reflective, found in the remaining two quadrants. These tools occupy a middle ground and can be dialled up towards more reflective engagement if designed accordingly. In the top-right cell are tools involving passive reflection but resulting in conscious experiential learning. These include certain system 2 nudges such as commitment devices or norms-based interventions, which may not require deep deliberation at the outset but still prompt recipients to reflect enough to form stable, conscious associations with their new behaviours. These tools rely on moments of cognitive engagement, even if not continuously or effortfully sustained.

In the bottom-left cell are tools involving active engagement but that result in unconscious learning. A good example is the use of navigability nudges like GPS systems. These require active decision-making during first or failed encounters, prompting problem-solving and trial-and-error. Over time, however, users develop an intuitive familiarity with the system that allows them to rely on it almost automatically. Reflection, in this case, transitions from conscious to unconscious as the experiential learning consolidates. Importantly, when the tool fails (e.g., due to signal loss or incorrect directions), users are pushed back into active cognition—drawing on previous learning to devise alternatives. Such tools demonstrate a dynamic interplay between reflection and automation, between cognitive effort and fluency.

This taxonomy of reflection in behavioural tools helps clarify the mechanisms by which policy interventions shape not just decisions but the thinking behind them. It also underlines the importance of designing for reflection explicitly—recognising that both the quality of engagement and the nature of the learning it produces critically determine a tool's long-term effectiveness.

Conditions for Reflection

Pure reflection is arguably the most cognitively demanding form of reflection. When individuals are required to engage actively in this process, they must expend significant mental resources in order to undergo perspective transformation. Yet, as discussed earlier, it is not easy to sustain such a demanding activity. People frequently find better uses of their time than to deliberate deeply on every decision. Even more fundamentally, individuals may be constrained by their own psychological or situational limitations that prevent them from fully completing a process of reflection. We propose that two important caveats underlie the capacity for reflection.

The first caveat is foundational: to engage in reflection, one must begin with a thought. Yet this seemingly basic requirement is not trivial. Reflection, as noted earlier in the chapter, risks becoming an infinite regress of introspection unless anchored in a specific stimulus. While it is reasonable to assume that most people engage in some degree of thinking, the depth and quality of such engagement varies greatly across individuals and contexts. The second caveat follows from the first: assuming that one initiates reflection, a meaningful transformation of perspective also requires the willingness to follow through with the implications of this new understanding. These two challenges suggest that there are core conditions that must be met for reflection to lead to beneficial behavioural change. The ability to meet these conditions may distinguish more reflective individuals from others. We discuss these conditions below.

Returning to the earlier example of buyer's remorse, we observed that guilt or regret may trigger a cognitive stimulus that sets off the process of reflection. However, not all decisions provoke this kind of reflection. People frequently make impulsive purchases—such as buying a new smartphone or gaming console—without experiencing subsequent regret. This is often because such decisions do not violate any internal moral standard or perceived norm. In the case of the car buyer, for instance, if the individual is extremely wealthy, the emotional impact of the purchase may be negligible. Even if others point out the irrationality of the decision, the buyer may remain unmoved, unwilling to question their own judgement. This illustrates a failure to enter into a reflective state despite receiving relevant social cues. Alternatively, a person may have come into unexpected wealth—such as through a windfall gain—and may lack a sense of stewardship that often accompanies earned income (Oliver 2024). In such situations, there is little motivation to reflect because there is no felt moral conflict or perceived error in judgement.

These examples point to a lack of moral or practical conscientiousness—the sense that one's actions have implications that ought to be considered. This absence of inner moral dialogue, where individuals fail to examine the opportunity costs of their actions, can lead to poor self-regulation or to socially suboptimal outcomes. Sometimes these failures remain internal, but often they have externalities. Consider again the case of people who are unmoved by a norms-based intervention promoting plant-based diets. In such studies, a subset of individuals appears resistant to the social cue. This resistance likely stems from the same psychological dynamic as the car buyer: a diminished sensitivity to whether their actions have broader consequences. Although this behaviour might appear selfish, it is not necessarily irrational from a neoclassical economic perspective, where individuals are assumed to act in pursuit of their own preferences. However, when private actions have public consequences, as with diet and environmental sustainability, some level of conscientious awareness is necessary for reflection and change.

Conscientiousness, therefore, is a necessary condition for initiating reflection. Without an internal standard of what is right or wrong, good, or bad, individuals are unlikely to engage in self-directed deliberation. Put differently, in the absence of a conscience, long-term behaviour change is difficult—if not impossible—because individuals will consistently see their actions as justified. Importantly, conscientiousness is not fixed; it can be cultivated. Education, deliberation, and targeted informational interventions can help individuals become more reflective. For instance, climate education is increasingly linked to the rise of global moral concern. A multi-country study found that between 2013 and 2019, the proportion of individuals who saw climate change as a serious threat increased by 10 percentage points, largely attributed to rising awareness and educational efforts (Fagan and Huang 2019). In another survey across 17 developed economies, 80 per cent of respondents reported being willing to change how they live in order to mitigate climate change (Bell et al. 2021). This suggests that moral conscientiousness—when activated—is a crucial precondition for reflection to unfold.

However, conscientiousness alone is not sufficient. Some individuals may possess a conscience but still fail to act reflectively. This brings us to the second necessary condition: goal orientation. Reflection is unlikely to lead to behavioural change unless the goals of the individual are aligned—at least partially—with the goals of the policy or intervention. As Christine Clavien (2018) and Samuli Reijula and Ralph Hertwig (2022) argue, individuals are more likely to be moved by a reflective policy intervention when they share some of the values or preferences that the intervention seeks to promote. This alignment provides what they term a 'shared preference justification'. In our own study using a social norms intervention on vegetarian diets, we found that participants who already had weak or no intention to reduce meat consumption were those least moved by the intervention. Without an anchoring personal goal, the stimulus failed to activate any meaningful process of reflection.

It is certainly possible to possess a conscience without having goal orientation, but such cases often fail to produce lasting behavioural change. Conscientiousness allows people to judge whether something is right or wrong; goal orientation gives them the motivation to act upon that judgement. For example, many individuals may believe that reducing emissions is important but may not act on that belief unless their personal goals (e.g., health, finance, identity) align with the behavioural recommendations (e.g., eating less meat). Without that alignment, even the most morally aware individuals may fail to act. In this way, conscientiousness and goal orientation function jointly as preconditions for the kind of deep, deliberate reflection that leads to sustained behavioural change.

A final condition concerns the capacity to act after reflection has occurred. Even if individuals are both morally conscientious and goal-oriented, they may fail to follow through. Reflection must be accompanied by behavioural implementation. Returning to the car buyer, even if they come to recognise that their decision was imprudent, they must still exert the effort to cancel the transaction. Similarly, meat eaters persuaded by social norms still need to translate that shift in perspective into a change in dietary habits. This is where willpower and motivation become essential. Decades of research in psychology have demonstrated that the gap between intentions and behaviour is often wide (Ajzen 1991; Fishbein and Ajzen 2011). People regularly fail to do what they intend to, due to competing priorities, emotional temptations, or procrastination (Hassan et al. 2016). The ability to persist with goals requires self-regulation, including both self-control—resisting short-term temptations—and grit, the sustained effort over time (Duckworth and Gross 2014). At the core of both, however, is motivation. Motivated individuals are more likely to translate their reflections into consistent behavioural routines.

To summarise, three conditions shape the capacity for reflection: (1) conscientiousness—the internal moral or evaluative compass; (2) goal orientation—alignment between personal and policy objectives; and (3) motivation—the capacity to follow through with new perspectives. While the first two are necessary to initiate and guide reflection, the third is sufficient to ensure that reflection results in durable behavioural change. When these conditions are met, people are capable of engaging in the kind of active, conscious reflection that this chapter has examined.

The Need to Support Reflective Processes

We hope, by now, it has become reasonably clear what reflection is and what it entails. To summarise: reflection is an act of thinking which ultimately leads to newer perspectives. These new perspectives are either completely dissociated with our prior beliefs and therefore end up generating some cognitive dissonance where we might revoke our actions of the past in engaging with new behaviours, or they invigorate these prior beliefs, making us believe in them even more than what we did before. The process of reflection to fulfil perspective transformation must be active, although we discussed cases of passive reflection where this process might be prompted outside our control, and hence we do not own this process of behaviour change. Reflection also ends in a state of conscious or unconscious experiential learning, the former where we retain the knowledge of this process of perspective transformation and ably link our newer perspectives with stimuli of a similar nature if they were to arise in future. Such a conditioned reflex of experiential learning reduces the costs of reflecting for us. If unconscious, such reflexes decrease our likelihood of getting it consistently right.

We also discussed conditions that facilitate this process of reflection successfully, with conscientiousness and goal orientation being necessary to kickstart it, but motivation as sufficient to deliver on the goals of reflection and perspective transformation. Nonetheless, these necessary and sufficient conditions tell us, not everyone can be equally good thinkers. While some are naturally better at thinking, others might be less skilled. And this is where some signal and guidance from policy-makers, as we hinted towards this possibility, at the beginning of this chapter, might be helpful in enabling everyone to be at par with each other and equally engage with tools that require watchfulness and attention.

In the next chapter, we discuss avenues to dial up these pure- and quasi-reflective tools, so that people can always use them, even when they fail to fulfil all these conditions themselves. This is where the merits of nudge+ lie—they make reflection accessible to all as mini-reflective prompts embedded in a conventional nudge or one that follows full-blown reflective sessions.

References

Ajzen, Icek. 1991. The theory of planned behavior. *Organizational Behavior and Human Decision Processes* 50 (2): 179–211. https://doi.org/10.1016/0749-5978(91)90020-T.

Aksoy, Cevat Giray, Nicholas Bloom, Steven J. Davis, Victoria Marino, and Cem Ozguzel. 2025. *Remote work, employee mix, and performance*. National Bureau of Economic Research.

Anderson, John R. 1982. Acquisition of cognitive skill. *Psychological Review* 89 (4): 369. https://doi.org/10.1037/0033-295X.89.4.369.

Banerjee, Sanchayan, and Peter John. 2024. Nudge plus: Incorporating reflection into behavioral public policy. *Behavioural Public Policy* 8 (1): 69–84. https://doi.org/10.1017/bpp.2021.6.

Banerjee, Sanchayan, and Julien Picard. 2023. Thinking through norms can make them more effective. Experimental evidence on reflective climate policies in the

UK. *Journal of Behavioral and Experimental Economics* 106:102024. https://doi.org/10.1016/j.socec.2023.102024.

Banerjee, Sanchayan, Manu Savani, and Ganga Shreedhar. 2021. Public support for 'soft' versus 'hard' public policies: Review of the evidence. *Journal of Behavioral Public Administration* 4 (2). https://doi.org/10.30636/jbpa.42.220.

Banerjee, Sanchayan, Matteo M. Galizzi, Peter John, and Susana Mourato. 2023. Sustainable dietary choices improved by reflection before a nudge in an online experiment. *Nature Sustainability* 6 (12): 1632–1642. https://doi.org/10.1038/s41893-023-01235-0.

Bell, James, Jacob Poushter, Moira Fagan, and Christine Huang. 2021. In response to climate change, citizens in advanced economies are willing to Alter how they live and work. https://www.pewresearch.org/global/2021/09/14/in-response-to-climate-change-citizens-in-advanced-economies-are-willing-to-alter-how-they-live-and-work/.

Boud, D., & Walker, D. 1998. *Promoting reflection in professional courses: The challenge of context. Studies in higher education* 23(2), 191–206.

Brown, Alan S. 2004. *The déjà vu experience*. Psychology Press.

Bryan, Gharad, Dean Karlan, and Scott Nelson. 2010. Commitment devices. *Annual Review of Economics* 2 (1): 671–698. https://doi.org/10.1146/annurev.economics.102308.124324.

Camerer, Colin, Samuel Issacharoff, George Loewenstein, Ted O'donoghue, and Matthew Rabin. 2003. Regulation for conservatives: Behavioral economics and the case for "asymmetric paternalism". *University of Pennsylvania Law Review* 151 (3): 1211–1254. https://doi.org/10.2307/3312889.

Carrel, C., Gavard-Perret, M. L., & Caldara, C. 2023. Factors of effectiveness of green nudges for more ecoresponsible behaviour–Systematic review and research directions. Recherche et Applications en Marketing (English Edition), 38(3), 32–76.

Chi, Michelene T. H., Robert Glaser, and Marshall J. Farr. 1988. *The nature of expertise*. Psychology Press.

Clavien, Christine. 2018. Ethics of nudges: A general framework with a focus on shared preference justifications. *Journal of Moral Education* 47 (3): 366–382. https://doi.org/10.1080/03057240.2017.1408577.

Cranton, Patricia. 2006. Fostering authentic relationships in the transformative classroom. *New Directions for Adult and Continuing Education* 2006 (109): 5–13. https://doi.org/10.1002/ace.203.

Dewey, John. 1933. *How we think*. DigiCat.

Duckworth, Angela, and James J. Gross. 2014. Self-control and grit: Related but separable determinants of success. *Current Directions in Psychological Science* 23 (5): 319–325. https://doi.org/10.1177/0963721414541462.

Dunlosky, John, and Janet Metcalfe. 2008. *Metacognition*. Sage Publications.

Ericsson, K. Anders, and Andreas C. Lehmann. 1996. Expert and exceptional performance: Evidence of maximal adaptation to task constraints. *Annual Review of Psychology* 47 (1): 273–305. https://doi.org/10.1146/annurev.psych.47.1.273.

Fagan, Moira, and Christine Huang. 2019. A look at how people around the world view climate change. *Pew Research Center*. https://www.pewresearch.org/short-reads/2019/04/18/a-look-at-how-people-around-the-world-view-climate-change/.

Festinger, L. 1957. A theory of cognitive dissonance. *New York*.

Fishbein, Martin, and Icek Ajzen. 2011. *Predicting and changing behavior: The reasoned action approach*. Psychology Press.

Fitts, Paul M., and Michael I. Posner. 1967. Human performance. Brooks/Cole.

Fonagy, P., Gergely, G., & Jurist, E. L. 2018. *Affect regulation, mentalization and the development of the self*. Routledge

Flavell, J. H. 1979. Metacognition and cognitive monitoring: A new area of cognitive–developmental inquiry. *American Psychologist* 34 (10): 906.

Frederick, Shane. 2005. Cognitive reflection and decision making. *Journal of Economic Perspectives* 19 (4): 25–42. https://doi.org/10.1257/089533005775196732.

Gilovich, Thomas, and Victoria Husted Medvec. 1995. The experience of regret: What, when, and why. *Psychological Review* 102 (2): 379. https://doi.org/10.1037/0033-295X.102.2.379.

Hansen, Pelle Guldborg, and Andreas Maaløe Jespersen. 2013. Nudge and the manipulation of choice: A framework for the responsible use of the nudge approach to behaviour change in public policy. *European Journal of Risk Regulation* 4 (1): 3–28. https://doi.org/10.1017/S1867299X00002762.

Hattie, J. 2008. Visible learning: A synthesis of over 800 meta-analyses relating to achievement. routledge.

Hassan, Louise M., Edward Shiu, and Deirdre Shaw. 2016. Who says there is an intention–behaviour gap? Assessing the empirical evidence of an intention–behaviour gap in ethical consumption. *Journal of Business Ethics* 136 (2): 219–236. https://doi.org/10.1007/s10551-014-2440-0.

Hertwig, Ralph, and Till Grüne-Yanoff. 2017. Nudging and boosting: Steering or empowering good decisions. *Perspectives on Psychological Science* 12 (6): 973–986. https://doi.org/10.1177/1745691617702496.

Kahneman, Daniel. 2011. *Thinking, fast and slow*. Macmillan.

Kahneman, Daniel, and Gary Klein. 2009. Conditions for intuitive expertise: A failure to disagree. *American Psychologist* 64 (6): 515. https://doi.org/10.1037/a0016755.

Kolb, David A. 1984. *Experiential learning: Experience as the source of learning and development*. Englewood Cliffs, NJ: Prentice Hall.

Kolb, David A. (2014). *Experiential learning: Experience as the source of learning and development*. FT press.

King, P. M., & Kitchener, K. S. 1994. Developing Reflective Judgment: Understanding and Promoting Intellectual Growth and Critical Thinking in Adolescents and Adults. Jossey-Bass Higher and Adult Education Series and Jossey-Bass Social and Behavioral Science Series. Jossey-Bass, 350 Sansome Street, San Francisco, CA 94104-1310.

Korthagen, Fred, and Angelo Vasalos. 2005. Levels in reflection: Core reflection as a means to enhance professional growth. *Teachers and Teaching* 11 (1): 47–71. https://doi.org/10.1080/1354060042000337093.

Luyten, P., Campbell, C., Allison, E., & Fonagy, P. 2020. The mentalizing approach to psychopathology: State of the art and future directions. *Annual Review of Clinical Psychology* 16 (1): 297–325.

MacLeod, A., Gordon, J., & Mann, K. 2009. Reflection and Reflective Practice in Health Professions Education: *A Systematic Review.*

Mamede, S., Schmidt, H. G., & Rikers, R. 2007. Diagnostic errors and reflective practice in medicine. *Journal of evaluation in clinical practice, 13(1), 138–145.*

Mezirow, Jack. 1991. *Transformative dimensions of adult learning.* Jossey-Bass, 350 Sansome Street, San Francisco, CA 94104-1310.

Mezirow, Jack. 1997. Transformation theory out of context. *Adult Education Quarterly* 48 (1): 60–62. https://doi.org/10.1177/074171369704800105.

Moon, Jennifer A. 2004. *A handbook of reflective and experiential learning: Theory and practice.* Routledge.

Oliver, Adam. 2024. If you've earned it, you deserve it: Ultimatums, with Lego. *Behavioural Public Policy* 8 (2): 395–402. https://doi.org/10.1017/bpp.2021.29.

Parker, Sharon K., Caroline Knight, and Anita C. Keller. 2020. Remote managers are having trust issues. *Harvard Business Review.* https://hbr.org/2020/07/remote-managers-are-having-trust-issues.

Reijula, Samuli, and Ralph Hertwig. 2022. Self-nudging and the citizen choice architect. *Behavioural Public Policy* 6 (1): 119–149. https://doi.org/10.1017/bpp.2020.5.

Schön, Donald A. 1986. *The reflective practitioner: How professionals think in action.* Taylor & Francis.

Schraw, Gregory, and Rayne Sperling Dennison. 1994. Assessing metacognitive awareness. *Contemporary Educational Psychology* 19 (4): 460–475. https://doi.org/10.1006/ceps.1994.1033.

Squire, Larry R., and Adam J. O. Dede. 2015. Conscious and unconscious memory systems. *Cold Spring Harbor Perspectives in Biology* 7 (3): a021667.

Sunstein, Cass R. 2015. Nudges do not undermine human agency. *Journal of Consumer Policy* 38 (3): 207–210. https://doi.org/10.1007/s10603-015-9289-1.

Sunstein, Cass R. 2016. People prefer system 2 nudges (kind of). *Duke Law Journal* 66:121. https://doi.org/10.2139/ssrn.2731868.

Vygotsky, L. S. 1978. Mind in society: The development of higher psychological processes (Vol. 86). Harvard university press.

Taylor, Edward W. 2007. An update of transformative learning theory: A critical review of the empirical research (1999–2005). *International Journal of Lifelong Education* 26 (2): 173–191. https://doi.org/10.1080/02601370701219475.

Zeelenberg, Marcel, and Rik Pieters. 2007. A theory of regret regulation 1.0. *Journal of Consumer Psychology* 17 (1): 3–18. https://doi.org/10.1207/s15327663jcp1701_3.

Zimmerman, B. J. (2002). Becoming a self-regulated learner: An overview. Theory into practice, 41(2), 64–70.

CHAPTER 4

Reflection with a Nudge: Nudge+

It is not possible for all of us to think consistently and uniformly about a decision. In the last chapter, we showed how reflection often calls for different conditions to be met before people can engage with this process fully. It is necessary for us to be conscientious and goal-oriented to make use of psychological cues and kickstart perspective transformation. We also discussed that we must be motivated to go through with this process once it has begun. The difference in our ability to think creates diversity in our views and opinions. This, in turn, creates opportunities for us to think, and to choose from a new set of options. To some extent, differences in thinking abilities are important as it creates enough variance for deliberation. How would it look if all of us thought the same things at the same time? We would become a country of bots, all prone to the same errors of judgement. Fortunately, we are not like that.

However, there are also downsides of creating too large differences in the thinking ability of different citizens. If thinking differences are too wide, where some people lack the basic capability to reason and decide for themselves, we run the risk of widening existing inequalities in societies, especially when some public policies that require thinking are at play. A lot of our differences in thinking are to do with our genes (Plomin and von Stumm, 2018). Many others are to do with how we are educated to think or trained to live, or the environment and ecosystem we find ourselves to be in, while growing up, working, and living our adult lives

© The Author(s), under exclusive license to Springer Nature Switzerland AG 2026

S. Banerjee, P. John, *Nudge+*,
https://doi.org/10.1007/978-3-032-13261-1_4

(Bronfenbrenner, 1979). These disparities, attributed to differences in our abilities, in reasoning different issues, create situations where some people benefit more than others from stronger cognitive skills of reasoning. One could also loosely relate this idea to the theory of human capabilities developed by Amartya Sen and colleagues (Nussbaum and Sen 1993; Sugden 1993), which posits a person's social position to be an outcome of their own ability to do different things and function in the society. We take a reduced view of this capabilities approach in this book, where essentially, we focus on psychological capabilities of humans to think and reflect before they act.

Differences in our reflective capabilities make our task even harder, especially as we envisage a future of capable humans who must reason their own decisions and know when to switch between automatic and reflective cognition. What happens when someone fails to do this? Are we back to the beginning, where our thinking humans are demoted to being considered as the rational actor who is prone to errors and biases as typically conceptualised by a standard economics textbook? Then, are they people who simply amount to being flawed and irrational in the strictest neoclassical sense of economic decision-making? We argue that in these circumstances, appropriate signalling by policy-makers can guide thinking humans to decide effectively, and such tools should be agency building at the very least. If these tools bypass people's agency, under the false pretence that being watchful of these interventions preserves their autonomy and liberty, then they are simply unreasonable for people who already lack such psychological capabilities. If not, this creates a paradox: a policy designed to guide individuals who are assumed to be insufficiently capable of making such decisions on their own simultaneously relies on those same individuals to make an active choice to opt in or out.

This is a fundamental challenge of a policy like the nudge. While a nudge does not reduce available choices for anyone, its design manipulates people unknowingly, where only those who are watchful of the nudge exercise their agency to engage with it voluntarily. For the unwatchful, they run the risk of being anchored by the nudge. This is often what is known as the non-alien control of a policy (Schmidt 2017). It is as if you feel you oversee making your own decisions, but you have been permitted by someone else to make this choice. Consider two situations. Situation A: a friend calls you and asks you to donate to a charity. Situation B: a friend adds you to an online messaging forum with other common friends in the group. Then they call on you in the group and request your donation.

Situation B is markedly different from situation A. It has the added element of being watched—you are put in the spotlight (see Gilovich et al. 2000). One might argue that in both situations, your freedom to choose how much to donate, if at all anything, is the same. You could refuse your friend equally in both settings, which makes both situations liberty preserving. Yet they are not equivalent, for if you refuse your friend for a donation in situation B you run the risk of undermining your reputation in front of your wider social network. Being put in this spotlight nudges you in a way to donate, which might be against your personal preferences. Unless you think about this actively, you are likely to donate more in situation B than in situation A.

Often, when citizens are nudged, they are moved towards one decision more than the other, which unduly affects their choices to be made. So, even though a nudge does not limit people's available choices, they often manifest different anchors in their perceived choices. It requires some skills to then opt out of this nudge, that not all have. But does this mean reliance on policy tools like the nudge is always bad? No, not quite. But it is important to hold the nudge accountable of this prerequisite that citizens should be made watchful of the nudge to avoid non-alien control, if they are not already. We need to find a way that empowers citizens before we nudge them. One way of doing this, as we will discuss here, is to dial up the reflective capacities of thinking humans in society, so they can wilfully engage with a nudge, being aware of its limitations and effects fully.

When set up in this way, a policy tool that will empower people to build on their psychological capabilities to reflect and engage fully with a nudge will be called a nudge+. The nudge and its reflective plus are critical to this new hybrid tool we describe. This is because nudge+ is designed in a way where each standalone technique of behaviour change overcomes the limitations of the other, in some ways mutually reinforcing the effects each tool can have on citizens. We discuss the premise to nudge+ in this chapter. We do this, first by identifying ways in which reflective prompts can upgrade nudge into various nudge+ interventions. The discussion then turns to whether reflection happens inside or outside the remit of a conventional nudge. In the second half of the chapter, we elaborate on some of the varied roles that reflection has when it is combined with a nudge.

Reflection Outside the Nudge

It was the traditional view of nudge+ that reflection would occur outside the nudge rather than seeking to make nudge more reflective in itself. This had been the guiding principle to nudge+ since John et al. (2009) first put forward their idea of using lessons from enabling large-scale reflection by citizens, through panels and juries, to craft deliberative behavioural interventions called think. Think is a more targeted deliberative intervention designed to facilitate behaviour change. They later developed the idea of conveying a nudge with a think with the expectation that thinkers would be able to use and process a nudge better (John 2018; John and Stoker 2019). Such a nudge+, in its combination of a nudge with an external think, was expected to foster an active process of reflection in citizens, which could lead them to consider their behaviours in a wider context and would promote conscious experiential learning.

Early tests of such nudge and think combinations, based on this traditional conceptualisation of nudge+ policies, where the nudge was delivered separately to the process of reflection, were tested in a series of trials (John et al. 2013, 2019), using design and field experiments. An example was a community think with local councillors and officials around creating a video. Another was an online forum where citizens were encouraged to think about ethnic diversity and young people's anti-social behaviour, which had some positive effects. These results were later summarised in two editions of the book titled *Nudge, Nudge, Think, Think.*

But what could be the rationale for such reflection to happen outside of the nudge? A nudge bypasses people's volitional control and enables them to reach a decision that is thought to be welfare improving for them. Come to think of it, a nudge overcomes the requirement that individuals need to be motivated always to follow through with an action that can improve their welfare. This also happens to be a limiting factor for most thinking humans, in how they fail to translate their intentions into final actionable behaviours, the so-called intention-behaviour gap that we pointed out in the last chapter. For thinking humans to be motivated, it is critical that they engage with perspective transformation. Having reflected on the range of available scenarios to act and then having weighed them to come up with an alternative that reforms their perspective, they will have to engage eventually with such new behaviours. If someone lacks the willpower to do so, giving them a nudge is a practical way of enabling them to follow these new behaviours easily, without doing all the heavy cognitive lifting themselves. The nudge in this case acts like an SOS response that enables thinking humans to realise the full potential of reflection, a process that they might have just engaged with.

However, it is not just the nudge that aids the reflective process. Pure reflection that precedes a nudge also overcomes the ethical shortcoming of standard behavioural interventions, namely the problem of non-alien control. People who are not watchful enough to avoid the nudge can be disproportionately influenced by the nudge, but not when they have just reflected before it. A pure reflection exercise, such as one where citizens engage in juries or deliberations, enables them to think clearly about their prior choices and evaluate all available set of outcomes. If they retain the experience of this jury consciously, when such individuals are subjected to a nudge by the policy-maker, they can choose to go through with the nudge autonomously to achieve their goals. This is because after reflection citizens become aware of their own goals. Only if the nudge aligns with their new perspectives, as subsequently evaluated by them in the process of perspective transformation, they choose the nudge. Therefore, an external think that facilitates reflection can improve the uptake of the nudge by restoring agency in people to ultimately do what is best for them.

The relationship between reflection and nudge, in this case, can be thought to be mutually beneficial to both nudging and thinking, making nudge+ more than the sum of its parts. This uplift occurs because of synergistic association whereby the nudge overcomes the cognitive burden of translating intentions into actions towards the end of reflection, and the think empowers all nudge recipients to be equally watchful and builds their agency to use the nudge thoughtfully. This argument is not the same as saying that the sequence of this combination cannot be changed, with the plus coming after the nudge. We will discuss these sequencing effects in the next chapter when we carefully piece together the design features of a nudge+. For now, it is sufficient to say that the process of reflection can happen outside the remit of a nudge. In all such cases, pure reflection must evoke the conscience of citizens who can then choose to engage with a nudge that aligns with their own goals, thereby overcoming any barriers to perspective transformation imposed by a lack of willpower on their part.

While innovative, these traditional nudge+ policies were hard to scale up because of the associated high costs of organising such large-scale citizen deliberations. Eventually, this view of think, where reflection was actively organised at the level of population, gave in to a new conceptualisation of this tool, where reflection was embedded as a mini-think in or close to the nudge. Hence, nudge+.

The shift in this thought process of designing the new variant of this nudge+ needed theorising (Banerjee and John 2024). Following this work, we proposed the potential for small-scale reflection in nudge, which was to happen at the level of the individual now. This combination differed from its predecessor in that reflection was meant to happen independently for citizens, rather than some kind of group-led thinking, like a mini-think which is delivered alongside the nudge. The shift of focus to individual thinking, as laid out in recent work that we did with some other colleagues (see Banerjee et al. (2024)), also meant that such nudge and think combinations could be delivered at the same time, rather than having to sequence them one after the other using many different settings.

Some early tests spoke to the benefits of this new approach. The first came from Monika Mühlböck and colleagues (2022) published their findings on the effectiveness of combining an information nudge with a survey tool. The latter was designed to enable jobseekers to think about different strategies to seek employment opportunities. An interesting feature of this new nudge+ policy they tested was that it employed a mini-think, using their idea of a follow-up survey, in line with our new conceptualisation as explained above. This design made it possible to foster individual thinking on the information nudge. They deployed this nudge+ via e-mails to 7000 job seekers in Austria in collaboration with the Austrian Ministry of Social Affairs. Their experimental findings showed that those jobseekers who were made to reflect after the nudge were found to increase their chances to find employment by 3 percentage points or so, over a period of six months.

Around the same time, we were also designing and testing a wide range of nudge+ interventions (Banerjee et al. 2023) to promote the uptake of climate-friendly diets. In this experiment, we were interested in testing the whole spectrum of behavioural policies based on their inherent reflective potential. First, we designed a think. This think intervention was a modification of a commitment contract that introduced active reflection for citizens, as we have explained before. Using this think, people were encouraged to reflect twice, first about their own preferences and motivation before signing a pledge for climate-friendly diets. This was followed by an ask to think on the best way possible to follow through with their goals which involved a choice of two different kinds of nudge and the standard control setting. The conceptualisation of this think tool closely resembled the actual process of perspective transformation, where the initiation of this pledge first resulted in a stimulus, which made them think and consequently led people to evaluate all their options.

Next, we also tested two nudges independently in this experiment. A default nudge which set environmentally sustainable food items as the standard set-menu with an option to opt out to the main menu, and a labelling nudge which colour coded food items to reflect their carbon footprint to customers. In an attempt to create the nudge+, we modified these two groups of interventions, by combining the nudge with the think, such that once people had reflected on whether they wanted to adopt climate-friendly diets, they were provided with a nudge, which in this case was the default , to ease them into following through with their new choices. In this way, the nudge+ exploited features of our conceptualisation where reflection would happen outside the nudge, nonetheless, it would be deployable at the level of the individual. Our experimental findings validated our new conceptualisation as we found this nudge+ was more effective, on average, than either its standalone nudge or think counterparts in reducing intended orders of carbon-intensive meals.

This combination of pure reflection that happens outside the remit of a conventional nudge is called a two-part nudge+ (Banerjee and John 2024). In this hybrid tool, there are two clear and different components that are pieced together, hence the name, two-part. One of the components is a thinking device that prompts the process of active and conscious reflection in citizens, whereas the other is a nudge that enables citizens to follow through with their new perspectives post-reflection. While the conventional view of nudge+ implies that any two standalone interventions—think and nudge—can be simply put next to each other in the experiment, which then becomes the nudge+, our new approach differs considerably. Following our new conceptualisation, the think should be combined with the nudge in ways that retain some but not all features of either tool. Only then, the resulting hybrid tool can be thought to embody the best of both worlds while overcoming the limitations of the standalone tools.

When considering the nudge+ as described above in more detail, this point becomes clearer. In the think, the modified commitment device, people were prompted to think twice: first about their prior beliefs, their own preferences to eat meat-free diets before they could pledge. Second, as part of this reflective process, they were also asked to think about the best possible way to follow through their new perspectives resulting from their pledge. This pure reflection tool embodied two active decisions that people had to make. However, when the nudge was embedded into this think, the second reflective decision was withdrawn. Having decided whether to pledge, a nudge was readily available to customers to guide them along their new perspectives automatically. The default nudge used in this nudge+ tool is also different in its identity versus a nudge that is not to be preceded by such reflection. This is mainly because engaging in reflection makes participants more watchful of their own preferences before the nudge is delivered to them, therefore limiting chances of anchoring them to ends designed by the nudge (O'Connor 2023; Pennycook et al. 2020).

Reflection Inside the Nudge

A relatively new type of nudge+ is a one-part device, where the nudge and think are intertwined into a composite tool, rather than being made proximate to one other in some ways. Here it is not possible to piece out the nudge from a think, in how such tools are designed and how they function. Nonetheless, both these components retain their individual roles and complement the other, so they are more than the sum of their parts. The think enables users of the nudge to reflect actively, which then results in a conscious learning environment for the user. Then the nudge makes it convenient for the user to reflect and follow through with its resulting new perspectives. Examples of such one-part nudge+ policies were outlined in some of our earlier work (see Banerjee and John 2024), such as a dual-self pledge, where people are encouraged to make a short- and a long-term pledge at strategic intervals, thereby allowing them to finetune their long-term goal based on their ongoing performance. This is different from a standard commitment device where one makes a single pledge (the long-term target) which then makes the process of behaviour change quite inflexible. The dual-self version of this pledge allows for individual reflection to guide an individual towards their new targets along the process.

One way to design these one-part nudge+ tools is to dial up the reflective potential of quasi-reflective tools we outlined in the previous chapter. Recall, a quasi-reflective tool implies the process of reflection is passive or unconscious. Where passive, reflection happens outside the control of the thinker but ends up in a state of experiential learning where the users retain consciousness in effectuating new behaviours. An example of this was the commitment or the social norm nudge. In these cases, people are exempted usually from an active process of reflection, but the nudge results in a situation where people must take charge and act, to reinstate new behaviours.

We also discussed another type of a quasi-reflective tool in the last chapter. In this type, the process of reflection is active, such that people actively participate in the process of perspective information-processing. Nonetheless, based on how often this reflective process is repeated or not, the end state often becomes unconscious, and the same experiential learning is used again and again. An example of this, we said, was a navigational guide like the GPS which when goes astray often requires drivers to think actively of alternative means to use for navigation. However, if the GPS malfunctions repeatedly, people follow the same cues they used in the first instance, reducing this whole process to simple shortcuts.

Our idea of the one-part nudge+ relies on upgrading these tools of quasi-reflection to induce pure reflection alongside a nudge. It is possible to design nudge in ways that can prompt active reflection or can lead users to retain a conscious experience of how to respond to such new stimuli if they were to face them again in future. Let's consider a few examples here to drive this point home.

A social norm nudge relies on norm internalisation. This is the idea that when new norms are directed towards people, they mentally account for such norms by internalising them, which then steer them towards new behaviours. There is evidence that suggests that when processes of norm internalisation fail, it limits the effectiveness of a social norms nudge (Bicchieri et al. 2022; Entwistle 2021; Gross and Vostroknutov 2022; Hauser et al. 2018; Mols et al. 2015; Sunstein 2017). If this process of norm internalisation is made active, there is reason to believe that this nudge will deliver on its goals better. But making such a norm internalisation process explicit to users corresponds to dialling up the quasi-reflective potential of the nudge.

We tested this in an experiment with 5555 British individuals (Banerjee and Picard 2023) as we described earlier. In this experiment, we presented people with a social norm nudge randomly. This nudge emphasised on an increasing rate of vegetarianism among citizens in the UK. We expected this norm to increase intentions for orders over plant-based or climatarian diets versus the control condition in the experiment. Next, we wanted to evaluate the merits of norm internalisation as a mechanism of these treatment effects. So, pre-emptively, we designed two more treatment arms, where we delivered external reflective prompts to recipients randomly in helping them internalise these norms effectively. We did this in two steps:

first, we asked people to reveal their personal norms for climate-friendly diets randomly; then we prompted them to compare these norms and make an active decision to comply with the social norms. Here, we expected that signalling norm internalisation to people would improve the effectiveness of the social norms nudge.

Our experimental findings validated this, as we found people who were prompted to think actively on social norms responded better to this nudge—the overall effectiveness of social nudge almost doubled when people were made to think explicitly through norm internalisation. This social-norm nudge combined with a reflective prompt is an example of a one-part nudge+, where the sole purpose of the prompt is to dial up the thinking potential of this otherwise quasi-reflective tool.

Consider another example. Keppeler et al. (2025) tested the effectiveness of a nudge+ like intervention where they upgraded a nudge to increase its psychological ownership for citizens who were nudged with this intervention. They conducted a field trial in Germany where people were randomly entered into a mailing campaign to increase their intentions for COVID-19 vaccinations. In the treatment group, the authors upgrade the mailing campaign (a nudge in this case) by including possessive personal pronouns which in turn empowered people receiving this letter to relate personally to the nudge that was set in motion by the authors. In the control group, this campaign letter was mailed to people without such psychological ownership prompts. Their experimental findings showed that adding such reflective prompts to the nudge increased vaccination intentions of German people by 2.9 percentage points. Similar effects of using such psychological ownership mechanisms have been observed by Dai et al. (2021) using field trials to improve vaccination behaviours among citizens in the United States of America.

However, the effectiveness of the reflective prompt often depends on the strength of its signal to the receivers of the nudge, including the degree to which it dials up the reflective potential of the quasi-reflective tool. For example, in our first study to promote climatarian diets (Banerjee et al. 2023), we also tried to upgrade two quasi-reflective nudges, the default and the labelling nudge, by providing an additional information disclosure prompt alongside it. This information disclosure prompt was embedded into the nudge and worked by enabling people to think of the construct and design of the nudge. The expectation was that once people became aware of how the nudge was constructed, they will become more watchful of it too, complying with it if and only if it aligns with their own goals.

For the default nudge, where people were provided with shorter menus randomly, this one-part nudge+ then resembled the shorter menu but now with an additional disclosure on this menu that explained how it was constructed i.e., it said the menu was shorter because it had only environmentally sustainable items. Similarly, for the labelling nudge on menus, the additional disclosure prompt explained what the labelling scheme was and how it was designed. The change involved additional legends to the menu which explained the meaning of the green, amber, and red signs, and also discussed their rationale. For example, any food item which was marked red had emissions more than the average emissions of all items available on this menu. While such reflective prompts increased the choice of green items from the menu versus the control condition, they were no better than the quasi-reflective nudge. This is important when we think of dialling up reflection as a means to improve the effectiveness of quasi-reflective tools. If we fail to dial up reflection sufficiently, people cannot complete the entire process of perspective transformation. In this case, where people only evaluated if their goals were aligned with the nudge but did not go further, such a nudge+ is limited in its potential to deliver effective behaviour change.

These one-part nudge+ policies, nonetheless, if properly done have the added benefit that they can be scaled up in their applications. As technology aids the delivery of nudge, adding reflective prompts to existing nudge interventions becomes easier and more practical. Consider the example of a navigability nudge, like the GPS device. This quasi-reflective nudge can benefit from Artificial Intelligence-assisted tools like Alexa or Siri which then prompts drivers to think of their actions when the nudge fails. A GPS device not only reads out driving instructions to users, like when to turn left or right, but also creates a dialogue such as when it senses the GPS-device to be less reliable or more. In doing this it is expected that users relying on such devices can be inspired to think using their own cognition to navigate through a road system. Another example is bots at a restaurant through which people place their own orders and can deliver a reflective prompt that empowers people to think before they are given a nudge that suits their purpose. The possibilities of such nudge+ policies are large, though remain to be tested in real world settings.

But What Do We Reflect Upon?

By now, it must become clear that reflection added to a nudge can have many different purposes. To some extent, this depends on the type of behaviours that policy-makers want to target. Either way, while the premise and process of reflection remains broadly similar for these different types of behaviours, the outcome to which the nudge is guiding someone to can be very different. This variation in the kind of outcomes has implications for the effectiveness of nudge+ policies when they are compared to the nudge.

While nudge+ can lead to more effective outcomes, this is not always to be expected. Sometimes, nudge+ backfires when the nudge fails to deliver a positive behaviour change after people have engaged in reflection. But as we continue to argue in this book, this is not necessarily a bad thing to happen. Because some kinds of nudge are meant to fail (see Tor 2020). It is indeed problematic when a good nudge, one that is designed with the benevolence of the policy-maker and those that agree with the goals of most people, fails. But what is more concerning is when a bad nudge (such as a sludge) harnesses people's biases and disempowers them. They are manipulated to reach or deliver a particular outcome, which is against their own self-interest. The analogy here is to choose appropriate statistical thresholds to minimise type-1 (false positive) or type-2 (false negative) errors - one knows there is a trade-off and you cannot simply minimise them both, but it is much safer to limit type-1 errors, the false positives, even when they imply somewhat higher false negatives. A bad vaccine can harm many healthy individuals if allowed in the market which is morally way worse than a good vaccine being subjected to higher standards thereby delaying benefits to the unhealthy. In a similar way, embedding reflection within nudge+ serves as a protective filter, allowing robust, welfare-enhancing nudges to persist while exposing and weakening those that depend on manipulation. Such an error of policy-making, allowing the bad nudges to be free, can have widespread consequences in the long-run, including a loss of trust in government and policy-makers who effectuate such policies, as people come to realise the dark effects of nudge over time. It is here that reflection stands a true chance to allow people to see through the nudge, if they can be made to think through it sufficiently, assess whether they are worthy of relying on, and only then commit to it.

This reflection comes in many different forms. We describe them next and summarise the manifold purposes they have when they are combined with a nudge to transform it into a nudge+. We also list the testable predictions that arise from such a research agenda of nudge+.

Reflective Transparency

The most basic type of reflection that we will discuss here, is one that follows from transparency in the design of the nudge. We will call this reflective transparency. Research on the transparency of nudge, in some sense, is one of the building blocks of many programmes like nudge+ which have sought to address the challenges of designing a policy transparently,[1] where the operational knowledge of the policy remains in the domain of public knowledge. While it is necessary for governments to be open with its citizens about what they do, as one of the basic tenets of democracy, how they do so is equally important when it comes to building policy transparency. For the former, as Lades and Delaney (2022) argue (but also see Thaler and Sunstein 2008, 2021), nudge tends to satisfy the publicity principle (Rawls 1971) where governments tend to release public communication about nudge that they institute. However, on the latter, that is where policies are less transparent, as it requires governments to know why some kinds of nudge works if they do, and in turn, requires them to make citizens aware of these interventions. This is often what is known as the 'token transparency' (see Bovens 2009). Nudge is 'in-principle token-transparent' as watchful citizens can opt-out of the nudge. And we have already highlighted the pitfalls of in-principle token transparency in this chapter, where nudges can widen existing inequalities if it steers people away from their true personal goals just because they lack watchfulness.

Realistically, token transparency is hard to convey to citizens. There is wide scholarly debate whether policies that nudge are easy to spot in the wild, with concerns around them operating in the dark (Glaeser 2005; Rebonato 2012; Hansen and Jespersen 2013; Barton and Grüne-Yanoff 2015; Nys and Engelen 2017). There are several reasons why nudge appears to be opaque in its application. One, for instance, relates to the idea of who nudges. While it can be expected that governments can make their tools of governance visible to all, including nudge, a large number of

[1] Boosts, as we discussed in Chap. 1, refer to types of behavioural tools and techniques which enable people to use their reflective capacities better (Hertwig and Grüne-Yanoff 2016, 2017). Boosts improve skills, update existing heuristics through better rules, and enable citizens to implement their intentions with goal plans.

nudges that we experience everyday come from commercial choice architects. Examples include search engines on the internet and messages from a grocery store or coffee chain. Such organisations have no obligation to engage with any publicity principle, let aside strict (moral) obligations to deliver token transparency. Often nudge can end up being sludge, where the policy-maker manipulates receivers for their own interests. Also, benevolent entities can fail to understand why a nudge works, hence limiting the extent to which it can convey such information to public. Moreover, it might be distracting to inform people about how a nudge works, as our example in Chap. 2 shows about signage on narrowing roads which increased road accidents unlike it intended to. For some cases, it is possible that token transparency is actually impractical to deliver to people.

Nonetheless, these concerns have prompted researchers in this field to consider actively transparent nudges over the last decade or so. As a result, there are now nudge taxonomies that address this problem (see Hansen and Jespersen 2013), helping to understand when tools are transparent or not. Cass Sunstein (2016) has also contributed to this debate by showing that most people like to be nudged, more often preferring a system 2 (the educative and thinking) nudge than the system 1 (the automatic) one. A major thrust to this direction of research came from Steffel et al. (2016) who showed across seven different experiments that transparency did not reduce the effect of a default nudge, in fact, citizens appreciated such an open nudge very much. Loewenstein et al. (2015) also validated this with their experimental findings to show when people were informed about a default nudge transparently, with an information disclosure, they did not revise their choices under the nudge—the nudge was not rendered ineffective.

Following these early tests of transparency, Bruns et al. (2018) tested the role of disclosures on the effectiveness of default contributions to reduce carbon emissions. They generated similar findings from the lab where information on the purpose of the nudge, its influence, or both combined, failed to reduce its efficacy. In our own experiments (Banerjee et al. 2023), as discussed earlier, we found that adding information disclosures about the construct and presence of a default nudge did not hamper its effect. While these studies proved transparency was not detrimental to the nudge, it was Paunov et al. (2019a) who first found, across three different experiments, that pro-active signalling of transparency in the default nudge increased the retention rate of the nudge. Later, in follow-up experiments to understand the mechanisms, the authors pinned this down to transparency about the purpose of the nudge and target behaviours of people, with observed increases in compliance with the nudge (Paunov et al. 2019b, 2020).

But these results were hard to generalise across other kinds of nudge, as Kantorowicz-Reznichenko and Kantorowicz (2021) showed with the social norms nudge. In their experiment, reflective transparency on the purpose of the nudge and its targeted effect decreased the impact of the nudge. So how can we make sense of these contextual treatment effects that transparency seems to have on nudge?

A reasonable explanation comes from the differences embodying these transparency treatments in the two cases. For instance, on a closer investigation, it became clear that Kantorowicz-Reznichenko and Kantorowicz (2021) motivated their decision to be transparent by stating that these kinds of nudge are generally seen to 'influence decision' which 'follows evidence from behavioural studies that demonstrate people are strongly influenced by the actions and beliefs of other people' (Table 1, p. 369). Contrarily, Paunov et al. (2019b) motivated defaults by highlighting the benefits that default policies have in helping people achieve better decisions. It turns out to be a simple case of framing, where the latter is more empowering. The transparent disclosure in Paunov et al. (2019a, 2019b, 2020) runs the risk of invoking negative sentiments, like anger from people who can be provoked to think of themselves as objects under a scanner in the study. In more recent studies, for example, as discussed previously in this book, similar negative findings appear. In the study led by Just and Gabrielyan (2025), when people were told to eat less junk food, participants in the transparent condition ate 133% more junk food than those in the untreated group.

However, that is not all. Even if two nudges are subjected to the same transparency treatment, could it be that the default nudge would be different to another nudge? The short answer is yes. And this is not just particular to the default as every nudge works very differently to another. But some, like the default, are just stronger in harnessing the biases of people under its influence. To a certain extent, this explains why only transparency will have limited benefits in a research programme like the nudge+. Transparency increases the confidence of people when receiving the nudge. It does make them think but it does not get people to reflect fully on the specifics of their bias that the nudge leverages. The power of thinking is that it can ultimately empower people to realise their own shortcomings and work towards addressing them. The process of perspective transformation does not emerge under the simple case of transparency because receivers of the nudge cannot evaluate all their options and are restricted to an unbalanced consideration of the nudge. We can consider this point in more detail, making our case with defaults again.

Defaults target people's biases much strongly than other sorts of nudge, we argue. Is there evidence for this claim? In the study led by Berger et al. (2022) discussed earlier the effects of default carbon offsets hold even under rising financial costs. Their research speaks to the stickiness of defaults, which endow people with some options that lead to a status quo bias. Here, transparency cannot undo the endowment effect of the nudge. Even when people recognise being under the influence of the nudge they are unduly influenced to move along with it. Steffel et al. (2016) demonstrate this strikingly, as they show 'preference articulation' besides transparency is what actually allows people to debias themselves from this unbalanced influence of the default nudge. In one of their seven experiments with 690 participants, they randomly prompted some to jot down their thoughts in favour of a green or a premium amenity. Their findings revealed that debiasing methods attenuated the default effects. Debiasing, when upgraded as a form of reflection (Slovic and Fischhoff 1977; Fischhoff 1982; Lord et al. 1984; Arkes 1991; Tetlock 1992; Sieck and Yates 1997; Mussweiler et al. 2000; Larrick 2004; Milkman et al. 2009; Morewedge et al. 2015; Soll et al. 2015) and combined with a default nudge, can empower people to build up their agency and thereby accept or reject a nudge in a programme of nudge+.

Similarly, besides the endowment effect, defaults are also seen to be strong when they work through endorsement (Jachimowicz et al. 2019). If policies like nudge are endorsed by choice architects that receivers of the nudge seem to trust, they are more likely to go along with it. Here, transparency, merely on the design, presence, or construct of the nudge has limited effects in reforming perspectives. People are rendered incapable under the nudge to reflect on their bias that makes them go along with this nudge. This endorsement bias is seen to mediate the true effects of the nudge (see Sunstein et al. 2019).

While transparency is important to policy design and can help people to evaluate policies like nudge based on its merits, most of the time the thoughts they provoke are unknown to the researcher or the policy-maker, which then does not help in token transparency. If the true goal of nudge+ is to support people in making an informed case of whether they want to be steered by a nudge, so that they can own this process of behaviour change, reflection must be directed at the biases that nudge is meant to harness, like our example with the default nudge shows. Only then, it is possible to reconcile these in nudge+. Transparency is undeniably important to make nudging more legitimate, but its reflective potential is probably quite limited. Other types of reflection combined with nudge offer greater benefits than simple reflective transparency.

Self-Reflection

An alternative is to reflect on one's own self. Such a reflection where one can think about their own preferences and articulate it openly is called self-reflection. For the time being, for the sake of argument, assume that such human preferences are stable and consistent over time. This does not need to be true always. But if it is, what would this act of self-reflection look like? Many of the examples in this chapter conform to this idea of self-reflection already.

Consider, for instance, our example of enabling people to think about their meat-eating preferences, either when they were asked to sign a commitment contract (Banerjee et al. 2023), or when they were asked to consider social norms about eating (Banerjee and Picard 2023). In both these cases, when people think of their own preferences, what they are doing is thinking about what they believe are their preferences for the current decision in that moment. This process of preference articulation is core to identity formation and it is very important to take place before subjecting citizens to a nudge. Why? Because if people do not realise their true personal self and their goals, and they commit to a nudge, then this nudge can disproportionately affect the realisation of their own identity, which is the precursor to agency (Banerjee et al. 2024). Here, nudge can have negative welfare effects on those with weak or transient preferences (for a discussion, see Sunstein 2017). This is because the nudge does not inhibit someone's actual choices. For example, a nudge does not prevent them from eating meat, but it compromises their agency to exercise their true abilities to decide without the nudge. When the nudge is taken away, people cannot fully follow through with their nudged behaviours because they never owned the behaviour to begin with.

This imbalance in the effects of a nudge on those who do not realise their identity can go a long way in reshaping how people think of themselves in society. It simply undermines their autonomy to make decisions without the nudge. It may be important to make individuals realise that they like eating meat, even when such behaviours can have negative impacts on the environment. These are two very different realisations, and unless this cognitive dissonance is made imminent to them, expecting a long-term shift in their behaviours is hopeless. Tricking people to not eat meat when they truly want to, can only work a limited number of times, but at what cost? Not targeting the right biases makes a nudge seem like a quick fix, the effect of which will fade away with time.

But when people self-reflect, it allows them to articulate their preferences clearly to themselves, and in this process, they realise what and how they want to do things. For instance, if people want to do good things, like reduce meat-eating, and agree with the goals of the nudge, they will choose the nudge autonomously to help them along the way. If this is what nudge was designed for, then self-reflection will only enhance the effectiveness of the nudge and deliver to its own goals. This is what we found in the social norms experiment, when people who had intentions to change themselves, benefitted increasingly from the uptake of the nudge. On the contrary, there are some people who might have the same goals as the nudge but who might not want to go along with it. Alternatively, there might be some whose goals are completely different to the nudge. Self-reflection allows these people to become watchful of the nudge and reject it. It is for these types of people that nudge is not the right tool—but we will discuss the ethics of such behaviour change later on in the book.

Next, we consider what happens if people change their preferences over time. If we relax the assumption of consistency and stability of preferences, and assume that people have different short- and long-term goals for them, then it makes the case for self-reflection even stronger. Consider any standard commitment nudge, without any active reflection preceding it. This nudge works by prompting people to sign a contract, which then harnesses their psychological biases in which people are expected to stick with it (Bryan et al. 2010). But if people have different goals, then such commitment devices can work better when people are allowed to reflect. We proposed such a nudge+ tool earlier where we combine different versions of this commitment contracts together (see Banerjee and John 2024). Recall, in simplest form, this could be thought of as a dual-self pledge, where people sign two different commitment contracts—one for the short term and one for the long term, with the idea that as people's preferences evolve over time, these pledges can be adjusted, which builds in room for reflection on what is the best course for them to achieve their own goals.

Consider obesity, as an example. A conventional commitment nudge would tie people into a contract to reduce weight forever. But this does not give the individual an opportunity to think through the contract and its effectiveness for themselves over time. Failing the contract at any time could also imply negative consequences on their own well-being. On the contrary, if individuals were allowed to make a long-term weight reduction plan, such as your healthy weight target after a year, and then split this target into 12 monthly instalments, with possibilities to revise these targets at the end of every month, they could harness the effectiveness of the commitment device better. If the individual, for instance, realises at the end of two months, they are constantly underperforming on their small targets, they no longer need to bear the stress to deliver on the longer target. In turn, they think again and revise to what they feel is an achievable goal.

Self-reflection, therefore, allows people to understand themselves more and in consequence use the nudge in better ways. It also implies that those who do not judge the nudge's target behaviour to conform with their own preferences, will reject it outrightly. Set up this way, self-reflection combined with the nudge limits the need to make the assumption that the policy-maker needs to decide for the individual, when the individual is not aware what they truly prefer. By enabling people to articulate their preferences, this nudge+ makes the nudge more agentic and libertarian in its design.

The effectiveness of a nudge+ comes about when people conform with the target behaviour of the nudge upon self-reflection, and will be greater than its standalone nudge. We expect the effectiveness of a nudge+, when people do not conform with the target behaviour of the nudge upon self-reflection, will be lower than a standalone nudge.

Reflection on the Mechanism of the Nudge

Another possibility is to reflect on the mechanism of the nudge itself. This type of reflection can be based on the design of the nudge, such as its intent and purpose, or the biases it harnesses from people. Reflection on the mechanism of the nudge builds on our discussion on token transparency earlier, such that citizens are not just informed of the nudge simply but are empowered to think about how such a nudge works as well and what implications it has for themselves. At the end, such a reflective process ends with people reviewing how they view a nudge, and whether they think it can work for themselves in achieving some target behaviours.

It is possible that this kind of reflection on the mechanism of the nudge is strongly correlated with people's approval of the nudge in itself. Here it is important that framing effects do not bias people's reaction to the nudge, otherwise an approval (or not) could be biased by the frame in which such a nudge is presented, as we discussed in the case of Paunov et al. (2019a, 2019b). Or as shown in experiments previously (Bang et al. 2020; Michaelsen et al. 2021), where the evaluation of the nudge changes based on whether the nudge is presented jointly with other policies or not.

It is, therefore, important, that any reflection on the mechanism of a nudge is supported by appropriate debiasing techniques that allow people to articulate their true and unbiased preferences over the nudge, given their understanding of this policy. In such debiasing methods, people should be made to consider other policies jointly with the nudge, so that one has an informed decision about the policy type that they prefer. After this, if people fundamentally disagree with the relevance of the nudge for themselves, at the end of the reflective process, they will respond less favourably to it. On the contrary, if then people agree that such a nudge is conducive to their own goals of achieving an end behaviour, they will respond more favourably to the nudge. This reasoning leads us to believe the effectiveness of a nudge+, when people judge it favourably after reflecting unbiasedly on its mechanism, will be greater than its standalone nudge. Moreover, the effectiveness of a nudge+, when people judge it unfavourably after reflecting unbiasedly on its mechanism, will be lower than its standalone nudge.

Reflection on the Source of the Nudge and Their Goals

A fourth possibility is to reflect on those who deliver the nudge and their perceived goals. This is important, because reflection on the source of the nudge, could generate forms of reactance, such as through unintended backfire effects, that can act as signals to nudgers to enable them to better understand citizen preferences. In turn, choice architects can revise policies to make them coherent with citizen preferences. This is crucial both for social choice architects, like governments and policy-makers and commercial ones, who nudge for profit. Let's consider one at a time.

For governments, wrong policies do not necessarily reflect non-benevolence. A fundamental limitation of nudging for good is that governments often lack complete information of what is best for all its citizens. They may know the best interests of the general population, such as not to foster an obese society, or to limit crime, or mitigate climate change impacts, but they probably do not know the welfare and interests of specific segments of the population. It is an unrealistic demand to make of them as well. Nonetheless, if that is the case, then enabling citizens to reflect on the source of the nudge, not simply in who delivers them, but also thinking about their rationale for doing so, could generate useful signals which can then communicate these latent preferences to governments. In turn, reshaping policies based on this appropriate feedback from the citizen community can increase compliance with the nudge.

Policy approval for a nudge when aligned to its effectiveness also implies that governments might be less hesitant to try, test, and adapt new policies (Haynes et al. 2012; Halpern 2015), as they can do so without negatively affecting their own ratings in the long-run. It is this citizen dialogue, fostered in the process of deliberation, that opens up new possibilities for more mature policy-making.

Consider this example. In 2022, we ran an experiment with colleagues based in Canada, the UK, and the USA (Banerjee et al. 2022) on more than 24,000 people across the G7 countries. Here we evaluated the impact of citizen reflection on default vaccination appointments. We measured the effect of this policy on people's intentions to get vaccinated and their support for the policy. We did this by comparing four treatment conditions in which they were randomly assigned against a scenario where COVID-19 cases were rising in the future. Then, those who were randomly assigned to the control condition were left on their own to choose a vaccine that was made available to them by their government. In the nudge condition, people were informed randomly that a vaccine appointment would be automatically scheduled for them conveniently, at the behest of their government, by their local clinic. Each of these conditions were then coupled with a reflective prompt on the source of the nudge. In the think condition, people were instead prompted to reflect on government's vaccination strategy in the control condition and then articulate these thoughts using a text box. In the nudge+ condition, we asked people to reflect on the government's strategy to default people into vaccination appointments, following which they defaulted into it. In each case, we asked people to self-report their intentions to be vaccinated and of their policy approval.

What we found was unexpected relative to the general findings in the literature and to our own pre-conceived notions of the effectiveness of these vaccine defaults, which we had pre-registered prior to the experiment. Typically, automatic scheduling of appointments leads to an increase in the uptake of the vaccine. Our experimental findings showed that the default nudge reduced individual vaccination intentions compared to the control condition. But people approved of this nudge by the government compared to the condition when it was left up to them to take the vaccine. There was a disparity here that an ineffective nudge was de-facto approved by citizens, on average. Nonetheless, for the nudge+ condition, when citizens were made to think about the government's actions using this nudge, this paradox seemed to disappear. In the nudge+ condition, thinking about the government's actions using the nudge completely washed out its public support, as the nudge continued to remain ineffective in promoting vaccination intentions. Thinking here enabled people to communicate their true preferences to the government for a policy that could be then revised based on this new information (see Banerjee et al., 2023).

If this type of reflection were to be scaled up across different public policies, what could happen? First, any reflection of this kind will increase people's watchfulness of the nudge employed by commercial choice architects. Imagine you are buying a ticket. At the end of the checkout, somewhere in fine print, you have been opted in to donate to a charity, owned and operated by the airlines you are about to fly with. The amount is insubstantial to your flight ticket price, and you are too lazy to opt out, so you go along with it. Maybe you do not care about the charity you just donated to? Or maybe you do? Your preferences are immaterial to the donation.

But suppose, a friend pointed this out to you. You have now become watchful of the nudge. Then you will be attentive to this every time you book a ticket. Not thinking about the source of the nudge makes you vulnerable to behaviours that you probably do not want to engage with. They also make you vulnerable to sludges when commercial choice architects could take advantage of your biases to engineer you towards outcomes that reduce your welfare inadvertently. Thinking about the source of the nudge and its goals is a sludge audit, which you as an individual employ by being thoughtful about it. Such sludge audits can be useful in reducing these unnecessary friction costs that commercial choice architects employ (Soman 2020; Sunstein 2022). Set up this way, we propose that a citizen's view of their choice architects would moderate the effect of the nudge in a nudge+.

Reflection on Our Bigger Problems with Nudge+

In this chapter, we discussed two different schools of thought, to combine reflection with a nudge. The first, a conventional view of nudge+, comes from the early works of John et al. (2009), in combining a group-led think with an individual nudge using field and design experiments. In these nudge+ interventions, the thinking typically happens outside the nudge, and at the population level, such as with citizen juries and forums, deliberative democracies and so on, following which the population is administered a nudge to change their behaviours. The more recent formulation of nudge+ embodies the idea of a mini-think embedded into the nudge (John and Stoker 2019; Banerjee and John 2024; Banerjee 2021). For these nudge+ interventions, it is fundamental to the design of the nudge+, that both reflection and nudging are deployed at the level of an individual. These tools can be two-part, where a pure reflective prompt is made proximate to a nudge, combining them in ways that it retains some features of either tool but not all. Or they are one-part in which quasi-reflective prompts are dialled up with nudge and turned into a composite tool. For both types, the nudge and the think mutually reinforce each other as the nudge eases the process of perspective transformation by making reflection more compliant for citizens. Think builds agency into the nudge and empowers citizens to break free from all disproportionate influences of the nudge.

Then, we discussed the different ways in which citizens can reflect. The basic form of reflection comes from transparency, but as said, reflective transparency is often limited in its potential. Here, other types of reflection, for example, on the nudge, on oneself, or on the source of the nudge, its goals and mechanism, can be stronger. But reflection does not need to be restricted on only one of the types above. It is quite natural to expect that reflection starts by thinking about the nudge and its mechanism; then thoughts turn to other dimensions, such as who is delivering the nudge or how personal preferences relate to the task primed by the nudge. It is also possible that some of this reflection can generate negative emotions and affect one's own well-being. The more reflection one engages in, the greater is the cognitive burden imposed on citizens. This can be challenging particularly as we suffer from limited attention spans. Often reflection or deliberation has been critiqued on grounds that reflection leads people into echo-chambers, polarising people further, strengthening their views and opinions they already hold, without necessarily correcting them. While this criticism has some justification, it speaks to cases when reflection is left unstructured. Our hope is that policy-makers and practitioners will be able to harness appropriate moments to inculcate a reflective prompt in the nudge in ways that do not make it too burdensome for citizens. Left this way, nudge+ still remains open to some critiques of ethical manipulation, such as when people are given a false sense of agency, an illusion of sorts. We will discuss this point in greater detail in Chap. 6.

To conclude, reflection, as we define above, must be well-designed to help citizens evaluate a nudge fully and engage with it better. It must be embedded into a policy in structured ways by experts who have gauged the possible remits of the given nudge. Focus groups, consultants, and pilot studies are therefore crucial before a reflective element is embedded into the nudge. Being unaware of the dimensionality that reflection results in is detrimental to the merits of a policy like nudge+. It is here that more work is needed to validate the testable hypotheses presented in this chapter further and expand the domains in which nudge+ interventions have been tested. In the next chapter, we will unpack the cognitive underpinning of nudge+ and outline how reflective prompts, varied in their objectives, could be sequenced with a nudge.

References

Arkes, Hal R. 1991. Costs and benefits of judgment errors: Implications for debiasing. *Psychological Bulletin* 110 (3): 486. https://doi.org/10.1037/0033-2909.110.3.486.

Banerjee, Sanchayan. 2021. Rethinking the origin of the behavioural policy cube with nudge plus. In *Behavioral-based interventions for improving public policies*, 1–16. IGI Global Scientific Publishing.

Banerjee, Sanchayan, and Peter John. 2024. Nudge plus: Incorporating reflection into behavioral public policy. *Behavioural Public Policy* 8 (1): 69–84. https://doi.org/10.1017/bpp.2021.6.

Banerjee, Sanchayan, and Julien Picard. 2023. Thinking through norms can make them more effective. Experimental evidence on reflective climate policies in the UK. *Journal of Behavioral and Experimental Economics* 106:102024. https://doi.org/10.1016/j.socec.2023.102024.

Banerjee, Sanchayan, Andrew Hunter, Peter John, Richard Koenig, Blake Lee-Whiting, Peter Loewen, John McAndrews, Brendan Nyhan, and Manu Savani. 2022. Citizen reflection reduces support for default vaccination appointments. Evidence from G7 countries. https://doi.org/10.21203/rs.3.rs-1964391/v1.

Banerjee, Sanchayan, Matteo M. Galizzi, Peter John, and Susana Mourato. 2023. Sustainable dietary choices improved by reflection before a nudge in an online experiment. *Nature Sustainability* 6 (12): 1632–1642. https://doi.org/10.1038/s41893-023-01235-0.

Banerjee, Sanchayan, Till Grüne-Yanoff, Peter John, and Alice Moseley. 2024. It's time we put agency into behavioural public policy. *Behavioural Public Policy* 8 (4): 789–806. https://doi.org/10.1017/bpp.2024.6.

Bang, H. Min, Suzanne B. Shu, and Elke U. Weber. 2020. The role of perceived effectiveness on the acceptability of choice architecture. *Behavioural Public Policy* 4 (1): 50–70. https://doi.org/10.1017/bpp.2018.1.

Barton, Adrien, and Till Grüne-Yanoff. 2015. From libertarian paternalism to nudging—And beyond. *Review of Philosophy and Psychology* 6 (3): 341–359. https://doi.org/10.1007/s13164-015-0268-x.

Berger, Sebastian, Andreas Kilchenmann, Oliver Lenz, Axel Ockenfels, Francisco Schlöder, and Annika M. Wyss. 2022. Large but diminishing effects of climate action nudges under rising costs. *Nature Human Behaviour* 6 (10): 1381–1385. https://doi.org/10.1038/s41562-022-01379-7.

Bicchieri, Cristina, Eugen Dimant, Simon Gächter, and Daniele Nosenzo. 2022. Social proximity and the erosion of norm compliance. *Games and Economic Behavior* 132:59–72. https://doi.org/10.1016/j.geb.2021.11.012.

Bovens, Luc. 2009. The ethics of nudge. In *Preference change: Approaches from philosophy, economics and psychology*, 207–219. Springer.

Bronfenbrenner, U. 1979. The ecology of human development: Experiments by nature and design (Vol. 352). Harvard university press.

Bruns, Hendrik, Elena Kantorowicz-Reznichenko, Katharina Klement, Marijane Luistro Jonsson, and Bilel Rahali. 2018. Can nudges be transparent and yet effective? *Journal of Economic Psychology* 65:41–59. https://doi.org/10.1016/j.joep.2018.02.002.

Bryan, Gharad, Dean Karlan, and Scott Nelson. 2010. Commitment devices. *Annual Review of Economics* 2 (1): 671–698. https://doi.org/10.1146/annurev.economics.102308.124324.

Dai, Hengchen, Silvia Saccardo, Maria A. Han, Lily Roh, Naveen Raja, Sitaram Vangala, Hardikkumar Modi, Shital Pandya, Michael Sloyan, and Daniel M. Croymans. 2021. Behavioural nudges increase COVID-19 vaccinations. *Nature* 597 (7876): 404–409. https://doi.org/10.1038/s41586-021-03843-2.

Entwistle, Tom. 2021. Why nudge sometimes fails: Fatalism and the problem of behaviour change. *Policy & Politics* 49 (1): 87–103. https://doi.org/10.1332/030557320X15832072208458.

Fischhoff, Baruch. 1982. Debiasing. In *Judgement under uncertainty: Heuristics and biases*, ed. Daniel Kahneman, Paul Slovic, and Amos Tversky, 422–444. Cambridge University Press.

Gilovich, Thomas, Victoria Husted Medvec, and Kenneth Savitsky. 2000. The spotlight effect in social judgment: An egocentric bias in estimates of the salience of one's own actions and appearance. *Journal of Personality and Social Psychology* 78 (2): 211. https://doi.org/10.1037/0022-3514.78.2.211.

Glaeser, Edward L. 2005. *Paternalism and psychology*. Cambridge, MA: National Bureau of Economic Research.

Gross, Jörg, and Alexander Vostroknutov. 2022. Why do people follow social norms? *Current Opinion in Psychology* 44:1–6. https://doi.org/10.1016/j.copsyc.2021.08.016.

Grüne-Yanoff, Till, and Ralph Hertwig. 2016. Nudge versus boost: How coherent are policy and theory?. *Minds and Machines,* 26(1), 149–183.

Halpern, David. 2015. The rise of psychology in policy: The UK's de facto Council of Psychological Science Advisers. *Perspectives on Psychological Science* 10 (6): 768–771. https://doi.org/10.1177/1745691615609917.

Hansen, Pelle Guldborg, and Andreas Maaløe Jespersen. 2013. Nudge and the manipulation of choice: A framework for the responsible use of the nudge approach to behaviour change in public policy. *European Journal of Risk Regulation* 4 (1): 3–28. https://doi.org/10.1017/S1867299X00002762.

Hauser, Oliver P., Francesca Gino, and Michael I. Norton. 2018. Budging beliefs, nudging behaviour. *Mind & Society* 17 (1): 15–26. https://doi.org/10.1007/s11299-019-00200-9.

Haynes, Laura, Ben Goldacre, and David Torgerson. 2012. Test, learn, adapt: Developing public policy with randomised controlled trials. *Cabinet Office-Behavioural Insights Team*. https://doi.org/10.2139/ssrn.2131581.

Hertwig, Ralph, and Till Grüne-Yanoff. 2017. Nudging and boosting: Steering or empowering good decisions. Perspectives on Psychological Science, 12(6), 973-986.

Jachimowicz, Jon M., Shannon Duncan, Elke U. Weber, and Eric J. Johnson. 2019. When and why defaults influence decisions: A meta-analysis of default effects. *Behavioural Public Policy* 3 (2): 159–186. https://doi.org/10.1017/bpp.2018.43.

John, Peter. 2018. *How far to nudge?: Assessing behavioural public policy*. Edward Elgar Publishing.

John, Peter, and Gerry Stoker. 2019. Rethinking the role of experts and expertise in behavioural public policy. *Policy & Politics* 47 (2): 209–225. https://doi.org/10.1332/030557319X15526371698257.

John, Peter, Graham Smith, and Gerry Stoker. 2009. Nudge nudge, think think: Two strategies for changing civic behaviour. *The Political Quarterly* 80 (3): 361–370. https://doi.org/10.1111/j.1467-923X.2009.02001.x.

John, Peter, Sarah Cotterill, Liz Richardson, Alice Moseley, Graham Smith, Gerry Stoker, Corinne Wales, Hanhua Liu, and Hisako Nomura. 2013. *Nudge, nudge, think, think: Experimenting with ways to change civic behaviour*. A&C Black.

John, Peter, Sarah Cotterill, Alice Moseley, Liz Richardson, Graham Smith, Gerry Stoker, and Corinne Wales. 2019. *Nudge, nudge, think, think: Experimenting with ways to change citizen behaviour*. Manchester University Press.

Just, David R., and Gnel Gabrielyan. 2025. On nudging and psychological reactance. *Applied Economic Perspectives and Policy* 47:1600.

Kantorowicz-Reznichenko, Elena, and Jaroslaw Kantorowicz. 2021. To follow or not to follow the herd? Transparency and social norm nudges. *Kyklos* 74 (3): 362–377. https://doi.org/10.1111/kykl.12274.

Keppeler, Florian, Martin Sievert, and Sebastian Jilke. 2025. Increasing COVID-19 vaccination intentions: A field experiment on psychological ownership. *Behavioural Public Policy* 9 (1): 16–35. https://doi.org/10.1017/bpp.2022.16.

Lades, Leonhard K., and Liam Delaney. 2022. Nudge Forgood. *Behavioural Public Policy* 6 (1): 75–94. https://doi.org/10.1017/bpp.2019.53.

Larrick, Richard P. 2004. Debiasing. In *Blackwell handbook of judgment and decision making*, 316–338.

Loewenstein, George, Cindy Bryce, David Hagmann, and Sachin Rajpal. 2015. Warning: You are about to be nudged. *Behavioral Science & Policy* 1 (1): 35–42. https://doi.org/10.1177/237946151500100106.

Lord, Charles G., Mark R. Lepper, and Elizabeth Preston. 1984. Considering the opposite: A corrective strategy for social judgment. *Journal of Personality and Social Psychology* 47 (6): 1231. https://doi.org/10.1037/0022-3514.47.6.1231.

Michaelsen, Patrik, Lina Nyström, Timothy J. Luke, and Martin Hedesström. 2021. Downstream consequences of disclosing defaults: Influences on perceptions of choice architects and subsequent behavior. *Comprehensive Results in Social Psychology* 5 (1–3): 25–48. https://doi.org/10.1080/23743603.2021.1983720.

Milkman, Katherine L., Dolly Chugh, and Max H. Bazerman. 2009. How can decision making be improved? *Perspectives on Psychological Science* 4 (4): 379–383. https://doi.org/10.1111/j.1745-6924.2009.01142.x.

Mols, Frank, Alexander Haslam, Jolanda Jetten, and Niklas Steffens. 2015. Why a nudge is not enough: A social identity critique of governance by stealth. *European Journal of Political Research* 54 (1): 81–98. https://doi.org/10.1111/1475-6765.12073.

Morewedge, Carey K., Haewon Yoon, Irene Scopelliti, Carl W. Symborski, James H. Korris, and Karim S. Kassam. 2015. Debiasing decisions: Improved decision making with a single training intervention. *Policy Insights From the Behavioral and Brain Sciences* 2 (1): 129–140. https://doi.org/10.1177/2372732215600886.

Mühlböck, Monika, Fabian Kalleitner, Nadia Steiber, and Bernhard Kittel. 2022. Information, reflection, and successful job search: A labor market policy experiment. *Social Policy & Administration* 56 (1): 48–72. https://doi.org/10.1111/spol.12754.

Mussweiler, Thomas, Fritz Strack, and Tim Pfeiffer. 2000. Overcoming the inevitable anchoring effect: Considering the opposite compensates for selective accessibility. *Personality and Social Psychology Bulletin* 26 (9): 1142–1150. https://doi.org/10.1177/01461672002611010.

Nussbaum, Martha, and Amartya Sen. 1993. *The quality of life*. Clarendon Press.

Nys, Thomas R. V., and Bart Engelen. 2017. Judging nudging: Answering the manipulation objection. *Political Studies* 65 (1): 199–214. https://doi.org/10.1177/0032321716629487.

O'Connor, A. 2023. Behavioural insights for online safety: understanding the impact of video sharing platform (VSP) design on user behaviour.

Paunov, Yavor, Michaela Wänke, and Tobias Vogel. 2019a. Ethical defaults: Which transparency components can increase the effectiveness of default nudges? *Social Influence* 14 (3–4): 104–116. https://doi.org/10.1080/15534510.2019.1675755.

Paunov, Yavor, Michaela Wänke, and Tobias Vogel. 2019b. Transparency effects on policy compliance: Disclosing how defaults work can enhance their effectiveness. *Behavioural Public Policy* 3 (2): 187–208. https://doi.org/10.1017/bpp.2018.40.

Paunov, Yavor, Michaela Wänke, and Tobias Vogel. 2020. Combining defaults and transparency information to increase policy compliance. *Social Psychology*. https://doi.org/10.1027/1864-9335/a000419.

Pennycook, Gordon, Jonathon McPhetres, Yunhao Zhang, Jackson G. Lu, and David G. Rand. 2020. Fighting COVID-19 misinformation on social media: Experimental evidence for a scalable accuracy-nudge intervention. Psychological science, 31(7), 770–780.

Plomin, Robert, and Sophie von Stumm. 2018. The new genetics of intelligence. Nature Reviews Genetics, 19(3), 148–159.

Rawls, John. 1971. A theory of justice. In *Applied ethics*, 21–29. Routledge.

Rebonato, Riccardo. 2012. *Taking liberties: A critical examination of libertarian paternalism*. Palgrave Macmillan.

Schmidt, Andreas T. 2017. The power to nudge. *American Political Science Review* 111 (2): 404–417. https://doi.org/10.1017/S0003055417000028.

Sieck, Winston, and J. Frank Yates. 1997. Exposition effects on decision making: Choice and confidence in choice. *Organizational Behavior and Human Decision Processes* 70 (3): 207–219. https://doi.org/10.1006/obhd.1997.2706.

Slovic, Paul, and Baruch Fischhoff. 1977. On the psychology of experimental surprises. *Journal of Experimental Psychology: Human Perception and Performance* 3 (4): 544. https://doi.org/10.1037/0096-1523.3.4.544.

Soll, Jack B., Katherine L. Milkman, and John W. Payne. 2015. A user's guide to debiasing. In *The Wiley Blackwell handbook of judgment and decision making*, vol. 2, 924–951. https://doi.org/10.1002/9781118468333.ch33.

Soman, Dilip. 2020. Sludge: A very short introduction. *BEAR. [Online]*. https://www.rotman.utoronto.ca/-/media/Files/Programs-and-Areas/BEAR/White-Papers/BEARxBIOrg-Sludge-Introduction.pdf. Accessed 18 September 2020.

Steffel, Mary, Elanor F. Williams, and Ruth Pogacar. 2016. Ethically deployed defaults: Transparency and consumer protection through disclosure and preference articulation. *Journal of Marketing Research* 53 (5): 865–880. https://doi.org/10.1509/jmr.14.0421.

Sugden, Robert. 1993. Welfare, resources, and capabilities: A review of inequality reexamined by Amartya Sen. *JSTOR*.

Sunstein, Cass R. 2016. People prefer system 2 nudges (kind of). *Duke Law Journal* 66:121. https://doi.org/10.2139/ssrn.2731868.

Sunstein, Cass R. 2017. Nudges that fail. *Behavioural Public Policy* 1 (1): 4–25. https://doi.org/10.1017/bpp.2016.3.

Sunstein, Cass R. 2022. Sludge audits. *Behavioural Public Policy* 6 (4): 654–673. https://doi.org/10.1017/bpp.2019.32.

Sunstein, Cass R., Lucia A. Reisch, and Micha Kaiser. 2019. Trusting nudges? Lessons from an international survey. *Journal of European Public Policy* 26 (10): 1417–1443. https://doi.org/10.1080/13501763.2018.1531912.

Tetlock, Philip E. 1992. The impact of accountability on judgment and choice: Toward a social contingency model. In *Advances in experimental social psychology*, 331–376. Elsevier.

Thaler, Richard H., and Cass R. Sunstein. 2008. *Nudge: Improving decisions about health, wealth, and happiness*. Penguin.

Thaler, Richard H., and Cass R. Sunstein. 2021. *Nudge: The final edition*. Penguin.

Tor, Avishalom. 2020. Nudges that should fail? *Behavioural Public Policy* 4 (3): 316–342. https://doi.org/10.1017/bpp.2019.5.

CHAPTER 5

Thinking Fast, but Slowly

So far, we have set out the basic features of reflection, which form the building blocks of nudge+. For example, in Chap. 3, we discussed what reflection means and what it entails, the conditions under which citizens can engage in a meaningful reflective process so it transforms their perspectives, and whether contemporary tools of behaviour change embed some elements of reflection in them. Then in Chap. 4, we outlined the ways in which nudges can be upgraded to incorporate reflection in them. This is the premise of the nudge+ framework, whereby a nudge and a think are combined, such that, they are either made proximate to each other in the form of a two-part hybrid or are carefully moulded into a one-part device, where the nudge complements the reflective plus and vice versa. We concluded this discussion by exploring the realm of possibilities associated with reflection, such as thinking about one's own preferences and articulating them clearly to debias oneself from the unbalanced influence of the nudge or thinking about the source of the nudge, its mechanisms, and goals more broadly. These different possibilities further suggested that the effectiveness of the nudge+ intervention compared to the standalone nudge depends on the exact type of reflection undertaken by citizens alongside the nudge. A careful process of selection, therefore, must be employed when deciding to choose an appropriate form of reflection that is to be combined with the nudge in a nudge+ policy.

© The Author(s), under exclusive license to Springer Nature Switzerland AG 2026

S. Banerjee, P. John, *Nudge+*,
https://doi.org/10.1007/978-3-032-13261-1_5

From this discussion so far, it is clear that thinking and nudging are fundamental to the design of a nudge+ intervention. Citizens must be subjected to both these forms of behaviour change in a nudge+ world, if they are expected to take advantage of them mutually, and then improve their behaviours. Yet these techniques rely on different channels of cognition. They also demand different cognitive resources. Thinking is more demanding than nudging. To think, we must slow down, evaluate the pros and cons of engaging with an action. But to be nudged, we can simply become objects of our own shortcuts, where we keep doing what we do, act fast, and the nudge changes how elements of choice are presented to us, so we can engage with better decision-making. At first glance, it seems that to nudge+ is paradoxical. How can we ask citizens to think fast and slow at the same time? Is it even possible that such a combination makes any sense? Further, is it even needed, for does it not defeat the purpose of dual thinking if we know that slow cognition is more costly to us? To think fast but slowly seems paradoxical at first. But it is quite natural of us, as we will discuss in this chapter. This form of cognition, as citizens constantly monitor their fast responses, often cueing slower responses when needed, is also increasingly suggested in newer working models of cognitive processing (De Neys 2023). Such insights also make nudge+ appealing as a new framework of behaviour change.

But before we get into the details of how and when this seemingly paradoxical phenomenon can arise, let us think about scenarios when we have switched between fast and slow thinking, rather quickly, using both to our advantage. Consider driving. You are on the motorway, cruising comfortably at a reasonably fast speed (especially high if you're on German motorways). In the next moment, you realise the tanker in front of you is turning towards its side, almost changing lanes. You have two responses now, either you continue speeding, in fact you speed up even, so you can stay on the same lane and comfortably overtake the tanker before it blocks your lane. Or you switch lanes now. Albeit this latter strategy requires some careful manoeuvring, for your action is likely not expected by other drivers in the adjoining lanes. Which one of these two intuitions do you follow? Naturally, you have some thinking to do, and you must switch from being comfortably fast (not just with your car speed but also your brain) to being reasonably slow! This example can be generalised to other instances of driving as well, where you are under the influence of fast reflexes normally (especially if you are an experienced driver), but occasionally, you must slow down to make conscious decisions before you can go back to being comfortably fast, such as when responding to navigation by maps or taking the next left when you have missed your turn and so on.

Such switching between fast and slow thinking also happens for other actions, say, when cooking a meal. As you start a new dish, you follow a recipe book down to all its ingredients listed. As you cook more frequently, you become savvier with the ingredients you need, occasionally pausing, tasting what you cook, and thinking what could have made it better! You can even make small adjustments to the recipe that still keep it as the same dish but closer to what you like to eat. In a way, you personalise the rules and shortcuts that are generally prescribed as a recipe for a good meal to suit you better. Occasionally, we find ourselves in situations, when we employ a thoughtful slow process in addition to what we are doing fast already. It could be the other way around too, where we can become fast thinkers in the midst of thinking very slowly. In the example of cooking, if you find something is spicier than you wanted it to be and you are thinking of how to make it more conducive to your palate, you can rely on shortcuts that you have used in the past, such as adding milk or water to tone down the spiciness of your food. This is akin to driving, where if you are considering when to brake, you often employ shortcuts based on your previous experiences, which tell you how hard you should brake to stop before you crash. This process of switching between fast and slow thinking is more natural than we anticipate it to be. Often, we do not realise this, thereby, making it seem more like a paradox. Yet it is not a paradox, as the switches are very natural for us as to cope with what the world throws at us every day. In fact, it is this switching feature of the human brain that saves us time and our cognitive resources—imagine thinking about everything all the time, what a tiresome hellish life we would lead!

The basis for these different routes of thinking comes from a long account of dual process theories in psychology, often recalled from the more popular book by Daniel Kahneman (2011), *Thinking, Fast and Slow*. The central proposition of dual process theories is that humans often rely on two very different types of cognition—one which is fast, which does not drain our mental resources, relies on shortcuts, and produces reactions quickly. This has been called differently but is most colloquially referred to as the reflexive or fast type of cognition. Then there is the opposite kind—which is slow, thoughtful, burdensome, and more time-consuming in producing reactions, referred to as the reflective or slow type of cognition. These cognitive resources work together in reacting to different cues that we encounter.

In this chapter, we will review the different modes of interaction that have been proposed between fast and slow cognition, especially with a focus on what explains the switch between slow and fast thinking coherently. We will reason that nudge+, which relies on slow and careful thinking alongside fast nudging, is supported by a very recent notion of dual process theory, often dubbed as the dual process theory 2.0 (De Neys 2018), which does not presume exclusivity in the response of the fast and slow type of human brain. Exclusivity, as the label implies, suggests that a fast and slow response is cued exclusively by the fast (type-1) or slow type (type-2) of the human brain. In other words, it denies the proposition that type-1 cognition can cue a rational or deliberative type 2 response and vice versa. As we will discuss, it is this denial of the exclusivity assumption that allows for a more coherent switch between our fast and slow systems of thinking.

A discussion of this duality will enable us to understand fully the role of sequencing in combining the nudge with its plus to design nudge+. It is possible to deliver the think alongside the nudge, such that reflection cues monitoring of the response which is generated under the nudge.

Dual Process Theories of Cognition

The dual process theory of cognition has been a standard workhorse model in social psychology that has sought to explain how humans respond to the various cues they encounter in their everyday lives. A common way to understand the working of this model is to ask people 'what's your name?'. In almost all cases (except for infants), all human beings will respond immediately to this question with their name without much thought. Similarly, ask someone 'what's two times two?' and they will answer four immediately. So, there is something unique about our brain, in that it can respond very quickly to certain prompts.

These quick reactions usually involve decision-making over cues that we associate with strongly, such as our name which is associated with our identity ever since birth, or actions that are repeated frequently, like the basic mental math for two times two which we have practised innumerable times as a child in school. When the same tasks become slightly more complex, where our shortcuts fail, we become slow, taking much longer to reason, analyse, and answer. For instance, if we change the questions above to asking, 'what's your name in Mandarin (or any other language)?', assuming you are not an expert in that language, or 'what's 983 × 564?', we tend to pause and rely on our analytical thinking skills to come up with a response, or perhaps saying you do not know (or maybe guessing the times table if you are familiar with large numbers). This bifurcation of cognition and its categorisation into two different types of brain processes is the centrepiece to a dual process model, where this fast response is traditionally referred to as the output of system 1 and the slow one of system 2.

There exist many different accounts of the dual process models (for an evolutionary review, see Gawronski et al. (2013)), The essential features of these cognitive processes most prominently featured in the work of Jonathan Evans and Keith Stanovich (Evans and Stanovich 2013). The need for these cognitive processes to be defined in this way came from a wake-up-call in psychology, as growing research showed that not all properties of a certain type of cognition were satisfied simultaneously during any given task. Then there was also increasing evidence in neuroscience that failed to map these cognitive responses to definitive parts of the human brain. The absence of strict neural correlates decimated the idea that any dual cognition posited to be happening inside the brain could be related to any physical cluster of brain parts (the so-called system). On the contrary, there could be multiple brain systems, in fact, which were activated during different fast or slow tasks (Stanovich 2009a, 2009b). Ever since then, there has been a growing consensus that has favoured the understanding, that these dual processes, at best, represent types rather than systems of cognition, which can share common properties, where not all are defining (Evans and Stanovich 2013). The brain is not simply partitioned, like dual systems theory seemed to suggest, in two halves. This is what marked the transition in semantics from a 'system 1 versus system 2' typology to a 'type 1 versus type 2' one (Wason and Evans 1974; Evans 2009).

However, despite these critiques to dual process theory, the rationale for two different types of cognition remains strong and 'irrefutable' (Pennycook 2017). Evans and Stanovich (2013) proposed that a fast type of cognition must be autonomous—that is, it represents those parts of the brain, and their corresponding cognition, which generates responses automatically when subjected to a certain cue. Our cognition that follows questions like 'what's your name?' or 'what's two times two?' would fall under the remit of this type 1 brain processing. On the other hand, a slow type of cognition must satisfy cognitive decoupling, which is the ability of the human mind to engage into thinking and reasoning, and if needed, use algorithms necessary to respond to certain cues. Answers to questions like 'what's your name in Mandarin' or 'what's 983 × 564?', would induce cognition that would be classified as type 2. These dual process models hold a critical place in different domains of social psychology for decades, as Pennycook (2017) notes, such as reasoning (Evans 1989; Sloman 1996; Stanovich and West 2000), decision-making (Frederick 2005; Barbey and Sloman 2007; Kahneman 2011), cognition and cognitive development (Chaiken and Trope 1999; Epstein et al. 1996; Barrouillet 2011; Brainerd and Reyna 2002; Klaczynski 2001), clinical psychology (Beevers 2005; Pyszczynski et al. 1999), and cognitive neuroscience (Greene et al. 2001; Goel 2007; Lieberman 2007). Further, as De Neys (2023) notes, they have also appeared prominently in the popular media (Shefrin 2013; Lemir 2021; Tett 2021), and also in policy recommendations on topics ranging from economic development (World Bank Group 2015), greenhouse gas emissions (Beattie 2012), to COVID-19 pandemic (Sunstein 2020).

But what has remained an open question in this literature is not whether such a theory can be useful. Many would agree it is, given the influence it has had, for it explains the two main ways in which humans are seen to respond when they react to different cues. But mainly how to understand the ways in which these different brain processes interact with one another. What causes one to prevail over the other, necessitating the switch. Consider the pair of questions, 'what's your name?' and 'what's your name in Mandarin?'. Or for that matter the easy versus hard multiplication problem. How is it that our brain knows which type of cognition to employ successfully in each case? How can it necessarily switch between our fast and slow response? That's the million-dollar question, at least to dual process theorists. As if there is another meta-thinking resource, that we are endowed with, and which directs one type of cognition over the other?

If we were to believe (falsely) that the responses generated by the two types of cognitive resources are unique to themselves (called 'exclusivity' in modern parlance) i.e. type 1 generates a fast response and type 2 generates a slow response but not both, then this will lead to an infinite regress. For example, where type-1 is only capable of generating a fast response and similarly type 2 is only capable of generating a slow response, is it not paradoxical to think of another meta-resource that will determine a switch between these types, for such a process will first need to activate type-2 cognition. The infinite regress under the presumption of exclusivity has often called into question the coherence of the switch feature, an unavoidable prediction of model dual process theories. Questions like these have motivated particularly dual process theorists for a long time. But to better understand this, and how the presumption of exclusivity concerns the matter of switch, we must consider the different mechanisms that have been proposed to understand the interaction of these processes. Here, we review a prominent typology by Evans (2007, 325–329) that gives insights into the conflict resolution mechanisms of the different types of cognitive processes.

The conflict resolution mechanism by Evans (1977) demonstrates the tussle between our fast and the slow type of cognition. It does so eloquently by using a statistical model of predicting a right response to a deductive reasoning task. We assume that there are different probabilities with which these fast and slow brain processes are engaged to act. As far as the task is concerned, it is further assumed that a person can come up with a binary response of some sorts. Solving this simplistic model, Evans (2007) shows that there can be multiple plausible psychological explanations that deduce the same deterministic response to the task. It is through compelling explanations that we understand how the two brain processes might engage with one another.

Consider, the first psychological explanation to this. It is called the 'pre-emptive conflict resolution' mechanism. In this, our brain processes, fast or slow, are thought not to conflict, when a certain task comes up. Instead, there are some overarching selection rules that help decide which type of cognition will be employed when facing a certain task. Think of this as you are participating in a pub quiz with your friend as a duo. You and your quizzing partner have decided pre-emptively that you will divide the rounds in which you will answer. Maybe this is based on your expertise of the subject matter. When these rounds pop up, you simply fall back on your arrangement and submit answers to the questions as a team. The brain, thus, pre-emptively comes up with a decision, made by any one type, that is then collectively considered its final response to a certain cue. As Evans (2007) points out many early dual process theorists thought of dual process interactions in this way, with a particular reference made to the works of Klaczynski (2001) in the selective scrutiny of belief biases.

Another explanation of how this deterministic response comes through is the parallel-competitive mechanism of conflict resolution. Here, it is assumed that there are no pre-decided rules, which then determine the appropriateness of a certain type of cognition given a task. Instead, both fast and the slow types of cognition come up with a response simultaneously to any cue. If the responses from both types of brain processes match and are in sync, the overall response is the same. There is no conflict which is detected. This is trivial. However, if there is conflict, then a resolution mechanism kicks in, and one type emerges as the more appropriate response. Such a cognitive architecture has been seen in accounts of dual process theories by Chaiken (1980), Chaiken and Trope (1999), and later also by Epstein (1994); Epstein et al. (1996). However, this mechanism has been critiqued often on grounds that faster type-1 cognition is more likely to come with a quicker response than our slower type-2 cognition. Then, there is the chance that the faster response is delivered first, which is later verified by the response from the slower type. This conceptualisation relates to a sequential model of conflict resolution where system 2 acts as the validator of the responses generated by system 1.

This mechanism is what forms the basis of a third psychological explanation of conflict resolution, in which one type of cognition always, by default, acts as the validator of the other's response, intervening and correcting these responses when they are incorrect. Hence, the name, 'default-interventionist' mechanism. But, as Evans (2007) argues, with experimental evidence, it is not necessary that our slow system always acts as the validator. Sometimes, it is the case that system 1 brain processes are normatively rational and offer a better response than type-2. This mostly relates to the quantity versus quality debate of cognitive reasoning, where what matters is not only the quantity of cognition for a rational response, but also the quality of the analysis such cognition delivers (see De Neys 2021).

For instance, without advanced math skills, it is a bit naïve to expect that we will get the right answer from type 2 brain to our question, 'what's 983 × 564?', just by thinking about it. Cognition from type 2 is derived from education and training, besides other factors. In these cases, type 1 cognition, is probably just as good as type 2 cognition is. Consider another example. If you ask someone, who's never been to the United Kingdom, to make an educated guess of which city has the bigger population: London or Derby, they might choose London based on their gut feelings, simply because London sounds more familiar to them over Derby. Here, their type 2 cognition is more likely to be flawed if they are not educated on the demography of the UK. This is where simple heuristics shine, as Gigerenzer and Todd (1999) showed with the availability heuristic. The fast response is better in many such cases—not to say always. It does fail at times as well. But this should not be generalised.

In summary, we have multiple accounts of interaction of the faster type 1 cognition and the slower type 2 cognition. While the pre-emptive model of interaction posits that the brain and its different types of cognition work according to some pre-determined rules and thereby avoid conflict, the other accounts suggest otherwise. In this, the parallel competitive structure would argue that both brain processes work in parallel, almost competing with one another for the right response to a problem, but the default-interventionist structure suggests that one of these two processes is always set into motion, by default, the other acting as a validator of responses and taking charge only when things seem to be going wrong.

Conflict Resolution Mechanisms

So which psychological explanation makes most sense? Well, for starters, all these mechanisms of conflict resolution have enjoyed some level of empirical support, in which they have emerged better than the others. Nonetheless, the sequential pathway of cognition, the default-interventionist structure, has been favoured over the others by many prominent scholars. For example, Evans and Stanovich (2013), after theorising on the defining characteristics of the two types of brain processes, sided with the default-interventionist structure as an optimal pathway of conflict resolution. Similarly, Daniel Kahneman in his work with Shane Frederick endorsed the slow system as a rectifier, where neither process was thought to be passive (Kahneman and Frederick 2002). This explanation was also reflected later in Kahneman's account of the two systems in his book, *Thinking, Fast and Slow*. While to many, the interaction between the fast and slow cognition still remains an open question, some psychologists such as Grayot (2020, 105) claim that '[behavioural and neuro economists should] either stick to their purported ambitions to give a realistic description of human decision-making and give up the narrative, or they revise and restate their scientific ambitions.'

Recall the fundamental problem with some of these accounts is that we have limited understanding of what decides the switch between the two types of brain cognition. In recent work, psychologists have also suggested the role of an advanced cognitive process, a three-process model, which attributes a meta-thinking role to a third type of brain processes that facilitates between type 1 and type 2 brain processes. Some have called this the executive function of the brain (Stanovich 2009a; Diamond 2014). However, as Wim De Neys (2023) points out it is implausible to explain the switch between these two types of cognition if we do not do away with the presumption of exclusivity. Recall, exclusivity is the 'tendency to associate intuitive and deliberate processing with the computation of unique responses. system 1 is believed to be responsible for generating a response X and system 2 is responsible for generating an alternative response Y. Critically, here is the underlying exclusivity: Generation of the alleged deliberate response is by definition believed to be beyond the capacity of the intuitive system 1. This simple exclusive dichotomisation is appealing' (De Neys 2023, 2) yet misleading as there is rare empirical evidence that supports this notion. It is the presumption of exclusivity which clouds our understanding of the switch in all leading accounts of such cognitive processing. This is explained eloquently by De Neys (2023) in one of his recent articles on 'Advancing theorising about fast-and-slow thinking'. In this paper, De Neys addresses the main arguments and findings about the cognitive architecture for addressing the relationship between intuition and deliberation. The paper discusses the roles of system 1 (type 1) and system 2 (type 2) processing, the detection of response conflict, and the mechanism controlling the switch between intuitive and deliberative processing. We will summarise this next, before relating it back to the workings of the nudge+.

De Neys' Working Model of Dual Process Theory 2.0

De Neys critiques the foundational assumptions of influential fast-and-slow dual process models, focusing on the exclusivity and switch feature. The exclusivity feature refers to the assumption that intuition and deliberation generate unique responses, while the switch feature concerns the mechanism by which reasoners decide to shift between more intuitive and deliberate processing. De Neys argues that traditional switch accounts, such as the conflict monitoring system 2 and low-effort deliberation, are conceptually problematic as they presuppose exclusivity and fail to present a viable internal switch mechanism. To see how, let's consider some of the prominent conflict resolution mechanism discussed above and see how they might be paradoxical in their working due to exclusivity.

Consider, for example, a no-conflict or a pre-emptive conflict resolution mechanism. As we have discussed, in pre-emptive conflict resolution strategies, each type is associated to work under a specific cue. As De Neys writes, such a model proposes that individuals may not internally switch from system 1 to system 2 thinking and instead always stay in system 1 mode. According to the 'no switch' model, people use system 2 only when system 1 doesn't cue a response or when they are externally prompted to do so. This model explains why individuals often give a system 1 response, attributing it to a failure in detecting the need to activate system 2. However, it fails to account for those who give a system 2 response, highlighting the need to explain how these individuals detect the necessity to engage system 2. The model is considered conceptually coherent but covers only part of the cognitive processes involved.

Next, consider the 'default-interventionist' perspective, which suggests a serial/sequential processing architecture. According to this view, people default to relying on system 1 and only engage the more deliberate system 2 when necessary. This setup raises the 'switch question', referring to the transition between the two systems. The common solution posits that system 2 monitors system 1 output and intervenes in case of conflict. However, this seemingly straightforward idea leads to a paradox, as De Neys points out. Detecting a conflict between system 1 intuition and unique system 2 considerations requires engaging system 2, but the decision to activate system 2 cannot rely on the activation of system 2 itself. This creates a logical problem, challenging the prototypical conflict monitoring system 2 account as it seems to beg the question.

A similar problem also arises with the parallel model, where two of the types of cognitive processes are competing with one another. De Neys criticises the parallel account in dual process models, arguing that it eliminates the cognitive advantage of such models. It suggests that in cases where system 1 aligns with system 2 and yields sound decisions, activating the demanding system 2 is unnecessary and burdensome on cognitive resources. The parallel model is deemed implausible from a cognitive economy standpoint as it may waste resources when not needed. The critique extends to situations where conflicting responses arise, asserting that the fast system 1 must wait for the slower system 2 to resolve conflicts, compromising quick reasoning and action. De Neys notes conceptual inconsistencies and an inability to provide a functional processing account, while clarifying that the issue lies in the continuous parallel activation of both systems, not in their parallel activation per se. The critique also notes a similar assumption in the serial default-interventionist account regarding parallel running once system 2 is activated.

Finally, De Neys discusses a challenge in dual process models where system 2 is expected to both generate a deliberate response and monitor for conflicts between systems 1 and 2 to make switch decisions. A proposed solution involves attributing monitoring and switch decisions to a third system or process, referred to as system 3. In this scenario, system 2 computes a deliberate response, and system 3 compares the outputs of systems 1 and 2. System 3 operates automatically and doesn't require the same cognitive resources as system 2. However, De Neys argues that this solution still raises questions and leads to an infinite regress. Recall, as we have discussed before, to determine if there's a conflict between systems 1 and 2, system 2 needs activation to compute a response, and even an automatically operating system 3 cannot discern conflicts without engaging system 2.

So, if none of these models work, where are we headed? As De Neys argues, the problem seems to lie with the assumption of exclusivity. If we do away with that, we can reasonably explain the switch feature. De Neys does this by proposing a new cognitive architecture where system 1 (or type 1) brain is capable of generating multiple responses, not just the fast type as was previously assumed but also a logical slow response. In fact, in De Neys' working model, system 1 is 'conceived as a collection of intuitively cued responses' (p. 8). This working model incorporates the notion of multiple intuitions as attention to multiple cues defining alternative decision options and includes components such as intuitive activation, uncertainty monitoring, and deliberation, and proposes that a reasoner switches to deliberation when the uncertainty between multiple activated intuitions reaches a critical threshold. By discarding the exclusivity feature and allowing the alleged system 2 response to be generated intuitively, it leads to a more viable dual process architecture. Let's consider the working of this model in more detail below.

De Neys (2023) outlines the first component of a model, presenting system 1 as a collection of intuitively cued responses, focusing on cases with two competing intuitions labelled as intuition 1 (I1) and intuition 2 (I2). Each intuition is identified by the response it cues and characterised by its activation level or strength, which can change over time. The activation strength reflects how strongly an intuition is tied to its eliciting stimulus. The model suggests that intuitions and strength differences primarily emerge through an automatisation or learning process, with repeated exposure and practice leading to the compilation and automatisation of responses. This process applies not only to the alleged system 1 response but also to the alleged system 2 response, assuming exposure through education and daily life experiences. The passage emphasises that strength differences may arise, affecting how well an eliciting stimulus cues the associated response in system 1. The eliciting stimulus can be any specific problem feature, and the illustration provides examples from ratio bias and moral reasoning problems to illustrate the concept.

The second component of this model involves an uncertainty monitoring process within system 1. System 1 continuously calculates the strength difference between activated intuitions, resulting in an uncertainty parameter (U). When the competing intuitions are similar in strength, the uncertainty is high, and if it reaches a critical threshold, system 2 is activated. If one intuition dominates in strength, the uncertainty is low, and no deliberation threshold is reached, allowing the reasoner to remain in system 1 mode. The model explains that the strength differences among competing intuitions vary for different individuals and situations, influencing whether the alleged system 2 response is chosen. The monitoring process applies even when there is only one or no intuition cued, with the uncertainty factor being maximal in entirely new problems. De Neys clarifies that uncertainty monitoring is a core system 1 process, operating without system 2 supervision. Deliberation is optional and only engaged when the uncertainty monitoring deliberation threshold is reached. In this way, it is clear in De Neys' working model, system 1 is capable of two different tasks, generating one or multiple intuitive responses and constantly monitoring them, such as when there arises an uncertainty, it activates system 2 processing.

Consequently, the third component of De Neys' model involves system 2 activation, marking the stage where reasoners engage in slow, demanding deliberation. One of the less developed parts of this working mode is that deliberation can serve various functions, such as response inhibition, algorithmic processing for rule-based tasks, and justification or rationalisation processes. system 2 allows for the active suppression of competing intuitions, the generation of new responses through algorithms, and seeking justifications for intuitions. Deliberation does not guarantee a correct or normative response; instead, it signifies that a reasoner has taken the time to think explicitly about their answer. Deliberation's roles, such as suppression, generation, justification, or others, may coexist. The critical outcome is that deliberation operates on system 1 by modulating the strength of activated intuitions or generating new responses. While it's possible to have system 1 activation without system 2 activation, the reverse is not true. During deliberation, system 1 remains activated, and deliberation acts on its strength representations, providing a mechanism to stop system 2.

Finally, De Neys' architecture takes one further step to explain why and when system 2 processing will stop, for if we allow it to run forever once it has started, we might be quickly depleting our cognitive resources. As such, he introduces the feedback loop as the final component of the model, addressing the question of when to stop system 2 engagement. The proposed feedback loop involves system 2 operating on strength representations in system 1, and the outcome of system 2 processing is fed back into system 1, affecting the uncertainty parameter. Deliberation in system 2 influences the activation levels, modulating the uncertainty parameter. When the uncertainty falls below the deliberation threshold, system 2 engagement stops, and the reasoner returns to pure system 1 processing. The uncertainty parameter serves as the critical determinant of system 2 engagement, with deliberation extending as long as the uncertainty remains above the threshold. The feedback loop illustration demonstrates this concept over time, showing the activation strength of competing intuitions and how system 2 engagement is initiated and stopped based on the uncertainty parameter. As De Neys notes, deliberation may not necessarily lead to decreased uncertainty; it can increase uncertainty and lead to further deliberation. The feedback mechanism ensures that deliberation has the potential to reduce uncertainty and stop system 2 engagement. Both the feedback and uncertainty monitoring components are functionally isolated but do not require postulating a different type of system or processing. The feedback process is considered a system 1 process, emphasising the continuous dynamic interaction between system 1 and system 2 activation during reasoning.

De Neys' working model builds on a default interventionist mechanism. However, as noted, towards the end of this exposition, there remain many areas to improve on, a reason De Neys prefers to call this as a 'working model'. While we do not pursue these areas of improvement here, we refer the interested reader to the research article and the series of commentaries that followed it. Instead, we now turn towards our understanding of nudge+ and how we can explain its cognitive underpinnings using this working model postulated by De Neys.

The Cognitive Underpinnings of Nudge+

What does this dual process model 2.0 of cognition tell us really about the workings of nudge+? Let's take a step back and put this back into context. Reconsider the questions: 'What's 2 × 2?' versus 'What's 983 × 564?'. It is obvious from our discussion so far that the first question will harness an intuitively cued response '4', which is likely the only response, so there will be no uncertainty, and slow response will not be monitored. Similarly for the second question, unless we have been trained in extensive mental math skills, we are not likely to generate any response with confidence. One could also come up with different responses, which then also leads to high uncertainty. As such, by De Neys' logic, system 2 will be cued, and once a satisfactory response is generated, the uncertainty will disappear, and we will revert back to our fast thinking.

Now consider, how one may respond under the influence of a nudge. Here we consider a classic nudge which generates an intuitive response (albeit it does also cue some passive reflection as discussed earlier in Chap. 3). After all, isn't that what a nudge is supposed to do? Take the case of the 'fly in the urinal'. Seeing this fly painted on urinals instinctively arouses men's desire to aim at it, thereby lowering spillage rates and improving sanitation hygiene. Using the model, it is clear that when one is faced with the fly in the urinal, they cue an intuitive response to shoot at it. This response is so strong, like many of our other responses under the nudge, that we often face no uncertainty. As we have discussed before, even though a nudge of this kind mainly generates an intuitive reaction, mainly driven by automatic processes, it does to some extent also cue a passive reflection (recall the distinction between kinds of reflection in Table 3.1).

Take another example. Sam wants to eat healthy but is often tempted by the chocolates. When Sam walks into the cafeteria, he often fails to stick with his healthy eating intentions when he sees the chocolates at the till. As is exemplified by De Neys' working model, it is clear that in this case, Sam generates a response that is cued by the visibility of the chocolates at the till which is 'I want to eat a chocolate'. A classic Thaler and Sunstein option of dealing with such a choice architectural problem will be to present a counter architecture where the chocolates are not so visible at the till. Repositing the chocolates so they are no longer at the eye level will often not generate the above cue. Where it does generate such a cue, it might be weaker to not be pursued by the individual. However, does this always work as such? Do we always have the benefit of a benevolent choice architect to guide us to where we want to be? What happens if we find ourselves in situations where the nudge is absent? Or if the nudge is indeed delivered but we would really want to override it and maintain our autonomy? This is where the 'plus' comes in.

Recall, a reflective plus works on the basis of 'perspective transformation' which suggests that when we prompt reflection, it enables us to articulate our true preferences and in return transform our beliefs. This process of perspective transformation can be clearly explained by the working model proposed by De Neys. When a person receives a specific prompt, this information cues a new intuitive response. Recall the example of where you have only recently been to a showroom. In this example, as had been described, the salesperson had shown you a number of different cars, of which they convinced you to sign up for buying one. Your excitement of seeing these different models got the better of you, and you agreed to sign up and buy one in haste. As you walked out of the showroom, you called up a friend or your financial advisor, who made you question your choice, and you started thinking if this was the best investment you made. You were trapped in buyer's remorse! What is really happening here is that in the first instance, when the salesperson convinced you to buy, you generated an intuitive response 'Let's buy'. However, when you speak with your friend or advisor, the new information, cues another intuitive response 'Should I really buy?'. These intuitive responses oppose each other, generating some form of cognitive dissonance (or 'uncertainty' in De Neys' parlance), that then activates your deliberation until we make a final choice. More precisely, when a reflective 'plus' is delivered, it cues a new response which leads to uncertainty and triggers deliberation.

In our proposition for the nudge+, we claim that any reflective plus simply cues the uncertainty monitoring process underlying system 1. If there is the slightest chance, that some people will not be watchful of the nudge, simply because their reflective capacities of the uncertainty monitoring type are weaker, then introducing the reflective plus can minimise these concerns by generating an additional opposing cue that kickstarts the uncertain monitoring and prompts system 2 deliberation. All reflective prompts delivered alongside the nudge ensure that they activate this second component of De Neys' cognitive architectural model. From then onwards, the individual takes charge and once resolve this uncertainty, they return back to an auto-pilot mode under the influence of the nudge. Thus, subjected to a nudge+, an individual can autonomously decide whether they want to go forward with the nudge or reject it, based on a reflective evaluation of what they are subject to.

Way Forward

Most psychologists would argue that activating the slow cognitive system is effortful (Pennycook 2017). It often requires a cue to get us analytically started. It is possible that the switch is naturally made based on some natural cues in the environment around us. It is also possible that this switch is easier to make for some people more than others, especially if their logically intuitive system is more developed. But there are situations, when it is quite plausible to imagine delivering an external prompt to cue an opposing intuition that eventually engages this system 2 thinking. So, the engagement of system 2 cognition, particularly in a multi-stage cognition process like the one described above, is either situationally or instructionally cued (Pennycook et al. 2015; Pennycook 2017).

Consider an example from De Neys to drive this point forward. De Neys' (2018) Speaks of a local cafeteria that serves both ice-cream (let's say unhealthy option) and blueberry cupcakes (healthy option) for lunch. In this world, there are two kinds of people: John, who likes ice-cream more than cupcakes and when faced with both these choices will take an ice-cream hands down; and Steve, who likes both ice-cream and cupcakes equally, so when faced with the choice, generates two different intuitive responses which eventually kickstarts the uncertainty monitoring process and sets deliberation in. Ultimately Steve chooses one. In this example, it is clear that for some reason Steve is better at activating multiple intuitions and thereby deliberate. Good for Steve, but for all the Johns that we have around us, an external prompt, like the one provided by the reflective plus can help them kick start and engage system 2 cognition—especially when it is needed or when John is not sure if it is latent or passive in the whole process.

This, however, can happen in many ways, as we have seen in the different examples so far. In some cases, people might receive these cues along with a nudge simultaneously, as with our example of using information disclosures that prompt reflective transparency about the nudge. In some other cases, the reflective cue can also be delivered before or after the nudge itself, like the example of combining a pledge with a default nudge. The timing of delivering the nudge and its reflective plus depends on the context of decision-making. Set up this way, it also brings in flexibility for the policy-maker as some sequences might be simply better than others. Ultimately, which sequences work best need to be validated through tests designed to evaluate their impact and effectiveness. But in all these cases, the cognitive underpinnings of the nudge+ engage fast thinking, slowly!

To summarise, the seemingly paradoxical phenomenon of engaging fast and slow cognition at the same time, when working with a nudge+, should not seem paradoxical any longer. Our idea of the nudge+ is supported by the notion of a De Neys' version 2.0 of dual process theory. In its truest sense, the applications of nudge+ speak to the merits of our brain, where we can navigate between slow and fast thinking effortlessly, with the help of an inbuilt logically intuitive power. This is what explains the seamless switch between the two types of cognition, just like when we are faced with different questions such as 'what's 2 × 2?' and 'what's 983 × 564?'. This ability to be logically intuitive can help people to become good thinkers. It is here we think the reflective plus is psychologically situated.

References

Barbey, Aron K., and Steven A. Sloman. 2007. Base-rate respect: From ecological rationality to dual processes. *Behavioral and Brain Sciences* 30 (3): 241–254. https://doi.org/10.1017/S0140525X07001653.

Barrouillet, Pierre. 2011. Dual-process theories and cognitive development: Advances and challenges. *Developmental Review* 31 (2–3): 79–85. https://doi.org/10.1016/j.dr.2011.07.002.

Beattie, Geoffrey. 2012. Psychological effectiveness of carbon labelling. *Nature Climate Change* 2 (4): 214–217. https://doi.org/10.1038/nclimate1468.

Beevers, Christopher G. 2005. Cognitive vulnerability to depression: A dual process model. *Clinical Psychology Review* 25 (7): 975–1002. https://doi.org/10.1016/j.cpr.2005.03.003.

Brainerd, Charles J., and Valerie F. Reyna. 2002. Fuzzy-trace theory: Dual processes in memory, reasoning, and cognitive neuroscience. *Advances in Child Development and Behavior* 28:41–100. https://doi.org/10.1016/S0065-2407(02)80062-3.

Chaiken, Shelly. 1980. Heuristic versus systematic information processing and the use of source versus message cues in persuasion. *Journal of Personality and Social Psychology* 39 (5): 752. https://doi.org/10.1037/0022-3514.39.5.752.

Chaiken, Shelly, and Yaacov Trope. 1999. *Dual-process theories in social psychology*. Guilford Press.

De Neys, Wim. 2018. *Dual process theory 2.0*. New York: Routledge.

De Neys, Wim. 2021. On dual-and single-process models of thinking. *Perspectives on Psychological Science* 16 (6): 1412–1427. https://doi.org/10.1177/1745691620964172.

De Neys, Wim. 2023. Further advancing fast-and-slow theorizing. *Behavioral and Brain Sciences* 46:e146. https://doi.org/10.1017/S0140525X23000559.

Diamond, Adele. 2014. Executive functions: Insights into ways to help more children thrive. *Zero to Three* 35 (2): 9–17.

Epstein, Seymour. 1994. Integration of the cognitive and the psychodynamic unconscious. *American Psychologist* 49 (8): 709. https://doi.org/10.1037/0003-066X.49.8.709.

Epstein, Seymour, Rosemary Pacini, Veronika Denes-Raj, and Harriet Heier. 1996. Individual differences in intuitive–experiential and analytical–rational thinking styles. *Journal of Personality and Social Psychology* 71 (2): 390. https://doi.org/10.1037/0022-3514.71.2.390.

Evans, Jonathan. 1977. Toward a statistical theory of reasoning. *Quarterly Journal of Experimental Psychology* 29 (4): 621–635. https://doi.org/10.1080/14640747708400637.

Evans, Jonathan. 1989. *Bias in human reasoning: Causes and consequences.* Lawrence Erlbaum Associates, Inc.

Evans, Jonathan. 2007. On the resolution of conflict in dual process theories of reasoning. *Thinking & Reasoning* 13 (4): 321–339. https://doi.org/10.1080/13546780601008825.

Evans, Jonathan. 2009. How many dual-process theories do we need? One, two, or many?. https://doi.org/10.1093/acprof:oso/9780199230167.003.0002.

Evans, Jonathan, and Keith E. Stanovich. 2013. Dual-process theories of higher cognition: Advancing the debate. *Perspectives on Psychological Science* 8 (3): 223–241. https://doi.org/10.1177/1745691612460685.

Frederick, Shane. 2005. Cognitive reflection and decision making. *Journal of Economic Perspectives* 19 (4): 25–42. https://doi.org/10.1257/089533005775196732.

Gawronski, Bertram, Dillon M. Luke, and Laura A. Creighton. 2013. 12 dual-process theories. In *The Oxford handbook of social cognition*, 282.

Gigerenzer, Gerd, and Peter Todd. 1999. Fast and frugal heuristics. The adaptive toolbox. In *G. Gigerenzer/PM Todd/ABC Research Group, simple heuristics that make us smart*, 3–34. Oxford.

Goel, Vinod. 2007. Anatomy of deductive reasoning. *Trends in Cognitive Sciences* 11 (10): 435–441. https://doi.org/10.1016/j.tics.2007.09.003.

Grayot, James D. 2020. Dual process theories in behavioral economics and neuroeconomics: A critical review. *Review of Philosophy and Psychology* 11 (1): 105–136. https://doi.org/10.1007/s13164-019-00446-9.

Greene, Joshua D., R. Brian Sommerville, Leigh E. Nystrom, John M. Darley, and Jonathan D. Cohen. 2001. An fMRI investigation of emotional engagement in moral judgment. *Science* 293 (5537): 2105–2108. https://doi.org/10.1126/science.1062872.

Kahneman, Daniel. 2011. *Thinking, fast and slow*. Macmillan.

Kahneman, Daniel, and Shane Frederick. 2002. Representativeness revisited: Attribute substitution in intuitive judgment. In *Heuristics and biases: The psychology of intuitive judgment* 49 (49–81): 74.

Klaczynski, Paul A. 2001. Analytic and heuristic processing influences on adolescent reasoning and decision-making. *Child Development* 72 (3): 844–861. https://doi.org/10.1111/1467-8624.00319.

Lemir, J. 2021. This book is not about baseball but baseball teams swear by it. *The New York Times*.

Lieberman, Matthew D. 2007. Social cognitive neuroscience: A review of core processes. *Annual Review of Psychology* 58 (1): 259–289. https://doi.org/10.1146/annurev.psych.58.110405.085654.

Pennycook, Gordon. 2017. A perspective on the theoretical foundation of dual process models. In *Dual process theory 2.0*, 5–27. Routledge.

Pennycook, Gordon, Jonathan A. Fugelsang, and Derek J. Koehler. 2015. What makes us think? A three-stage dual-process model of analytic engagement. *Cognitive Psychology* 80:34–72. https://doi.org/10.1016/j.cogpsych.2015.05.001.

Pyszczynski, Tom, Jeff Greenberg, and Sheldon Solomon. 1999. A dual-process model of defense against conscious and unconscious death-related thoughts: An extension of terror management theory. *Psychological Review* 106 (4): 835. https://doi.org/10.1037/0033-295x.106.4.835.

Shefrin, Hersh M. 2013. When CFOs think fast.... *The Wall Street Journal*. https://www.wsj.com/articles/SB10001424127887324299104578531561852942612.

Sloman, Steven A. 1996. The empirical case for two systems of reasoning. *Psychological Bulletin* 119 (1): 3. https://doi.org/10.1037/0033-2909.119.1.3.

Stanovich, Keith E. 2009a. Distinguishing the reflective, algorithmic, and autonomous minds: Is it time for a tri-process theory. In *In two minds: Dual processes and beyond*, 55–88. https://doi.org/10.1093/acprof:oso/9780199230167.003.0003.

Stanovich, Keith E. 2009b. *What intelligence tests miss: The psychology of rational thought*. Yale University Press.

Stanovich, Keith E., and Richard F. West. 2000. Individual differences in reasoning: Implications for the rationality debate?-Open Peer Commentary-Three fallacies. *Behavioral and Brain Sciences* 23 (5): 665–665. https://doi.org/10.1017/s0140525x00003435.

Sunstein, Cass R. 2020. *Too much information: Understanding what you don't want to know*. MIT Press.

Tett, Gillian. 2021. Mood and emotion are driving market swings. *Financial Times.* https://www.ft.com/content/89c95e78-ec7f-4d06-9ea8-a9b19a5ed6da.

Wason, Peter C., and Jonathan Evans. 1974. Dual processes in reasoning? *Cognition* 3 (2): 141–154. https://doi.org/10.1016/0010-0277(74)90017-1.

World Bank Group (2015). World Development Report 2015: Mind, Society, and Behavior. Available at: https://doi.org/10.1596/978-1-4648-0342-0

CHAPTER 6

Why Nudge *Forgood* When You Can Nudge+?

Having explored the design of nudge+, it is important not to ignore some of the potential pitfalls of thinking. This is not to knock down thinking as a goal of policy-making. But it is possible to address concerns with a critical perspective which might entail questioning the original rationale of nudge+, though in a way that strengthens rather than undermines this useful policy tool. In so doing, it is possible to consider ways to approach citizen reactions that do not conform to the expectations of the policy-maker. One of the consequences of encouraging people to think is that they realise that what is best for them may not be in line with the aims of the policy. If someone rejects a nudge, after thinking through it, should the policy-maker withdraw the nudge and try another way of influencing behaviour? Does the state have the right to override our bad choices? We argue against this view in a way that strengthens nudge+.

In practice, the costs of so-called wrong decisions over nudging are not as high as for other government policies. Even though the nudge might not suit everyone's preferences, people can voluntarily choose to reject nudge without a lot of cost to themselves. With accepting the nudge or not, the benefit of being able to think about the nudge is that people are in control of their actions and their responses to it. Consequently, people are not so gullible to the influences of the nudge which makes the choice to accept the nudge more credible. This is a way to avoid choosing an option that is not always in our best interests (Schnellenbach 2012).

© The Author(s), under exclusive license to Springer Nature Switzerland AG 2026

S. Banerjee, P. John, *Nudge+*,
https://doi.org/10.1007/978-3-032-13261-1_6

However, that is not to say that the thinking self will always resist a nudge that is viewed as liberty threatening. It may so happen that people believe the nudge is in the general interest of others and they choose to put everyone else above their personal gains. Or they come up with no better alternative and rather be steered. The point is that both decisions require thinking and in both cases, people get to choose. This is all facilitated by the plus. Facilitating the power to think and decide for the same outcome autonomously is a step towards embracing agency. If need be, autonomous citizens can and will side with paternalistic regulation, or they may not, and each choice is to be valued by the policy-maker.

When personal interests are seemingly overlooked, or when people feel helpless, bypassing personal autonomy is acceptable given perceptions of the reality. That is not the same as saying, 'nudge and be done with it'; but the policy is carried out with respect to the individual and keeps the door open to further deliberation. Being open in design about the nudge is as important as just publicly announcing the nudge. This relates to Bovens' (2009) point about token transparency, as discussed earlier in the book. It is important to bring in the plus. It comes in as useful and at minimal cost to the policy-maker as outcomes can remain unchanged; but its reflective potential facilitates watchfulness in the thinking person (Lades and Delaney 2022), who may act in a more self-guided way.

Consider a few examples. The outbreak of COVID-19 changed the socio-economic fabric of the society during 2020–2023 period and beyond. It forced citizens to alter their routines and habits. Communities, some which were predominantly libertarian in their outlook and preferences, have willingly supported and invited hard, liberty-threatening measures on account of full disclosure (Banerjee et al. 2021, 2025). This was mostly driven by the feeling of being helpless but was still reflective. One explanation could also be that this was motivated with an aim to minimise regrets (Banerjee 2020). But the outcome is quite clear. Autonomous citizens have often willingly accepted greater regulation, even if that means an infringement of their personal rights.

Of course, there is a long way to go in understanding the stability of these newfound preferences and the factors that influence them. COVID-19 might have been an outlier. The containment measures were also more paternalistic than most nudges will ever be. But the point remains that humans can collectively decide, in rare circumstances, to side with policies that infringe on their freedom. It does not make them any less autonomous. But that inevitable outcome does not preclude a lack of transparency in policy design, then or in the future. Instead, policy design must enable citizens to think about the course of the action. Participation based on transparent decisions, ensuring an engaged collective voice, is a fundamental feature of a democracy, though can happen in other regimes too. The proposition of nudge+ makes thinking humans reflective of what's in place and around them. The think in the nudge+ fosters this reflective process, at low cost to the recipient and the practitioner.

There can also be a parallel world to what we have just described. Authoritarian regimes can sometimes be associated with long-term, stable preferences for economic welfare and political stability where citizens might value liberty and autonomy as less desirable. In such societies, regardless of whether it is a nudge or any other regulatory measure, these policies can amass huge support. This could be related to different beliefs (Sunstein et al. 2018). Even in this world, it will still be imperative to facilitate thinking.

Consider the case where deliberation will ultimately lead to a different outcome to the policy goal. If thinkers resist the nudge they will digress from what the state (or the policy-maker) desires for them. There will be trade-offs between getting to what is perceived as efficacious by the policy-maker and what the thinking person brings to the table in terms of their decisions for themselves. In this setting, the moral implications of embedding a think into a nudge can be elaborated. The reflective plus is still the ethical way to proceed, even if it is not always the most effective means of driving behaviour change.

Reflective Empowerment

A natural starting point for defending the proposition of embedding think into nudge is to ask whether thinking humans can be immune to the biases of the policy-maker. The policy-maker may not be so benevolent as the nudge architect considers them to be. Another way of viewing this proposition is not to assume that the government is inherently malicious, but that popular beliefs differ from what the government wants to deliver, a stance that appears to encourage paternalism (Salanié and Treich 2009). These make up broadly the goals of the policy-maker, we will come back to this later in the chapter. But we must remember, there can also be limits to information (Downs 1972), such that policy-makers can be biased and misinformed about public policies (Hallsworth et al. 2018; McConnell and 't Hart 2019).

In these cases, there remain concerns that building in agency into the design of the nudge might undermine its efficacy as devised by the biased policy-maker, if the thinking person ultimately does not side with the nudge. The discussion started in the last section, relating to these trade-offs of what is perceived to be desirable by the policy-maker regarding the thinking person is too convenient a line as it cannot deal with the world where the policy-maker is behaviourally biased. And chances are they will mostly be so (Kuran and Sunstein 1998). The defence to this cannot plausibly be, 'a great deal of nudging is inevitable' (Sunstein 2018, 62). While coercion is the least good outcome when public officials are misinformed, it is not by any means the standard to limit transparent policy design. What we suggest as an alternative is the reflective empowerment of citizens.

Thinking humans may become reflectively empowered. These non-thinkers may become thinking humans when facilitated by the plus in the nudge: an active reflection which empowers them to evaluate the nudge and decide what is in it for them. If and when this happens, is reflective empowerment. In this context, it is not hard to reason that reflective empowerment, therefore, is nothing but the consequence of perspective transformation, the cognitive undertone to how the plus works.

Given reflective empowerment, can we reasonably argue that the power of reflection bestowed in humans make them superior to the policy-maker in choosing what is best for them? If their goals are not aligned to the nudger, do they fare well in overriding them, at least costs to other agents? What we are asking of the nudge+ then, is that when our policy-maker is not bereft of biases or misaligned intentions, the thinking person can unregrettably decide for themselves. Analysing outcomes under these circumstances, befits a moral exposition of the ethics of nudge+.

To dig deeper into the idea of reflective empowerment, it is useful to take a psychological discourse of why we need to move away from the idea of an excessive reliance on policy-makers as sole actors to nudge for good. Why instead should we facilitate a greater dialogue between the citizens and the policy-maker with the help of the nudge+? Here we take a day in the lives of Homer and Marge, favourite characters from the popular TV series Simpsons. For convenience, and in the true spirit of the television series, we identify Homer as the non-thinking individual, one who acts on their reflexes and is not intuitive or logical. Marge, on the other hand, resembles our ideal thinking human, she is intuitive and reflective in her actions.

We pick a specific event in their lives and the television series. Say, we are dealing with a case of regulation in Springfield, home to the Simpsons. Fondly recollected as *The Trouble with Trillions*, this twentieth episode, aired in season nine, shows how regulation can often fall through. In this episode, all hell breaks loose as Homer realises, he has not filed his annual income tax. Would a nudge have helped him? As much as Thaler and Sunstein (2008) would have agreed to this, the writers, and producers of the commercial clearly disagreed. Because, as it turned out, Marge had repeatedly put the taxes, as a reminder, on the top of Homer's to-do list, for a month to the deadline. Sadly, the reminder had clearly failed in invoking its salience to nudge Homer into filing his tax returns.

What is worse, irrational Homer was manipulated into assisting the government in spying on others. In return, he would be spared from financial implications and penalties. As Homer found himself in the middle of this severe tax audit, exposing his fraudulency, he took the way out. Agent Johnson (from the FBI) got Homer to uncover the long lost 'one-trillion-dollar bill'. History had it that President Truman handed this bill to Mr. Burns to help the Europeans, which ever since had been nontraceable. The only conclusion: Mr. Burns (the owner of the nuclear power plant) had hidden it, which Homer traced with a microphone in a sting operation. What happened next, was fraught with tragedies for our irrational Homer; for Burns blamed the US government to oppress the average American and instructed gullible Homer against letting the government push him around. Homer responded by freeing Burns from the FBI. The episode ended, with the dollar bill finding home with Fidel Castro who promised the characters land in Cuba, but clearly reneged on his promise, with Homer and Burns left in no-man's land (on a raft!).

This story leaves us to imagine what could have been done differently to help Homer. Certainly, it is not only that nudge failed! They failed because Homer lacked any attention, whatsoever, to respond to the reminder. Had Homer been reflectively empowered, he would have known what is in it for him with the reminders. To do things differently, for instance, the tax authority could have enticed Homer with a scheme where his prior tax audits would nudge him into the process of his next audits, a process of reflective feedback akin to our dual-self pledge discussed earlier in Chap. 3. Homer clearly remembered having done his taxes for last year. If every tax bill that he paid, would tie Homer down with a system to do his next, he would be attentive enough to the reminder when nudged! There is more to behaviour change than simply changing the choice environment (Hallsworth and Kirkman 2020). When we add to these tweaks with other incentives or information, such as the plus, we can stand to benefit from a more targeted intervention.

Marge's reminders would have been useful to conform him to his pledge! Or worse, Homer could be schooled by Marge into the consequences of non-compliance. However, this is not all. Homer was also gullible to his sentiments and fear, sans his reflection. Agent Johnson and Mr. Burns took reasonable advantage of his emotions. Our notion to reflectively empower Homer to a thinking person could well have avoided this outcome. First because if Homer had not failed compliance, given reflection on its consequences, there would have arisen no opportunities to be manipulated! But hypothetically, even after compliance, if Agent Johnson tried enticing him, the sheer power invested in him to think could have helped him bypass those directives! In a way, Homer was coerced to voluntarily agree to spy. His consent was manipulated. Empowering Homer reflectively is the key; not just to respond to nudge, but also to avoid unnecessary manipulation by the government, when it is not in his best interests.

There will be more about this later.

And we must not be fooled to think that it is only the Homers who fail to make use of nudge. In multiple field experiments, Kristal and Whillans (2020) show that nudge fails to nudge commuting behaviours of many individuals. Sunstein (2017) also acknowledges that nudge can fail, although for reasons different from what we say. When weighed up, nudge is often found to overestimate effect sizes of these interventions (DellaVigna and Linos 2022).

The Ethics of Manipulation

A recurrent theme of this chapter is to evaluate the nudge+ on its merits of restoring autonomy and reinstating agency in citizens. There will be, by extension, a discussion of the trade-offs between efficiency and autonomy; because what's good for the policy-maker might not always be perceived as good for the citizen, and if this happens, citizens can reliably fall back on their power to reflect and decide on what is best for themselves. Any gains of reflection, can add on to the pure nudge administered to people. While the nudge must be for good, the nudge+ benefits from reflective empowerment. It is just with the latter any prerequisites of watchfulness are absolved (Banerjee and John 2024).

These value additions come along several ethical dimensions—fairness, openness, respect, and goals (Lades and Delaney 2022). We discuss these now.

Fairness

Nudge can often have very localised, heterogeneous treatment effects on economic agents (Bao and Ho 2015; Mrkva et al. 2021). Homer and Marge, for instance, will respond very differently when exposed to the same nudge. The reasons are, first, that the nudge requires one to be watchful and apprehend if the nudge is any good for them. Besides this, lacking reflective empowerment, some nudges will be totally missed by Homer, just like the reminders failed to nudge him to comply with the taxes. If the world was only as simple as to having Homers and Marges, we could simply guesstimate the distributive losses of delivering nudge! Unfortunately, it is more complex than that. And whilst we have our Homers and Marges, we also have a wide spectrum of varying levels of cognitive engagement in citizens. What is worse is that their reflective capacities vary all the time. Sometimes they vary by socio-demographic characteristics as well. So, whether you are at home or at office, drinking coffee over a leisurely read or running errands, fighting with your partner or not, your reflective capacities are moderated. If we really live in a world where a great deal of nudge is inevitable, sadly, the distributive losses from these differences are insurmountable. Any economist possibly lacks the resources to measure them.

But even beyond these personal differences, nudge applications can also lead to behavioural spillovers (Damgaard and Gravert 2018). These unwarranted effects can occur either when the individuals feel morally licensed to compensate for their one-off good behaviours or are induced to act against their interests by the nudge. Pure nudge, one that changes the situational factors only (that is only the choice architecture), fails to correct for such issues, and is, therefore, unfit as a 'one size for all' policy. Sunstein (2017) elicits conditions under which a nudge like the default can fail or generate reactance at times. How can the nudge, which derives its success solely from an extrinsic change in the environment, therefore, lead to Pareto-improvements?

This begs the question: can we not design a nudge that is self-corrective of these differences? The answer is yes. We bring in the plus. We take our Homer to being a Marge, such that, when nudge is delivered, they do equally well in responding to them. Such a self-correcting device is fair. If citizens can be engaged with the behaviour change process and be effectively empowered to deliberate on the nudge, we can limit the concerns of ineffectiveness due to ignorance and spillovers. Homer now acts, not because he is tricked to behave well, but because he thinks and wants to behave well genuinely. That is the difference with the plus. Let's consider an example.

We compare a default with its default plus. Consider how they work differently in terms of fairness. Say we are in a restaurant. The default makes the desired option salient to the diners. When diners choose from this menu, they are prompted, at times unwillingly, to choose from the list of items cued by the policy-maker. It takes a reflectively empowered diner to find that they can opt out; or to feel the need to be co-opted into the desired choice. Otherwise, if individuals lack an understanding of the means and ends of this intervention, chances are that they might morally compensate for their forced dietary choice in the current instance by binge eating unhealthy food in their next meal. The action of doing good, without understanding the need for it, creates a false warm glow (Cain et al. 2014). A simple reflective tool, such as a prompt, can empower people to choose the menu that is best for them. In our world, this is the two-part, nudge plus. What this can do is as follows: when the nudge is made transparent to the receiver; it takes away the opportunity to manipulate, because the customers will have self-selected themselves into it!

And in terms of scalability, the plus need not impose substantial costs. How many times have we all interacted with servers to seek their suggestions when at a restaurant? It is a conversation with them. A similar conversation can happen with the bot when you walk into a fast-food outlet, trying to choose your meal by filtering out your allergens! If it is for environmental sustainability, it can start out by enlisting your target emissions for the meal, in return giving you a carbon budgeted meal that fits your target. If it is for health reasons, there could be an indicative calorie meter! Options abound. But once you have reflected on your preferences and listed them explicitly through the prompter, the default kicks in, because you asked for it! By being open about the nudge, the nudge+ is asking the nudger to be honest as well. There is nothing wrong with being presented with a nudge so long as the consumer knows what the nudge does to them and why they need it.

There remain two important caveats. First, while it is true that the nudge+ is unequivocally fairer to the nudge; it can, nonetheless, lead to null effects. This goes back to our concerns of trade-offs between perceived efficaciousness and the ethics of manipulation. For instance, prompting a diner to consider their dispositional factors through the prompt can strengthen their prior beliefs. Reflective empowerment makes the diner even surer of what they wanted before. If this happens, then the nudge will fail to moderate any priors. In the restaurant example, this would amount to unsustainable or unhealthy dietary patterns. So what is a better way of approaching this problem? A one-off behavioural change where the nudge tricks the customer into one good behaviour with a series of compensatory negative behaviours, or just leaving them to their priors? The answer to this requires full accountability of all actions (Nafziger 2020). Unfortunately, the evidence is inconclusive to make further claims (Ghesla et al. 2019).

The second caveat relates to the design of the plus. If the plus fails to facilitate reflective empowerment that is worthy of the demands of meeting such behaviour change, then such a nudge+ can also fail, on the presumption that individuals do not stand to gain and be empowered from the reflection to begin with, anyway. It is here that the policy-maker must co-design interventions, specific to the context we are in. This relates to the point in Chap. 4, when we discuss the sequencing of the plus to the nudge.

Openness

Regulatory openness is a theme that has been touched upon several times in this chapter already. A regulatory policy is deemed open only when citizens can identify the means and ends of paternalism. The moral permissibility of these interventions is, therefore, contingent on its transparency. As Bovens (2009) explains, transparency implies type and token interference. The former, in line with Rawls' (1971) publicity principle, says that the policy-maker must be able to publicise what it means to interfere with an agent's agency in influencing their behaviour while the latter makes it imperative for the agent to assert and understand the change in the choice architecture. Nudge is type and 'in principle' token transparent. While they easily satisfy the publicity principle (Thaler and Sunstein 2008), they place substantial cognitive demands of watchfulness when it comes to token transparency.

Many critiques to the nudge are based on the presumption that any greater demand on token interference transparency could potentially reduce the efficacy of nudge (Grüne-Yanoff and Hertwig 2016). Such an idea of token transparency also resonates closely with the idea of epistemic transparency put forward by Hansen and Jespersen (2013). These authors subsequently classify nudge by its transparency into type 1 and 2 nudges. Thus, not every nudge can be token (or, epistemically) transparent. Type (or, system) 2 is more likely to be transparent and therefore publicly acceptable than the type (or, system) 1 nudge (Sunstein 2016).

Recent empirical evidence refines this scholarly debate even further. Making nudge transparent does not reduce its effectiveness (Loewenstein et al. 2015; Bruns et al. 2018). There is also an overwhelming majority when it comes to the public palatability towards nudge (Sunstein 2016). If all of this were true, such that nudge is ex-post favoured by many, then why not make nudge open to begin with? Cultivating watchfulness (Ivanković and Engelen 2019) can go further in increasing the acceptability of nudge. Nudge+ promises a greater token transparency; for instance, when an agent sees a pledge that appeals to their disposition or a traffic lighting scheme that is compounded with an explicit labelling, it clarifies the purpose of the intervention in place. Therefore, it uses transparent means to achieve its ends. To this aim, Bang et al. (2020) show that revealing information about the design of the choice architecture improves the perceived effectiveness of the device, although more for others than for oneself.

Thus, nudge is open, yet conditional on watchful agents being able to block it if needed. On the contrary, nudge+ builds on the design by reflectively empowering all in cultivating watchfulness and respecting token transparency. When the policy-maker makes an option more salient with the pure nudge (default, reordering, et cetera), they are essentially 'celebrating their power' over their citizens. However, with the nudge+, citizens identify the means and ends of the paternalism and are free to choose otherwise fairly. The scholarly debate continues with most critics arguing for more transparency for nudges as a deliverable and non-controversial measure to introduce usually on a case-by-case basis (Schmidt and Engelen 2020).

Respect

A nudge that is fair and open in design must also respect the capacities of the recipient. Again, reflective empowerment is key. This line of argument follows the legitimacy of interventions and is reasonably more nuanced;

for nudge often violates the principle of consumer sovereignty (Schnellenbach 2016). Human preferences have been dubbed inconsistent, opaque, variable, and modifiable, and as such policy-makers, in following the rules of thumb, might either fail to note what is best for agents or can only make a fair approximation. This often runs the risk of misappropriation; for the social planner, in the behavioural world, also faces an information problem given their cognitive limitations (Hayek 1945). We will turn to this in the next section.

In such cases, because 'people know their personal preferences (or interests) better than anyone else, they promote their well-being better by making their own choices than by having them made for them' (White 2013, 83). Nudge, in this world, might lead to value substitution by replacing an agent's ends with those of the social planner.

But the nudge+ engages with the dispositional factors of an individual, respects their autonomy and agency. Consider the default, once again. A default compromises on the agent's capacity to engage in the exercise of self-formation of their preferences. Without any change in mere construct, the individual would choose otherwise. However, if such a nudge were to be combined with a plus, like the prompt, it would respect the citizen's agency in making an adept decision for themselves.

Citizens are also impatient. The plus acknowledges that they can have multiple selves and therefore short-term preference orderings can be different from long-term preference orderings. Both remain equally valid. Why is that so? Because what appears to be irrational might not be so since reasoning under scarcity could involve a different set of norms for individuals. This point has recently received a lot of attention in the works of Morton (2017) and Mullainathan and Shafir (2013).

Does this, however, mean that people who are not reflective stay the way they are always? Without any help, maybe this is the case. But if they are reflectively empowered, exposed to a world of multiple prompts, better choices may ensue. Recent evidence backs up this claim. For example, experiments by Ackert et al. (2020) show that emotional and cognitive intelligence matter significantly when it comes to determining risk and time preferences. Individuals with high emotional intelligence (EQ) are more patient. Similarly, individuals with high IQ are better utility maximisers. It would not be wrong to assume that when the plus upgrades Homer to Marge in reflective capacities, then dispositional factors associated with these cognitive skills are likely to be boosted (Hertwig and Grüne-Yanoff 2017).

A policy, like nudge, overpowers one's ability to grow and self-govern actions (Hausman and Welch 2010; White 2013). But the nudge+ sets out by accepting humans for who they are before they go on to empower them. So far in discussing the fairness and openness of a nudge and a nudge+, and in their respect for mental capacities, we have discussed the regulation of 'means' and 'ends' of engaging in certain behaviours. To distil this discussion of means and ends, we borrow from Engelen (2019) in acknowledging two distinct forms of rationality.

These are process rationality, which encompasses the processes that lead to certain behaviours (the means) and outcome rationality, which includes the final actions per design goals (the ends). When reflectively empowered citizens resist the nudge, they do what is best for them, not as intended by the nudge itself. There are two forces at play here targeting these different rationalities. First, reflective empowerment overcomes limitations to process rationality induced by the nudge. In this, it enables citizens to develop watchfulness. We have discussed this at length before. However, this happens in conjunction with identifying the ends of the nudge. The moral justification of doing what is best for oneself therefore rests on the outcome rationality, also induced by the plus. It is easy to relate that if the plus confers openness to the design of the nudge, then such a device cannot pervert outcome rationality. Even if goals are unidirectional, citizens will be informed of these goals. Respecting their mental capacities will enable them to opt out of any nudge should they wish.

Goals and Opinions

Influencing the means and ends of behaviour relates to the goals of the policy-maker. They might push us towards uni-directional targets, for example. These goals are unique, yet not mutually exclusive to their intentions. If this premise is accepted, where does it lead? To make things more complex, there can be a combination of cases. To simplify this, it is possible to reduce the possibilities of the policy-maker to a simple two goals and two intentions world.

These goals of the policy-maker can either be paternalistic or populist. A paternalistic goal is one that is set by the policy-makers themselves as they judge is best for the individuals. A populist goal is one that is set by the policy-maker based on what they judge citizens to deem appropriate for themselves. It is important to note that we are not subjecting these goals to any degree of moral evaluation, that is, we do not judge paternalistic or populist goals to be good or bad on moral standards. Let's take the example of abolishing private schools. The policy-maker decides to reform education system by folding all schools within a public system. This goal is paternalistic in nature if the policy-maker thinks that this is best for the citizens in the country. However, the same decision could also be made on a populist agenda if the policy-maker thinks that a majority of the citizens would favour abolishing private schools. In some sense, a populist goal is based on the anticipation of what the majority would prefer. Defined this way, populist goal is simply based on anticipated majoritarianism.

Similarly, the policy-maker can have two intentions: benevolent or selfish. Benevolence here is defined as undertaking an action that is in the reasonably best interest of citizens, subject to given conditions in which the policy-maker is making these decisions. Selfishness is defined as undertaking an action that serves some hidden goals of the policy-maker which are not necessarily always in the best interest of the citizens (see Table 6.1). Selfish goals can sometimes be benevolent. For example, increasing healthcare coverage to win votes in the next election could be a policy made with selfish intentions, but it is also benevolent if citizens end up getting better access to healthcare. Prestige projects such as building parks is also another

Table 6.1 Goals and intentions of policy-makers

Goals ↓ / Intentions →	*Benevolent (citizens' reasonably best interest)*	*Selfish (hidden/private interest of policy-maker)*
Paternalistic (policy-maker decides what's best)	**Example:** Abolishing private schools to reduce social inequality and improve equal opportunities **Logic:** Policy-maker judges it best for citizens' welfare	**Example:** Abolishing private schools to secure votes from a disadvantaged segment or to weaken elite opposition **Logic:** Goal framed as 'for citizens' best', but motivation is self-serving
Populist (policy based on anticipated majority preferences)	**Example:** Expanding healthcare coverage because citizens strongly prefer it and it improves their welfare **Logic:** Anticipated majority preference aligns with citizens' best interest	**Example:** Expanding healthcare coverage mainly to win re-election or boost popularity **Logic:** Policy-maker acts to secure office, but citizens still benefit (selfish yet benevolent outcome)

example of a policy that is made with selfish intentions but ends up with a benevolent outcome.

It is also interesting that the same goal could be motivated by different intentions. For instance, a paternalistic goal can arise out of selfish reasons or from benevolence. For example, in our previous example of banning private schools paternalistically—the policy-maker can do so with benevolence, if they are aiming to reduce social inequalities, or they can do so with selfish reasons, if they want to capitalise on the votes of a specific segment of the society. Therefore, it is essential to understand what the plus offers in addressing these different goals of the policy-maker (Clavien 2018).

To start out, consider the easiest case: when goals are paternalistic yet driven by benevolence. We have seen what happens here. Engaging the plus in the nudge leads citizens to side with the nudge under conditions of altruism or helplessness. If the risks of inaction or wrong actions are too high, nudges or nudge+ are not the most effective strategy for the policy-maker. The perils of deviation might outweigh the costs of infringement on liberty. Regulatory interventions, those that minimise this damage by erring on precautionary principles, must therefore be adopted. For instance, banning shark fins might be the best solution to protect endangered sharks. Phasing out fuel-based cars will be key to mitigating greenhouse gas emissions and addressing the net zero target. A nudge or a nudge+ can do little here.

Next is the case when goals are paternalistic yet driven by selfish motivations. In this world, there remains a chance that the nudge will co-opt process rationality (means) to steer citizens towards behaviours (ends) that are not in their best interests. Embedding the plus in the nudge is the stop valve that prevents these selfish goals from being realised with the nudge itself. We have also discussed this at length before.

We then move to the world where the goals are populist. These can be pursued with either selfish or benevolent intentions. In both cases, caution is needed, for there is a risk that majoritarian preferences will prove detrimental to society. Reflectively empowering citizens before embarking on this journey will act as a preventive measure. Let us see why. If society perceives the wrong goals, there will be substantial losses. When can this occur? In a world with a larger proportion of less reflective citizens compared to more reflective ones. If the policy-maker pursues unreflective citizens' goals with a nudge applied universally across society, we end up with damage costs, which totals the welfare losses for everyone. Why? Because more reflective citizens will resist this (remember they are normatively rational). Yet, we could minimise the loss to ordinary citizens as well if we were to use a nudge+ here. Because even if the government pursues the wrong goals of less reflective citizens with a nudge+ as a populist agenda, the plus stands to empower them reflectively. Ultimately, these citizens will reject the nudge and their ex-ante goals. In this way, the nudge+ is self-corrective, a key point in our research programme.

With a nudge, it is not always the less reflective citizens who are at risk of manipulation. This risk arises only in cases when the policy-maker is selfish and tries to promote paternalistic goals, or when they are benevolent but further a misaligned populist agenda. The more reflective citizens, given their strong preferences, are immune. Our discussion is summarised in Table 6.2 below.

Table 6.2 The ethics of manipulation in a 2-goal × 2-intention framework of regulation

Nudger goals ↓ / nudge intentions →	*Benevolent (citizens' reasonably best interest)*	*Selfish (hidden/private interest of policy-maker)*
Paternalistic (policy-maker decides what's best)	**Risk:** Nudges alone may be ineffective when deviation risks are too high (e.g., shark fin bans, fuel phase-outs) **Role of nudge+:** Improves over nudge when citizens face altruism/helplessness, but regulatory interventions may ultimately be more appropriate	**Risk:** Nudger may co-opt *process rationality*, steering citizens towards ends not in their best interest **Role of nudge+:** Works as a *stop valve*, embedding reflective empowerment so selfish goals cannot be realised unchecked
Populist (policy based on anticipated majority preferences)	**Risk:** Even with benevolence, misaligned majoritarian goals (a 'Homer-driven' agenda) threaten *outcome rationality* and may harm society **Role of nudge+:** Acts as a *self-corrective device* by empowering citizens to reassess and, if necessary, reject their own ex-ante goals	**Risk:** Pursuit of majoritarian goals for self-interest (e.g., votes, prestige) can generate outcome irrationality if citizens' preferences are unreflective **Role of nudge+:** Reflective empowerment mitigates manipulation, helping citizens reject misaligned populist nudges

Voluntary Consent

So far, we have argued that the ethical limitations to the nudge, in co-opting process and outcome rationalities, can be overcome with the design of a reflective plus. What the plus offers to the nudge then is a way out of it by the reflective empowerment of citizens. Set up this way, the nudge+ enables citizens to think about the nudge and its need for them, thereby helping them to choose whether they want to be under its influence or not. However, overcoming the resistibility of the nudge while building in transparency and restoring the rationality of citizens is not, by any means, necessary or sufficient to consent voluntarily to the nudge. Why is that?

In a hypothetical world, an unreflective citizen can be subject to a nudge that is open and transparent, easy to overcome when watchful and respects rationality, yet they may be illegitimately controlled to choose against their will by the nudge. This has been recently discussed by Kiener (2021), on the lines of 'manip necessary or sufficient to consent voluntarily to the nudge ulation' (Beauchamp and Childress 2019) or 'non-argumentative influences' (Blumenthal-Barby 2012). Take a step back to revisit our earlier example of Homer's tax non-compliance. When Agent Johnson presented Homer with a way out as a spy, this was an open and transparent choice to Homer. Homer knew what was in store for him, both as announced to him and in the design of the operation. However, was it easy to opt out? Pure semantics will answer yes. Homer could have turned down this offer and faced his consequences. His rational processes made him choose the way in, for he minimised his damages. Nonetheless, it was not as simple. The way out was designed in a way that Homer could do nothing else but take the offer. Fortunately, this was not a nudge, but had it been, we could not have called it ethical!

As Kiener argues, a nudge that illegitimately controls citizens, by leaving with no way out, just in the way it is presented to them, is not ethical. Even when consented to by citizens, ex-post, this cannot be taken to be as a valid reasoning to nudge; for the consent given in this case is influenced by the design of the nudge itself. Thus, besides these ethical justifications to address process and outcome rationality, a nudge must also secure voluntary consent: a process to remain uninfluenced by the design of the intervention!

Why not step back and assess the public palatability of nudge for a while. Sunstein (2015a, 2015b) defends the nudge position against the manifold critiques as a literal nonstarter; for humans are seldom but rational, functioning in non-neutral ecological environments where they are constantly influenced by unintended external cues. As such, the application of nudge seems inevitable but must be applied only 'for good'. And his defence rests on people consenting to the nudge when asked about its application, ex-post! We find it hard to accept this at face value. Why? Consider the framing of defaults for organ donation by Johnson and Goldstein (2003). The authors documented that framing organ donation as an opt-out default, versus an opt-in, dramatically increased consent rates to organ donation by almost two-fold. The massive success of defaults is almost always attributed to using citizen's inertia by exploiting their status-quo bias! Is this ethical? The nudge proponents would tend to argue in favour! The nudge is resistible, open in design and leads to outcome rationality! In any case, people who do not want the default strongly will reject it anyway (Sunstein 2017), we have discussed this. However, the framing vitiates consent here! What if the framing induces other biases at play? In the Johnson and Goldstein example, could consent arise from a desire to conform to norms, such that refusing the default was guilt-inducing? If this was true, the nudge is not ethically defensible for it manipulates the judgement to consent. Some, therefore, call nudging 'bullshit' (Simkulet 2018), where the goal is not rational persuasion, but only persuasion to get citizens to where they want them to be.

Consider another study by Venema et al. (2019) on the effectiveness of a nudge to promote the consumption of healthier diets. The authors experimentally manipulate the placement of different cup-sizes to test a centre-stage nudge. The idea: to assess if goals of the nudge, congruent or not to the respondents' beliefs, made a difference to their final choices. And the results tell us that the centre-stage nudge to choose the smaller cup-sizes was effective for those who wanted a healthier diet to begin with anyway; the presence of the nudge did not moderate these effects! Similarly, Sunstein (2017) finds North American women, after marriage, do not stick to the default rule of retaining pre-marriage surnames. This outcome comes about because of strong precedents. Thus, a nudge might not be 'the right instrument if the behaviour or the setting is tied to strong preferences'. How does one explain this? Clearly when preferences are strong, citizens do not get co-opted being manipulated for consenting illegitimately. It is only the weak-willed who fall prey to this.

Interpersonal justification, Kiener says, must be taken care of to avoid being in this dilemma. If we need to save our Homers from risks of manipulation, it is in the power of the plus to empower them to reflect on the goals of the nudger or on their misaligned priors. Often, opinions on nudge depend on whether citizens believe that the nudger or the policy-maker shares their same goals and whether they trust the intention of the nudger. This condition for the public palatability of nudge is otherwise known as a shared preference justification. Kiener calls it the interpersonal justification. Nudge+ is simply motivated along these lines. While the policy-maker initiates the policy, the plus can facilitate and restore capacities in agents to choose voluntarily the best for themselves. In the worst case of incompetence of the policy-maker, there remains no harm done to the citizens!

Some Counter Arguments

It is important to be aware that there are some counter arguments to more reflective forms of public policy, though of course they are not convincing in the end. They show that not every case of reflection is necessarily good. One classic argument rests on classic paternalist arguments of taking an initiative with someone and then convincing them afterwards, which is at the core of nudge. People might not see the logic of contributing to a pension scheme until they actually start as they would procrastinate otherwise. They learn by doing. This strategy is at the core of libertarian paternalism, going with the grain of preferences with light touch interventions. We accept some compulsion in many situations and do not think it violates autonomy long term. Take education—we often require people to take a course, such as a methods module in a social science degree, which students do not always like or appreciate, but once they are in the rest of the course they start to appreciate the instruction and say something like 'thank goodness I did this course, as I will get out a lot more out of my degree now that I have done it'. Being compelled causes more reflection after the event.

Thinking can be quite problematic sometimes, as people who think of lots of arguments at once, can become overwhelmed by thinking of both reasons to do something or not to do something. People can overthink things, which might involve an element of abstraction and hesitation as more information comes to bear. People might get confused and overloaded with arguments so it is possible that thinking about a problem can increase procrastination rather than lead to a decisive break through. The other issue is that many of the larger issues that are behind behavioural public policy choices can be alarming and worrying. If it were the case that these choices were more about personal taste and matching preferences so lifestyle choices, then it might be easy to think about them. But many of the big policy problems that make behaviour choices so important can disturb people's equanimity. They can get so caught up with the big issues that they cannot focus on the day to day or see their contribution as meaningless compared to the scale of the problem. One example is organ donation which reminds people of death and illness and arranging actions to prepare for an event that ends life, especially at a young age which is when organs are healthy, such as when recovered after a car crash.

So, it may be the case the health measures can backfire with more thinking. Organ donation was tested in the project reported in *Nudge Nudge, Think Think* (John et al. 2009). The project aimed to encourage students to put their names forward for the organ donation register. Using classrooms, the researchers randomly allocated students to a nudge group that received a number of behavioural prompts, then a think plus nudge group (nudge+) where they got the prompts but also were encouraged to think about organ donation in small groups. There was also a placebo group where the student received information on something quite different. The outcomes were best in the nudge group, followed by the placebo group, then the think group. We do not have direct evidence about what happened in the think group, but something managed to negate the effect of nudge, something about the think which may be to do with the worry about and thinking it all through that may have caused hesitation. In a project seeking to increase vaccine readiness, we found that a plus reduced vaccine intentions (Banerjee et al., 2024). It might mean thinking about health issues is not easy.

Delay and hesitation might be not what is needed. For example, the person who tries to save someone from drowning usually does not think through the options: they dive in and use the precious minutes to get the person ashore that might be lost by thinking it through while the person goes under. Now we should not condone reckless behaviour, and people helping others can get into difficulties themselves. In fact, a better outcome is to have someone trained who does not need to think through all the options but has the learning to put into place and can make (conscious) decisions quickly, thinking at the same time as using their learnt behaviours.

Conscious awareness is not an unconditional good. Consciousness can help people follow more undesirable goals than unconscious action because the depth of thinking can lead to more efficient delivery of worse outcomes from poor desires, such as the ruthless dictator who follows things through rather than someone just complies with a regime. Thinking might mean that self-interest plays a role.

When on research leave in another country, one of the authors (guess who?) was renting a garden apartment as part of the larger house. One afternoon he cut his finger badly when trying to slice some bread with large knife. Running with a bloody hand to the front door of the big house, he was shocked to see a slight hesitation in the response to the owners to his distress. In the nano-second just after when they opened the door, they seemed to be thinking the situation through before helping (worried about liabilities?). Thankfully, the hesitation did not last that long, and the owners were soon running to their medical store to apply bandages and creams to much thanking and appreciation. Thinking did help in this case then and no harm was done.

The more natural response to instincts and habits might be the product of a life chosen so that the individual does not need to think through each choice, but because they have decided on their moral compass, they know they will make the right choices, responding to cues in the right way. They can be happy in a kind of bumbling autonomy, preferable to an overcalculating assessment of immediate self-interest. Having set the course the individual can anticipate what nudge comes their way, which might contrast with someone who thinks they have autonomy but actually may be subject to more subtle forms of manipulation in the thinking environment. Deliberation theorists have become aware that forums and spaces to think are often subject to frames from those who run such forums (Ryfe 2005). The more automatic person might be less susceptible because they have not invested so much in autonomy. They might become subliminal critics of nudge, recoiling if they do not like something. Not expecting too much autonomy in the first place, they are sceptical, a bit like when people receive marketing information as opposed to a conversation with a friend making the same arguments. This is why face-to-face canvassing or peer recruitment is more effective than leaflets e-mails as people trust someone, they can have a conversation with (Green and Gerber 2019). The thinker might continue with the intervention because they are convinced, they are free when they are being subtly manipulated.

Ultimately these examples are exceptional cases and a long way from behavioural policy choices that are studied in this book. Or simply an exercise in author contrarianism. Overall, we believe that a choice made more freely and thoughtfully is better than one that is done unconsciously because we believe in agency as desirable in itself. In fact, it is consistent with this preference that we can accept choices from individuals that make them and society worse off (to a degree, providing no harm to others occurs), as we think that people have the right to make poor decisions, that they are their own best judge. That they should be allowed to make mistakes and then hopefully learn from them. We also have faith in humanity that people will make the right choices for themselves, in the long term with repeated conversations. It is hard for us to see what is in their interests (White 2013) but they can discover their interests through reflection. Overall, the intervention that increases agency is preferable to one that does not.

In summary, this chapter has mapped out the ethical dimension to reflective action on the part of individuals. The overall argument is intuitive, about preferring situations where an individual has the chance to reflect on something that is important to them rather than be subtly manipulated to do it. In other words, we celebrate more agency. But there are nuances along the way in how we see this happening in practice and some counter arguments to consider. Such contrary views can help us bolster our sense of ethical superiority of reflective interventions that help individuals achieve agency.

References

Ackert, Lucy F., Richard Deaves, Jennifer Miele, and Quang Nguyen. 2020. Are time preference and risk preference associated with cognitive intelligence and emotional intelligence? *Journal of Behavioral Finance* 21 (2): 136–156. https://doi.org/10.1080/15427560.2019.1663850.

Banerjee, Sanchayan. 2020. Reviving reciprocity to tackle behavioural anomalies during COVID19. Blog post, available here: https://www.orfonline.org/expert-speak/reviving-reciprocity-tackle-behaviouralanomalies-during-covid19-64243

Banerjee, Sanchayan, and Peter John. 2024. Nudge plus: Incorporating reflection into behavioral public policy. *Behavioural Public Policy* 8 (1): 69–84. https://doi.org/10.1017/bpp.2021.6.

Banerjee, Sanchayan, Manu Savani, and Ganga Shreedhar. 2021. Public support for 'soft' versus 'hard'public policies: Review of the evidence. *Journal of Behavioral Public Administration* 4 (2). https://doi.org/10.30636/jbpa.42.220.

Banerjee, Sanchayan, Peter John, Brendan Nyhan, Andrew Hunter, Richard Koenig, Blake Lee-Whiting, Peter John Loewen, John McAndrews, and Manu

M. Savani. 2024. "Thinking about default enrollment lowers vaccination intentions and public support in G7 countries." *PNAS nexus* 3 (4): 93.

Banerjee, Sanchayan, Manu Savani, and Ganga Shreedhar. 2025. Do the public support 'hard' or 'soft' public policies? In *Behavioural economics and policy for pandemics: Insights from responses to COVID-19*, 126–147. Cambridge: Cambridge University Press.

Bang, H. Min, Suzanne B. Shu, and Elke U. Weber. 2020. The role of perceived effectiveness on the acceptability of choice architecture. *Behavioural Public Policy* 4 (1): 50–70. https://doi.org/10.1017/bpp.2018.1.

Bao, Jiayi, and Benjamin Ho. 2015. Heterogeneous effects of informational nudges on pro-social behavior. *The BE Journal of Economic Analysis & Policy* 15 (4): 1619–1655. https://doi.org/10.1515/bejeap-2014-0125.

Beauchamp, Tom, and James Childress. 2019. *Principles of biomedical ethics: Marking its fortieth anniversary*. Taylor & Francis.

Blumenthal-Barby, Jennifer S. 2012. Between reason and coercion: Ethically permissible influence in health care and health policy contexts. *Kennedy Institute of Ethics Journal* 22 (4): 345–366. https://doi.org/10.1353/ken.2012.a495158.

Bovens, Luc. 2009. The ethics of nudge. In *Preference change: Approaches from philosophy, economics and psychology*, 207–219. Springer.

Bruns, Hendrik, Elena Kantorowicz-Reznichenko, Katharina Klement, Marijane Luistro Jonsson, and Bilel Rahali. 2018. Can nudges be transparent and yet effective? *Journal of Economic Psychology* 65:41–59. https://doi.org/10.1016/j.joep.2018.02.002.

Cain, Daylian M., Jason Dana, and George E. Newman. 2014. Giving versus giving in. *Academy of Management Annals* 8 (1): 505–533. https://doi.org/10.5465/19416520.2014.911576.

Clavien, Christine. 2018. Ethics of nudges: A general framework with a focus on shared preference justifications. *Journal of Moral Education* 47 (3): 366–382. https://doi.org/10.1080/03057240.2017.1408577.

Damgaard, Mette Trier, and Christina Gravert. 2018. The hidden costs of nudging: Experimental evidence from reminders in fundraising. *Journal of Public Economics* 157:15–26. https://doi.org/10.1016/j.jpubeco.2017.11.005.

DellaVigna, Stefano, and Elizabeth Linos. 2022. RCTs to scale: Comprehensive evidence from two nudge units. *Econometrica* 90 (1): 81–116. https://doi.org/10.3982/ECTA18709.

Downs, Anthony. 1972. Up and down with ecology: The "issue-attention cycle". In *Agenda setting*, 27–33. Routledge.

Engelen, Bart. 2019. Nudging and rationality: What is there to worry? *Rationality and Society* 31 (2): 204–232. https://doi.org/10.1177/1043463119846743.

Ghesla, Claus, Manuel Grieder, and Jan Schmitz. 2019. Nudge for good? Choice defaults and spillover effects. *Frontiers in Psychology* 10:178. https://doi.org/10.3389/fpsyg.2019.00178.

Green, Donald P., and Alan S. Gerber. 2019. *Get out the vote: How to increase voter turnout.* Brookings Institution Press.

Grüne-Yanoff, Till, and Ralph Hertwig. 2016. Nudge versus boost: How coherent are policy and theory? *Minds and Machines* 26 (1): 149–183. https://doi.org/10.1007/s11023-015-9367-9.

Hallsworth, Michael, and Elspeth Kirkman. 2020. *Behavioral insights.* MIT Press.

Hallsworth, Michael, Mark Egan, Jill Rutter, and Julian McCrae. 2018. Behavioural government: Using behavioural science to improve how governments make decisions. *The Behavioral Insights Team.*

Hansen, Pelle Guldborg, and Andreas Maaløe Jespersen. 2013. Nudge and the manipulation of choice: A framework for the responsible use of the nudge approach to behaviour change in public policy. *European Journal of Risk Regulation* 4 (1): 3–28. https://doi.org/10.1017/S1867299X00002762.

Hausman, Daniel M., and Brynn Welch. 2010. Debate: To nudge or not to nudge. *Journal of Political Philosophy* 18 (1). https://doi.org/10.1111/j.1467-9760.2009.00351.x.

Hayek, Friedrich August. 1945. The use of knowledge in society. *The American Economic Review* 35 (4): 519–530. https://www.jstor.org/stable/1809376.

Hertwig, Ralph, and Till Grüne-Yanoff. 2017. Nudging and boosting: Steering or empowering good decisions. *Perspectives on Psychological Science* 12 (6): 973–986. https://doi.org/10.1177/1745691617702496.

Ivanković, Viktor, and Bart Engelen. 2019. Nudging, transparency, and watchfulness. *Social Theory and Practice* 43–73. https://doi.org/10.5840/soctheorpract20191751.

John, Peter, Graham Smith, and Gerry Stoker. 2009. Nudge nudge, think think: Two strategies for changing civic behaviour. *The Political Quarterly* 80 (3): 361–370. https://doi.org/10.1111/j.1467-923X.2009.02001.x.

Johnson, Eric J., and Daniel Goldstein. 2003. *Do defaults save lives?* American Association for the Advancement of Science.

Kiener, Maximilian. 2021. When do nudges undermine voluntary consent? *Philosophical Studies* 178 (12): 4201–4226. https://doi.org/10.1007/s11098-021-01644-x.

Kristal, Ariella S., and Ashley V. Whillans. 2020. What we can learn from five naturalistic field experiments that failed to shift commuter behaviour. *Nature Human Behaviour* 4 (2): 169–176. https://doi.org/10.1038/s41562-019-0795-z.

Kuran, Timur, and Cass R. Sunstein. 1998. Availability cascades and risk regulation. *Stanford Law Review* 51:683. https://doi.org/10.2307/1229439.

Lades, Leonhard K., and Liam Delaney. 2022. Nudge Forgood. *Behavioural Public Policy* 6 (1): 75–94. https://doi.org/10.1017/bpp.2019.53.

Loewenstein, George, Cindy Bryce, David Hagmann, and Sachin Rajpal. 2015. Warning: You are about to be nudged. *Behavioral Science & Policy* 1 (1): 35–42. https://doi.org/10.1177/237946151500100106.

McConnell, Allan, and Paul 't Hart. 2019. Inaction and public policy: Understanding why policymakers 'do nothing'. *Policy Sciences* 52 (4): 645–661. https://doi.org/10.1007/s11077-019-09362-2.

Morton, Jennifer M. 2017. Reasoning under scarcity. *Australasian Journal of Philosophy* 95 (3): 543–559. https://doi.org/10.1080/00048402.2016.1236139.

Mrkva, Kellen, Nathaniel A. Posner, Crystal Reeck, and Eric J. Johnson. 2021. Do nudges reduce disparities? Choice architecture compensates for low consumer knowledge. *Journal of Marketing* 85 (4): 67–84. https://doi.org/10.1177/0022242921993186.

Mullainathan, Sendhil, and Eldar Shafir. 2013. *Scarcity: Why having too little means so much*. Macmillan.

Nafziger, Julia. 2020. Spillover effects of nudges. *Economics Letters* 190:109086. https://doi.org/10.1016/j.econlet.2020.109086.

Rawls, John. 1971. A theory of justice. In *Applied ethics*, 21–29. Routledge.

Ryfe, David M. 2005. Does deliberative democracy work? *Annual Review of Political Science* 8 (1): 49–71. https://doi.org/10.1146/annurev.polisci.8.032904.154633.

Salanié, François, and Nicolas Treich. 2009. Regulation in happyville. *The Economic Journal* 119 (537): 665–679. https://doi.org/10.1111/j.1468-0297.2009.02221.x.

Schmidt, Andreas T., and Bart Engelen. 2020. The ethics of nudging: An overview. *Philosophy Compass* 15 (4): e12658.

Schnellenbach, Jan. 2012. Nudges and norms: On the political economy of soft paternalism. *European Journal of Political Economy* 28 (2): 266–277. https://doi.org/10.1016/j.ejpoleco.2011.12.001.

Schnellenbach, Jan. 2016. A constitutional economics perspective on soft paternalism. *Kyklos* 69 (1): 135–156. https://doi.org/10.1111/kykl.12106.

Simkulet, William. 2018. Nudging, informed consent and bullshit. *Journal of Medical Ethics* 44 (8): 536–542. https://doi.org/10.1136/medethics-2017-104480.

Sunstein, Cass R. 2015a. The ethics of nudging. *Yale Journal on Regulation* 32:413.

Sunstein, Cass R. 2015b. Nudges do not undermine human agency. *Journal of Consumer Policy* 38 (3): 207–210. https://doi.org/10.1007/s10603-015-9289-1.

Sunstein, Cass R. 2016. Do people like nudges. *Administrative Law Review* 68:177. https://doi.org/10.2139/ssrn.2604084.

Sunstein, Cass R. 2017. Nudges that fail. *Behavioural Public Policy* 1 (1): 4–25. https://doi.org/10.1017/bpp.2016.3.

Sunstein, Cass R. 2018. Misconceptions about nudges. *Journal of Behavioral Economics for Policy* 2 (1): 61–67. https://doi.org/10.2139/ssrn.3033101.

Sunstein, Cass R., Lucia A. Reisch, and Julius Rauber. 2018. A worldwide consensus on nudging? Not quite, but almost. *Regulation & Governance* 12 (1): 3–22. https://doi.org/10.1111/rego.12161.

Thaler, Richard H., and Cass R. Sunstein. 2008. *Nudge: Improving decisions about health, wealth, and happiness.* Penguin.

Venema, Tina A. G., Floor M. Kroese, Emely De Vet, and Denise T. D. De Ridder. 2019. The One that I Want: Strong personal preferences render the center-stage nudge redundant. *Food Quality and Preference* 78:103744. https://doi.org/10.1016/j.foodqual.2019.103744.

White, Mark. 2013. *The manipulation of choice: Ethics and libertarian paternalism.* Springer.

CHAPTER 7

Who Is Nudge+ Done to and by Whom?

So far, we have discussed the general ethical implications of having citizens reflect alongside the nudge as opposed to just being nudged. However, the ethics of nudge+ also depends on who engages with nudge and whether it delivers on the scaling up opportunities for all groups of citizens. It is important to be aware that one of the preferred ways of directly engaging with citizens in deliberative mechanisms does not have massive reach. With the partial exception of deliberative polls (Fishkin 2009), the participants in these exercises have been limited in number and are usually not representative of larger populations. Nudge+ activities have the advantages of plugging in large numbers of citizens at scale but at the same time engaging them with large policy and political issues. Yet even with these more scaled-up activities, there is the challenge of ensuring that everyone participates on equal grounds.

Then who delivers this reflective plus to the citizens, whether citizens themselves, or the government, or a third-party agent. Nudge is traditionally administered by policy-makers, but can citizens have a more direct role? Can they get policy-makers to think? We consider whether it is feasible to use nudge+ to reverse the tables of who nudges and who is nudged to establish more of a level playing between policy-makers and citizens.

© The Author(s), under exclusive license to Springer Nature Switzerland AG 2026
S. Banerjee, P. John, *Nudge+*,
https://doi.org/10.1007/978-3-032-13261-1_7

Democratic Theory Concerning Nudging and Thinking

Discussion of ethics needs to be grounded in accounts of democratic citizenship. These debates have evolved from a reliance on conventional representative democracy based on long chains of delegation from principals to agents. The delegation is from citizens to representatives, and to their bureaucracies, and then to agencies and interest groups. The alternative is where the citizen is invited into direct dialogue with agencies and decision-makers (John et al. 2009). The classic nudge envisages a passive role for citizens as receptors of an intervention, as an object of policy-makers to use their discretion to improve social welfare. Citizens are rather like tax-payers who pay up their demands without really knowing why the rates have been set, and probably even more unaware of the exact rate of levy with sales taxes. This is still democratic as in western democracies the authorisation of nudge is like any other policies in that elected governments or executives are mandated to take executive action on and may use their majority in the legislature to ensure that this takes legal form. Within central governments there are usually portfolios or departments, which are the arenas in which nudge ideas are formulated, where ministers are the authorisers of new policies, such as nudge. Usually new legislation does not need to be passed to implement a nudge as it usually only requires changes in operating procedures that the government has discretion over as part of its general responsibility to run public services. In each ministry, a civil servant or state bureaucrat wanting to carry out a nudge can ask the minister for authorisation like any other policy, which can be done through drafting a proposal and putting it to the minister for sign off. Then it is up to the civil servant or bureaucrat to work with experts and other agencies to deliver the nudge and then report back to ministers, or parliamentary committees, or their equivalents at other levels of government. Democratic authorisation is in place because elected representatives may hold these ministerial office-holders to account. Governments earn legitimacy from winning an electoral contest when citizens choose candidates and programmes; then they are subject to parliamentary review and scrutiny.

The delegation model of democracy and policy-making has advantages as it devolves the running of government to experts but ensures the line of accountability to citizens who are the ultimate principal and can dismiss a government (Strøm 2000). But such a model has come under criticism as it relies on citizens being more than just passive receptors of information about the performance of the incumbent: they need to review it effectively, and we know that citizens are subject to the normal biases, such as time inconsistent preferences, when assessing government performance. For particular relevance for nudge is the vast size of the government machine and the difficulty for citizens to be aware what is happening, especially with the delegation of power to agencies (Flinders 2008), many of which are responsible for delivering nudges. This is the realm of political-bureaucratic relationships where the agent of the bureaucracy is hard for politicians to control (Weingast 1984). In terms of day-to-day politics, ministers (unless they have a special interest in nudge) are not going to see behavioural public policies as a key part of their political and policy agenda, compared to a major spending decision, for example. They are likely to see it as something good to happen and report on if successful, but they are not likely to be involved day-to-day. In practice, a nudge unit and behavioural policies are operating at the initiative of bureaucrats supported by their expert advisors.

The current operation of representative democracy has been seized on by critics who are keen to reinvigorate democracy and critical of the limited scope of party politics and the lack of responsiveness of the system (Barber 1984). Inspired by ideas of direct democracy, which go back to the Greeks, participation in policy-making carried out face-to-face with decision-makers is seen as a way to empower citizens. The direct control of policy is hard to achieve in most representative democracies so it requires some delegation on the part of policy-makers to alternative spaces where decisions may be discussed and advised, even mandated. Hence the popularity of mini-publics to debate public issues (Smith 2009), such as to discuss spending decisions (participatory budgeting) or engage in city-wide participation between service users and providers, called empowered participation (Fung 2004) or citizen governance (John et al. 2009). The idea is that coproduction with citizens, helping to produce services, generates more dialogue and interaction between citizens and the state, much more in the spirit of democracy than citizens' attempts to deal with long chains of delegation. It is possible to see nudge as helping coproduction between citizens and the state, with citizens being encouraged to do more by signals from the state. With this perspective, it is not a great step to see citizens more involved with collective endeavours alongside nudge. And if we accept the criticism, discussed earlier in this book by Chater and Loewenstein (2023) that nudges are too individualistic in conception (the 'i-frame'), a more collective form of nudge (the 's-frame') may be seen to be more consistent with collaborative policy-making. A conventional nudge tends to work on individual action and is less inclined to see the larger picture of collective action and partnerships associated with public policy. They deploy studies that show that using the i-frame can reduce attention to wider policy issues and proposals, such as to tackle climate change (Hagmann et al. 2019). A nudge that emphasises collective goals through think could have better success in ensuring adherence of policy goals when citizens understand those goals and engage with them.

A key aspect of the alternative to representative democracy is new institutions to facilitate more active roles for citizens to bring them in line with new democratic ideas. In this it is not enough for citizens to vote but they need to take active part, and for that they need to think about decision-making and the underlying issues, take on board new information, and then reason through the arguments in terms of their values. This is the virtue of a different model of democracy, deliberative democracy (Mansbridge 1983; Bächtiger et al. 2018). Here randomly selected citizens are facilitated to reflect and think about the big issues of the day, embracing wider policy issues, feeding directly into decision-making.

In many applications it is enough for deliberative democracy to take place as an alternative or complement to democratic debate. It can be directed to constitutional issues, such as electoral reform (Fournier 2011) or, for the UK, Brexit (Renwick et al. 2018). But deliberation is often tied to policy issues, such as a deliberative jury or deliberate polls on something specific (Curato et al. 2022), like the siting of a nuclear power plant or abortion rights. It is not that much of an extension to the argument to consider the kinds of issues addressed by nudge, such as to address climate change, have their equivalent in a think where the think becomes directed more to the actual behaviour. As explained in Chap. 3, such deliberations can be tied to behaviour change in a think or a deliberative nudge. Here nudge+ can take advantage of the deliberative side but scale this up to actual behaviour change in the ground rather than making recommendations to policy-makers that might not get implemented.

The key criticism of deliberative mechanisms is, first, the framing of the process (Zhong 2011), and possible manipulation by the designer of interventions, such as the form of facilitation, and the kinds of evidence that are brought to bear and by whom. This source of bias can bring think closer to nudge. Individuals are subject to the same pressures, such as from a benevolent policy-maker, to act in a welfare-enhancing way. Think-directed behaviour change is less obvious and not expected from citizens, so is possibly more powerful as a result. The second main criticism is the selection of people into these interventions that request a lot of time from them so causing differential attrition or even failure to recruit some participants. Mini-publics rely on random selection so can appear to be representative, and membership can be tweaked to ensure that certain kinds of people (such as minorities) sit on these institutional forums. Even with this attention to representation, many people do not want to get involved with these forums, leading to lack of attendance, even within certain categories. The person wanting to deliberate will have different orientations and attitudes to politics even within age, education, or social class categories, in ways that are hard to capture by measures of statistical representativeness, which tends to be done on demographics rather than orientations. Even with statistically representative samples, most mini-publics are too small to make inferences to general populations (Setälä 2017) and will be limited in policy impact in terms of practical change on the ground in the numbers affected compared to nudge interventions that can impact on many millions of people.

Internet-based forums provide one way to expand the reach of deliberation, as many more people can get involved on discussion boards than the classic citizen jury or assembly, which depend on people giving up whole days or a weekend to debate issues. Smith et al. (2013) invited people from a survey company's panel to debate issues on immigration/cohesion and young people's behaviour but found that even after selecting in respondents from the panel, there was a massive variation in who posted online or who were 'lurkers' in the background not saying anything but watching the debates.

The criticism applies to deliberative polling argued for by Fishkin and others (Fishkin et al. 2000; Fishkin 2009). With the deliberative poll, the deliberative element is embedded within a conventional survey so seeking to ensure representativeness and reach. These do in part address the issues of who gets involved with a think, though of course the question of who gets what and whether they are different from the general population in non-observed ways applies as before. Overall, the idea of scaling up think is consistent with the argument in favour of nudge+, but it is still important to realise that nudge and nudge+ also suffer from differential take up because of heterogeneity (Mertens et al. 2022). Nudge and nudge+ still suffer from the dilemma of inequality from social-economic status (Ponce de León Solís 2025).

Inequalities and Nudge+

One of the paradoxes of interventions designed to address equality and to reach all is that the very inequalities that are part cause of the public problem appear also in the remedies that are applied, hence middle-class benefits from the welfare state. Potentially nudge can address inequalities in ensuring that a wide range of citizens make good choices over their lives. Without being nudged, more wealthy and better-off citizens are able to use their personal resources to behave better for themselves or prosocially, as they have more free time to consider options, and more resources, for example to be able to buy foodstuffs that are healthy and also deliver on taste. Poorer populations do not have these. They also have lives that are characterised by stress and limited time as well as resource poverty, making take up of better choices harder. This is the argument in the book *Scarcity*, in which Mullainathan and Shafir (2013) argue that poor people have less attention capacity and cannot engage so well in planning, and they need to cope with the pressures of managing life under poverty with its day-to-day challenges. Nudge allows the policy-maker to reach these communities, helped by the low heterogeneity of these kinds of interventions. They cannot reach everyone but can get to a wide range of people in time-efficient ways.

Deliberative interventions and by implication think and nudge+ ideas put cognitive demands on individual to be able to do the thinking needed for a meaningful experience. They need to be able to process complex arguments and need to devote time to understand these issues, compared to a simpler nudge or political mechanisms that just need a vote. This is the reason the social inequality gradient of participation increases the more intense the activity: lower for voting; higher for membership of political parties and other forms of activism (Verba et al. 1995).

Of course, as argued by Young (2002), the space within deliberative mechanisms may be seen to enhance equality by allowing groups an equal right to speak and participate which they would not get in more conventional spaces such as assemblies or public consultation forums. A study of deliberative polls shows that there were no biases between high- and low-income participants, and men and women, in terms of who spoke, with mixed results for age and ethnicity (Siu 2017). Similar results using the discourse quality index, have been found for the Irish Convention on the Constitution (Mockler 2022). The design of deliberation through facilitation can help ensure access when citizens take part.

With nudge+ spaces the same kind of interruptions from more confident people or deference to others might not be directly applicable as nudge+ tends to be done on one's own, but citizens may still vary in cognitive capacity or at least the extent to which some groups find it easier to think. In the deliberative context it is possible through small numbers and facilitation to find representatives but as argued earlier these participants may not be typical of others, partly though having different levels of cognitive capacity or varying experiences in carrying out argument. If deliberations exclude many from thinking, nudge+ may be doing the same and even doing worse than nudge in this respect.

The main defence for nudge+ is that the think involved tends not to be burdensome as does not require massive time commitment, often taking a matter of seconds. It is less time-consuming than typical deliberation, so more likely to be taken up by a more representative sample than in a mini-public. The idea is that the think is closer in experience to what citizens might do in everyday life, which is to stop and reflect for a moment. These kinds of mini-think can be like when we are sitting in a bath or taking a shower and happen to reflect amid the soap suds, or those moment of pause that often happen every day, such as when waiting for a bus or train, when there is not much else to do (phones aside). People like to take the chance to reflect and nudge+ seeks to give this normal think a bit of structure. This is a long way from taking a day off work or caring to go to a special event where you meet people face-to-face, and have to speak out in front of others, or even do the equivalent online. That requires more courage and benefit from prior experience, such as doing such things in a work context which might be done by all or going to a school that privileges public speaking. Nudge+ then has more potential to offer equal participation in terms of reach of all citizens, so has one claim to be more democratic than deliberative mechanisms of mini-publics.

Who Delivers the Nudge+?

One important criticism of nudges is that they are too top down and deny agency for citizens. The relationship between citizens and the state is based on the deployment of technical expertise, where the citizen is the object to be manipulated, even if for the public good. The above sections have explored whether citizen deliberation can counter this agency-denying tendency of behavioural and other interventions, which it can do, and nudge+ takes advantage of this potential to increase autonomy. The real test of agency in these interventions is that they allow the citizens to say no to an intended behaviour change, so they do not have to follow the preferences of the policy-maker. Citizens can think through an alternative approach (e.g., saving in a different way for their pension).

But think only goes so far in countering passivity as the citizen has the chance to reflect but not such a great chance to influence matters. It is here that the deliberative mechanism would claim some advantage, but here the link to actual policy decisions is often slight, in spite of some influential deliberations taking place (Setälä 2017). Citizens debate but not much happens as a result as policy-makers have several influences on their decision-making which include parties, pressure groups, experts, interests of bureaucratic agencies, public opinion, and media agenda setting. Mini-publics find it hard to influence decision-making, which is a bit like writing an expert report and putting it in front of policy-makers, which is not the typical way in which public decisions emerge (Weiss 1977, 1998; John 2013). Once the jury disperses then policy-making carries on much as before. Nobody should be surprised by this.

An alternative is to put policy-makers on their toes to prompt them and to encourage them to engage in a practical way through feedback and interaction. More radical procedures in the policy-making process are needed to bring policy-makers closer to the perspective of citizens. Of course, policy-makers are citizens too with the same biases but also capacity to think if supported and encouraged to do so. Armed with the tools of behavioural science and using the power of the internet to send messages and do interventions, citizens can nudge and nudge+ as well.

A new vein of research into elites addresses these issues and is one where nudge+ can find a place. One important step forward is research by Peter Loewen and colleagues who test whether elites have the same biases of citizens when assessing information, testing out the famous Asian flu scenarios from Kahneman and Tversky on randomly assigned politicians in Belgium, Canada, and Israel (Sheffer et al. 2018), finding they share the same tendency to overweight sunk commitments, or tendency to overconfidence (Sheffer and Loewen 2019). Such studies back up the pre-behavioural and classic studies in public policy, which is that politicians and bureaucrats do not live up to the ideas of rational decision-makers, making decisions with reference to their group perceptions, or by hunches and intuitions (Allison and Zelikow 1999; Heclo and Wildavsky 1981).

It follows then that the designers of nudge cannot make a claim to moral superiority in terms of assessing welfare or interests of others than citizens, which is a key step in the more radical approach, embodied by more direct forms of democracy. It also follows that citizens can give a nudge to policy-makers, partly because when they appeal to more rational argument they tend to fail. Using the defaults of policy-makers and their biases might be a better way to get their attention. In their experimental study of using more rational and evidenced argument to politicians, Richardson and John (2012) found that there was no difference in responses between a more informed and better-argued letter and one that was not. Other experiments have shown that standard nudge techniques, such as making someone more visible can affect decision-making, such as legislators being subject to a 'you are being watched' intervention to encourage them to turn up to committees (Grose 2010). There is a danger, however, of such interventions falling into the same traps as the classic nudge of denying agency to the object of these researchers. Given the power of politicians and bureaucrats this is a surprising claim to make as they have many ways of realising agency. But the ferocity of their response to standard audit enquiries shows they believe they should have more agency with these experiments. This as shown in a case where Campbell and Bolet wrote randomly assigned e-mails to UK MPs testing out whether they would reply equally or according to the gender and race of the fictitious constituents. When the MPs were debriefed after the event—that is had a chance to think about it—they expressed anger at being deceived and the Speaker of the House of Commons wrote to King's College London and the research council to complain (Campbell and Bolet 2022). Even though there are defences of doing audit experiments on MPs to promote accountability, the episode illustrates the need to include powerful actors in a partnership between researchers or citizens and the politicians (Loewen and Rubenson 2022; John and Foos 2022). In this case, before the nudge, the politicians get a chance to think about the intervention and its meaning. The public remain pretty sanguine about the intrusive nature of these interventions (John et al. 2024), which does not mean that interveners could do better.

In Loewen's work it is possible to see evidence of the partnership approach where the relation between citizens and politics is two-way, each wanting to learn from each other. Given the importance of cognitions and of politicians and citizens being self-aware it is not much of a step to believe that nudge+ can play a role in this interactive relationship. Politicians and policy-makers may wish to carry out a reflective nudge to find out more about what their citizens are thinking on important issues, then citizens working with researchers may wish to nudge and help politicians think about the issues at the same time, which gets over the ethical issue that Campbell encountered.

There are no examples of these kinds of experiments and activities yet, but some research gets close. The main example is work on bureaucrats, crafting messages that create more feedback and interaction. Wittels (2020a) tested whether bureaucrats can be motivated to incorporate citizen input using non-financial incentives and value-based arguments. The main positive result is that messages that encourage motivation work more strongly. The research shows that participatory governance mechanisms can be entrenched in communications from citizens to bureaucrats. A second experiment sought to expose bureaucrats to scenario of conflict with citizens, but this forced them to observe professional rather than participatory norms (Wittels 2020b).

Conclusion

In this chapter, we discussed the role of the citizen to offer democratic reasons in favour of nudge+. Encouraging agency in a wider project of empowering citizens has many advantages, especially when traditional representative institutions do not offer much access. This is the reason we are interested in think and believe it to be ethically superior to nudge, because agency is an essential value in a democracy. Self-ownership, autonomy, and the translation of preferences into action are what democracy aims to do, and why we value it. The chapter gave some background to the wider debate and reviewed how deliberative democratic mechanisms or mini-publics is the route to use think and promote agency. Critical for democracy is its commitment to equality, which is about inclusion of all on equal terms. Deliberation does a good job at enshrining equality within mini-publics but its reach to all citizens is limited because of the small size of deliberation forums, and that their claims to representativeness are limited by the selection process of recruiting citizens. A nudge targeted to the wider population helps get over this problem, but nudged citizens lack the agency we are looking for. Hence, the nudge+ opportunity.

The chapter concludes with a prospectus about how to expand out nudge+ by asking who does the nudge and nudge+. The answer is to turn the tables and give the citizen the power to nudge as well as think. In this way, it is possible to envisage sets of relationships across the political system, which are inspired by ideas from behavioural science, because we need these cues to get people's attention and to get them to act, as they will not respond to rational argument alone. But think can be embedded alongside these behaviourally-targeted relationships. It can encourage reflection at the same time as citizens take action, which can then embed into their behaviour. Nudge+ helps the political system embody democratic ideals of reflective and response-led leaders and followers.

References

Allison, Graham T., and Philip Zelikow. 1999. Essence of decision: Explaining the Cuban missile crisis, 2nd ed. Longman.

Bächtiger, André, John S. Dryzek, Jane Mansbridge, and Mark E. Warren. 2018. *The Oxford handbook of deliberative democracy*. Oxford University Press.

Barber, Benjamin R. 1984. *Strong democracy: Participatory politics for a new age*. Univ of California Press.

Campbell, Rosie, and Diane Bolet. 2022. Measuring MPs' responsiveness: How to do it and stay out of trouble. *Political Studies Review* 20 (2): 175–183. https://doi.org/10.1177/14789299211038816.

Chater, Nick, and George Loewenstein. 2023. The i-frame and the s-frame: How focusing on individual-level solutions has led behavioral public policy astray. *Behavioral and Brain Sciences* 46:e147. https://doi.org/10.1017/S0140525X22002023.

Curato, Nicole, Jensen Sass, Selen A. Ercan, and Simon Niemeyer. 2022. Deliberative democracy in the age of serial crisis. *International Political Science Review* 43 (1): 55–66. https://doi.org/10.1177/0192512120941882.

Fishkin, James. 2009. *When the people speak: Deliberative democracy and public consultation*. Oxford University Press.

Fishkin, James S., Robert C. Luskin, and Roger Jowell. 2000. Deliberative polling and public consultation. *Parliamentary Affairs* 53 (4). https://doi.org/10.1093/pa/53.4.657.

Flinders, Matthew. 2008. *Delegated governance and the British state: Walking without order*. Oxford University Press.

Fournier, Patrick. 2011. *When citizens decide: Lessons from citizen assemblies on electoral reform*. Oxford University Press.

Fung, Archon. 2004. *Empowered participation: Reinventing urban democracy*. Princeton University Press.

Grose, Christian R. 2010. Priming rationality: A theory and field experiment of participation in legislatures. In *3rd Annual CESS-NYU Experimental Political Science Conference*.

Hagmann, David, Emily H. Ho, and George Loewenstein. 2019. Nudging out support for a carbon tax. *Nature Climate Change* 9 (6): 484–489. https://doi.org/10.1038/s41558-019-0474-0.

Heclo, Hugh, and Aaron Wildavsky. 1981. *The private government of public money: Community and policy inside British politics.* Springer.

John, Peter. 2013. *Analyzing public policy.* Routledge.

John, Peter, and Florian Foos. 2022. Introduction to symposium: Experiments with politicians: Ethics, power, and the boundaries of political science. *Political Studies Review* 20 (2): 169–174. https://doi.org/10.1177/14789299221075919.

John, Peter, Graham Smith, and Gerry Stoker. 2009. Nudge nudge, think think: Two strategies for changing civic behaviour. *The Political Quarterly* 80 (3): 361–370. https://doi.org/10.1111/j.1467-923X.2009.02001.x.

John, Peter, Kristina Kim, and Luis Soto-Tamayo. 2024. Using citizen voice to evaluate experiments on politicians: A UK survey experiment. *Journal of Experimental Political Science* 11 (1): 42–51. https://doi.org/10.1017/XPS.2023.3.

Loewen, Peter John, and Daniel Rubenson. 2022. Value-added and transparent experiments. *Political Studies Review* 20 (2): 243–249. https://doi.org/10.1177/14789299211059428.

Mansbridge, Jane J. 1983. *Beyond adversary democracy.* University of Chicago Press.

Mertens, Stephanie, Mario Herberz, Ulf J. J. Hahnel, and Tobias Brosch. 2022. The effectiveness of nudging: A meta-analysis of choice architecture interventions across behavioral domains. *Proceedings of the National Academy of Sciences* 119 (1): e2107346118. https://doi.org/10.1073/pnas.2107346118.

Mockler, Patricia. 2022. Measuring the inclusiveness of deliberation: Structural inequality and the discourse quality index. *Comparative European Politics* 20 (1): 53–72. https://doi.org/10.1057/s41295-021-00262-5.

Mullainathan, Sendhil, and Eldar Shafir. 2013. *Scarcity: Why having too little means so much.* Macmillan.

Ponce de León Solís, Viviana. 2025. Nudging and inequality: Examining the heterogeneous effects of behavioural interventions on low socio-economic status individuals. *Journal of Applied Philosophy.* https://doi.org/10.1111/japp.70015.

Renwick, Alan, Michela Palese, and Jess Sargeant. 2018. Discussing Brexit—Could we do better? *The Political Quarterly* 89 (4): 545–552. https://doi.org/10.1111/1467-923X.12595.

Richardson, Liz, and Peter John. 2012. Who listens to the grass roots? A field experiment on informational lobbying in the UK. *The British Journal of Politics and International Relations* 14 (4): 595–612. https://doi.org/10.1111/j.1467-856X.2011.00481.x.

Setälä, Maija. 2017. Connecting deliberative mini-publics to representative decision making. *European Journal of Political Research* 56 (4): 846–863. https://doi.org/10.1111/1475-6765.12207.

Sheffer, Lior, and Peter Loewen. 2019. Electoral confidence, overconfidence, and risky behavior: Evidence from a study with elected politicians. *Political Behavior* 41 (1): 31–51. https://doi.org/10.1007/s11109-017-9438-0.

Sheffer, Lior, Peter John Loewen, Stuart Soroka, Stefaan Walgrave, and Tamir Sheafer. 2018. Nonrepresentative representatives: An experimental study of the decision making of elected politicians. *American Political Science Review* 112 (2): 302–321. https://doi.org/10.1017/S0003055417000569.

Siu, Alice. 2017. Deliberation & the challenge of inequality. *Daedalus* 146 (3): 119–128. https://doi.org/10.1162/DAED_a_00451.

Smith, Graham. 2009. *Democratic innovations: Designing institutions for citizen participation*. Cambridge University Press.

Smith, Graham, Peter John, and Patrick Sturgis. 2013. Taking political engagement online: An experimental analysis of asynchronous discussion forums. *Political Studies* 61 (4): 709–730. https://doi.org/10.1111/j.1467-9248.2012.00989.x.

Strøm, Kaare. 2000. Delegation and accountability in parliamentary democracies. *European Journal of Political Research* 37 (3): 261–290. https://doi.org/10.1023/A:1007064803327.

Verba, Sidney, Kay Lehman Schlozman, and Henry E. Brady. 1995. *Voice and equality: Civic voluntarism in American politics*. Harvard University Press.

Weingast, Barry R. 1984. The congressional-bureaucratic system: A principal agent perspective (with applications to the SEC). *Public Choice* 44 (1): 147–191. https://doi.org/10.1007/BF00124821.

Weiss, C. H. (Ed.). 1977. Using Social Research in Public Policy Making. Lexington, MA: Lexington Books, D.C. Heath and Company.

Weiss, Carol H. 1998. Have we learned anything new about the use of evaluation? *American Journal of Evaluation* 19 (1): 21–33. https://doi.org/10.1177/109821409801900103.

Wittels, Annabelle. 2020a. The effect of politician-constituent conflict on bureaucratic responsiveness under varying information frames. *SocArXiv (4x8q2; SocArXiv)*. Center for Open Science. https://ideas.repec.org/p/osf/socarx/4x8q2.html.

Wittels, A. S. 2020b. Experiments on bureaucrat behaviour and public participation (Doctoral dissertation, UCL (University College London)).

Young, Iris Marion. 2002. *Inclusion and democracy*. OUP Oxford.

Zhong, Chen-Bo. 2011. The ethical dangers of deliberative decision making. *Administrative Science Quarterly* 56 (1): 1–25. https://doi.org/10.2189/asqu.2011.56.1.001.

CHAPTER 8

The Challenge of Nudge+ and How to Meet It

In this book, we have set out the prospectus for a new toolkit of behavioural public policy called nudge+. Nudge+, as we define it, is a modified nudge that incorporates an element of reflection into the delivery of the nudge. It intends to engage citizens in the process of behaviour change by inviting them to reflect on the nudge, its goals, its source, and/or more broadly on their own selves. Set up in this way, nudge+ makes nudges participatory, citizen-oriented, and bottom-up in design. The research programme of nudge+ builds on the strong foundations of classic behavioural nudges. As we have discussed earlier in this book, nudge+ interventions retain the many advantages that low-cost nudging toolkits have to offer. Yet, through their deliberative approach, these interventions also capture the benefits of large-scale thinks and overcome many of the ethical and effectiveness limitations of nudges. In this way, nudge+ captures the best of both worlds and promises a more empowering form of behaviour change. It also presents a radical agenda for policy change, citizen roles, and institutional reform.

Designing a nudge+ intervention can also be easy as all it takes is a simple prompt of reflection that is combined with the nudge. This deliberative cue ensures that citizens have a moment to think about what is good for them when they find themselves under the influence of a nudge. Nudge+ interventions can lead to perspective transformations which ultimately result in meaningful, long-term behaviour change.

© The Author(s), under exclusive license to Springer Nature Switzerland AG 2026

S. Banerjee, P. John, *Nudge+*,
https://doi.org/10.1007/978-3-032-13261-1_8

This process of discovering nudge+ has been elaborated across the previous chapters. Now the task of this conclusion is to pull the arguments together to help understand the concept more comprehensively and to see the benefits of this programme as an integrated project. To that end, we first offer a summary of the chapters to boil them down to their essences. Then we review some common criticisms of nudge+ and counter them thoughtfully where we can. This leads naturally to a discussion of the future for nudge+, both for researchers and for policy-makers.

The Book at a Glance

Chapter 1 gives the reader the essential context needed to understand how behavioural public policies have evolved over the last 25 years or so. The way in which behavioural economics emerged is very important as it transferred more sophisticated notions of human psychology into economics than those implied by the standard rational actor model. We review the nudge revolution in public policy, which came out of behavioural economics, turned into behavioural science and eventually became behavioural public policy. We note the dominance and prevalence of nudge, largely because it is so useful to policy-makers. We then move to some common criticisms of nudge, even though many of these are not so strong as contenders believe. But we do concur that the weakness of long-term effects and lack of legitimacy of nudge are crucial features that need addressing. We introduce the many alternatives to nudge that have been proposed, such as boost and the deliberative nudge, before discussing our preferred alternative of nudge+.

In Chapter 2 we set out our prospectus by arguing in favour of reflection as a desirable goal and for deciding oneself how to change behaviour, as we believe there are societal and welfare benefits from doing so. We argue against wanting to think all the time as that would be impossible, but in favour more of subliminal awareness, punctuated by a big think from time to time. Once we accept this approach, it is possible to envisage public policies that use such a mini-think and embed it into practice. This new direction to public policy is much needed as there are many intractable policy problems needing full citizen engagement if they are ever to be solved. Here a reflective kind of public policy can play a key role in addressing thorny public problems by engaging citizens for the long term. The chapter rounds off with an extended discussion of the meaning of reflection.

Chapter 3 is the heart of the book where we discuss the more practical element of nudge+ and dig much more into the detail. We elaborate on the nature of reflection and what that might entail, and whether standard nudge policies do in fact contain an element of reflection, making the plus or + part an amplification of something already there. We discuss whether reflection is conscious or not and conclude that it does not have to be, though this is important for big decisions.

Chapter 4 seeks to uncover what the plus or + is exactly, and whether it could occur within the nudge or alongside it. Developing the nudge+ idea, we claim that an element of reflection alongside the nudge but not part of it is core to the idea of nudge+ and the arguments we are presenting. We discuss the one-part nudge+ and what exactly do we reflect on, in particular the goal of the nudge and the policy context when delivering it.

In Chapter 5 we discuss what we think is happening when people are thinking or being nudged or nudge+. This requires critical examination of dual process theory, which is the foundation for considering that think and nudge rely on separate parts of the brain. While not disagreeing with this fundamental premise, especially as it is based on several decades of research in cognitive science, this chapter reviews work that indicates that the brain can be seen as much more complex when in play, so that fast and slow thinking can happen in coordination with each other and where there is swift movement between them. This fits neatly with the mechanism of nudge+, which operates on the margins of both systems and can help people address their whole selves. The plus allows citizens to kick start a monitoring response which brings in slow thinking to evaluate their intuitive responses under the nudge. Once system 2 either approves this nudge or proposes an alternative, it can safely go back to rest, and individuals can let the fast processes do most of the work. In some ways, the plus empowers people to do what the initial nudge was always assumed to do that is steer people towards welfare-improving behaviours as judged by themselves. This chapter roots the cognitive underpinnings of nudge+ in state-of-the-art literature on dual process theory.

In Chapter 6 we move to the ethics of nudge+, which rests on the superiority of its approach to encouragement of human agency. We argue that nudge suffers from the accusation of manipulation. They are not always fair and do not respect the individual. We seek to examine what is happening when someone is empowered and that they may still be manipulated by the designer of the nudge+ or think. Overall, nudge+ checks out in ethical terms, which is one of the main reasons for policy-makers and others to adopt it. It links policy much more to democratic processes. This might not rule out the ethical use of nudges in certain situations where it is not possible to reflect but suggests a more legitimate direction of travel for public policy towards more reflexivity and empowering citizens.

In Chapter 7 we continue to explore these ethical dimensions by considering the range of populations that are subject to nudge, nudge+, and think, which addresses the desirability of adopting policies that scale up to significant sections of the population, in particular the full range of groups to ensure representativeness and inclusion. We discuss the limitations of think through the self-selection and small numbers of participants. Nudge+ can be rolled out to more citizens and does not put such a cognitive burden on them as think does. The chapter discusses who does the nudging and nudge+ as another way to address the ethical challenge of policy-makers seeking to influence the behaviour of citizens. Asking citizens to use nudge and nudge+ interventions on elites can encourage a two-way dialogue between governed and governors. But nudge can suffer from the same problem when even done to powerful elites as it can deny autonomy and agency. Instead, by encouraging elites to think, citizens will be able to respect them as individuals too. And such a mini-think for elites can help them confront their own biases and make for a stronger democratic connection between citizens and the state.

Criticisms of Nudge+

The argument for nudge+ is based on its advantages across several dimensions. There are good ethical, cognitive, and policy-related arguments in favour of this new approach to behavioural public policy, which is supported by a fast-developing research programme and an emerging battery of tests. Researchers and policy-makers are increasingly ready to redesign their policies and create a new treatment arm in a randomised evaluation or survey experiment. Nudge+ gains strength from being part of a family of approaches that stress agency as part of behavioural public policy (Banerjee et al. 2024a) as there is an explicit link between transparency and nudge+. But academics and practitioners also have some reservations about nudge+. We want to acknowledge them fully and then come back with some powerful arguments to try to refute them.

The first attack on nudge+ is that it might undermine the power of nudge, either creating a null effect or even a backfire. This is because it used to be claimed that 'the psychological mechanisms … work better in the dark' (Bovens 2009). The whole point of nudge is that it operates on the automatic system 1 processes, which are the psychological cues that by definition are not conscious but happen without reflection. Introducing reflection might undermine this process, dampening the automatic because people are thinking. As we have discussed, this is not plausible because those biases might be operated by conscious thought. As we argued, studies of making nudge transparent, that is telling people they have been nudged, do not affect the efficacy of the nudge, at least in survey experimental work (Loewenstein et al. 2015). But thinking can be more than just making someone aware as it involves creating an inner debate, which transparency allows, but nudge+ interventions actively promote. Thinking may undermine the simplicity of the nudge and cause the participant to think of all the reasons for and against doing something so reducing themselves to indecision over something they may actually want to do. Or the nudge may cause them to worry about the topic, particularly if it is depressing, which again might cause no effect or a backfire. Earlier we discussed the example of organ donations from *Nudge, Nudge, Think, Think* (John et al. 2009), where the think caused a backfire when compared to the placebo. Maybe the topic of organ donation caused young people to worry too much and distract them from undertaking the prosocial behaviour? In our COVID research on the G7 (Banerjee et al. 2024b), we tested the effects of encouraging citizens to reflect on a hypothetical default nudge policy (automatic enrolment for COVID-19 booster appointments) on both vaccination intentions and policy support. Contrary to expectations, individuals report that they would be less likely to get the booster in the default nudge condition.

Of course, we can find and have cited many examples of the positive effects of nudge+ so maybe what matters is on average that it works. No intervention is foolproof, and this is why we test them with randomised controlled trials to select the context and populations where they do work. In fact, we should not be so fearful of the null effect or backfire, as they may show citizens to be thinking for themselves about the policy issues they face. This is interesting for two reasons.

The first reason is from the perspective of citizen engagement and empowerment. If citizens decide, upon reflection, that they do not want to follow the nudge it may be that they have decided for very good reasons, such as their personal circumstances, the desired behaviour is not for them. In which case the outcome is better for the individual as there is no one size fits all for any policy intervention. Even though the nudge is rejected, the policy could be welfare-enhancing. Even if not, at least they have thought through the consequences and decided against it. From the state's point of view, if such reactions were commonplace, then they might be welfare-reducing which is not what states are supposed to do with the expert knowledge they have and their wide mandate to manage public outcomes such as health. But the consequence of paternalism might be worse when citizens might find out that government was doing things they did not prefer to do. Such disregard for long-term preferences may cause reactance and the decline in trust, which may undermine even more obvious welfare-enhancing policies that ultimately require citizen cooperation. In fact, being given a chance to think might cause citizens to both reduce their intended behaviour but increase their confidence in the democratic procedures that got them to decide for themselves. This is just the type of relationship that underpins nudge+, which is about more long term and effective interaction between citizens and government than netting short-run welfare gains. Nudge+ can build trust and get citizens to nudge themselves, self-nudging in effect (Reijula and Hertwig 2022).

The second reason that these backfires are noteworthy is that nudge+ is still a young research programme, with only a limited evidence base on what works, when, and for whom. With nudges, there was a risk that the swift upswing in adoption as the initial surge of trials and applications took place before a solid proof of concept had been established across different domains. This created the false impression that early successes would automatically generalise to all contexts. As discussed earlier in the book, that phase of excitement has since given way to a more mature debate, informed by meta-analyses showing that the effectiveness of behavioural nudges varies widely across settings and populations. The same will almost certainly hold true for nudge+, perhaps even more so since it depends on specific conditions of operationalisation, as noted earlier in the book. Much remains to be studied: the cost-effectiveness of nudge+; its generalisability across behavioural domains, settings, contexts, and populations; and its sensitivity to socio-cultural change over time. While we currently know little about these factors, future trials can provide the answers.

The next criticism is the opposite argument that nudge+ is not free from the charge of paternalism and manipulation. It is usually very clear why the think has been commissioned as it is next to the nudge which is a clear policy choice. It is autonomy but with desired limits being conveyed, a form of enforcement autonomy. So there remains the possibility that citizens may be influenced by this choice making the nudge+ a framed rather than a neutral think. This is a more general problem of think that it is influenced by how they are structured particularly through their design and monitoring, which has been debated by researchers on deliberative democracy, and where procedures can also be put in place to deal with this potential source of biases. It could be the case that the problem is worse for nudge+ because it is so close to a nudge. If the nudge is clear then this is a clear signal for the citizen to act so citizens might be able to kick back if they want, as with the backfires discussed above, but it might also shift the citizen to where the policy-makers want them to be rather than where they would prefer to be autonomously, the manipulation charge once again. Discussed at several points in this book, the very freedom to think might lull the respondent into thinking they have the luxury of choice when they are being subtly manipulated, the repressive tolerance argument of Marcuse (1965). This is of course important because in the nudge+ world, the think is quite brief and happens when the person is on their own so has no chance to exchange views with others, as in the classic deliberation exercise, to double check the sense of what is being discussed. Overall, partly from the possibility of backfire, we do not think that meta-manipulation is a problem for nudge+, but it is important to acknowledge this potential criticism, partly because it is hard to detect.

This point leads to the next criticism that nudge+ is seen to enfold within rather than in criticism of existing socio-economic structures and is legitimated by how new innovations need a favourable, usually official, context to be adopted. In that sense, the strength of nudge+ in its utility for policy-makers is also a potential weak point in that it can fall into the slipstream of dominant understandings about how to do policy in western societies and reflects who controls that process. If the charge of manipulation is taken seriously, then nudge+ only appears to be bottom-up and embracive of citizen agency; but in fact it is really the tool of policy-makers designed to achieve specific politically determined ends. Overall, we reject this pessimistic scenario though much remains to be seen in how nudge+ interventions are developed. Our argument, going back to Chap. 1 is that nudge+ has the seeds of a more radical project partly from the empowerment of think. Once think is unleashed, then citizens can be critical of the very structures that commission and promote nudge and nudge+.

The final criticism is one of vagueness and lack of precision. This is a familiar problem with social science concepts, which can suffer from wanting to be all things, the practice of concept expansion identified by Sartori (1970) long ago, whereby concepts open up to encompass everything and thereby often end up meaning nothing as there is not much left to compare with the concept. In the nudge field, this is not helped by the profusion of concepts in recent years, which range from boost, to self-nudging, and to nudge+. Oliver (2025) complains about the profusion of buzzwords arguing that behavioural public policy should keep to its core more parsimonious definition originally offered by Thaler and Sunstein. Of course, Oliver (2018) has created his own fair share of these concepts from budge to shove! But it is useful to take stock of the large number of terms as behavioural public policy matures as a field.

By introducing a think alongside a nudge, it is important to be clear what the plus is and what is happening and at what point does a think happen. In a short space of time is there enough time to think to count as a think? Should we care more about outcomes than processes or procedures, that someone's mind has moved? And is the scope of the plus or + limited to the practical constraints of developing a plus alongside a nudge? This is easy if there is an internet application and one argument is that developing nudge+ is much easier where all transactions are online irrespective as to whether government or private (Dunleavy et al. 2006; Hood and Margetts 2007). With digital era governance, there are more opportunities for tweaking the delivery to introduce the plus which would have been much more difficult in earlier times. Delivering think is much harder to achieve in a paper-based world (e.g., tax letters) or face-to-face, such as in a doctor's clinic. But this kind of bias toward doing the easy things should reduce in future years as online dominates ever more. Chapter 3 sets out the different kinds of nudge+ as well as engaging in definitional precision in Chap. 2. Many of the current limitations are likely to be overcome as the research programme proceeds.

Future Research and the Policy Agenda

With the summary undertaken and the criticisms addressed, now is the time to say what is next for nudge+, first for research and then for policy. The first point is that there is a need for more tests of nudge+ owing to the early stage of the research agenda and despite the amount of research that has been done in a short space of time. Research will be useful in new domains, as well as more studies in the areas we have researched so far, the environment (especially food) and public health. We need tests over the economy, housing, and employment searches in particular. Interventions on political behaviour, such as voting and participation, would be particularly germane. As discussed in Chap. 7, tests that reverse the tables between citizens and the state could be designed, with citizens doing their own nudge+ interventions to help politicians and bureaucrats think. Such innovations could foster a spirit of collaboration between citizens and those who commission public services.

There also remains much to be said and done about scaling up active reflection prompts, especially with the help of AI which is becoming increasingly more dominant in public policy. We have not discussed this fully in this book and this is a future research agenda for nudge+. Using AI can be handy both in the successful design of new nudge+ tools as well as in understanding the dynamics of their applications. We will elaborate on both these types next.

Consider the example of personalisation of nudges where reflection is used as a starting point. Citizens can be asked to reflect on their own preferences or on barriers that prohibit them from taking up a certain behaviour. A sophisticated learning algorithm can then match the citizen with a nudge that is suited to their preference or helps them overcome their biases. In this way, reflection can become a starting point for tailoring many different kinds of behavioural tools, including nudges and boosts. Another potential area of application with AI is the help of chatbots. Reflection typically has been hard to scale up when it involves thinking with other individuals. This is precisely what led us to conceptualise 'mini-thinks' which will prevent the need for group thinking. However, chatbots can be developed today easily and these can be employed in various interactions. A well-designed chatbot that is trained to spark active reflection can also aid the delivery of many nudge+ tools. Finally, there remain applications of AI in the form of digital prompts which we have discussed in earlier examples, and these can be thought of as early prototypes of either these chatbots or personalisation techniques where the starting point is to think along with a supervised algorithm.

Next, AI tools can help to understand better the heterogeneity in the uptake of an intervention. Using various new computational social science methods, it is possible today to explore individual heterogeneity. Social scientists trained in these methods (Banerjee and Veltri 2024) can use these techniques to understand and identify clusters of individuals who behave in certain ways and then use behavioural and social characteristics to predict their likelihood of engaging in them (see Nikoloski et al. 2025 for an application in the energy sector). This ability to understand and predict behavioural responses using underlying behavioural characteristics using computational methods implies that a nudge+ practitioner will have ready information on reflective potential of citizens, following which they can better target the delivery of these interventions towards them.

While these examples suggest that participatory governance through reflection can be improved with AI tools and systems, there also remain many ethical challenges that researchers should be wary of. Tailoring or personalising nudge delivery by means of reflection runs that risk of extracting information about one's desired ends or barriers which makes them vulnerable to threats of manipulation. At the time of writing this book, we are not aware of national or international regulations that can regulate the delivery and application of behavioural insights. This makes such personalisation exercises even trickier in the absence of penalties for using them for non-benevolent purposes. Using chatbots to induce reflection also faces similar challenges where such AI models can be trained to induce echo chambers and further polarise people. Amidst growing concerns of political polarisation and misinformation, this will be an additional ethical challenge that public policy analysts and experts using AI for behaviour change should consider. These dangers of using AI for designing thinking-based interventions should not, however, deter us from the study of these newer tools as these can be promising and scalable, albeit with checks and balances in place.

We need more applications within the range of nudge+ interventions to add to our repertoire of a dual-self pledge card and a mini-think within a survey experiment. We are adding to this list over time, for example, with the idea that reflection can act as a starting point for personalisation, and we hope that more can be done here. Can nudge+ become more interactive, both with the policy-maker, and horizontally with other citizens? Can we get citizens not just to give their views about the nudge but about the processes that lead to nudge, the institutions people decide upon? In the endless tussle between a full-on think on the one hand and the more automatic nudge on the other, we can move a bit back towards think again once the early gains of nudge+ have been realised. The secret is the scaling up and the proximity to the nudge upon which further interventions can be made and refined.

These lessons apply to policy-makers too as they can use many applications tested in surveys and other experiments or done in partnership with researchers. There already has been a powerful set of influences from the academy to the practitioner world over nudge with a parallel but separate set of influences over deliberative democracy and mini-publics. The research and policy agenda of nudge+ see these two streams merging, becoming more than the sum of their parts. As governments and agencies work across many functional fields, such as energy, housing, environment, the economy, and community solidarity, so the range of applications can increase, as the discussion above indicates.

For policy-makers there are other benefits. We live in an age of distrust of government, suspicion of experts, and citizen discontent, which is mainly directed to the politicians but can spill over into the policy domains which they administer, such as public health. The nudge application can very much be seen as being part of more cynical practice whereby politicians are perceived to be keen to trick citizens to get them to do things that are not in their interests or reflect their stated preferences. This lack of transparency might in the long term undermine trust in the government, even though citizens support such measures when surveyed. Similarly, there is a danger that deliberative exercises are seen as the purview of a more articulate and well-educated minority, so neither popular nor generating more trust. In contrast, nudge+ is not designed to be manipulative and is intended to be the purview of the many. One consequence of the greater use of nudge+ ideas might reasonably be greater trust in government and a better relationship between policy-makers and citizens.

References

Banerjee, Sanchayan, and Giuseppe A. Veltri. 2024. Harnessing pluralism in behavioral public policy requires insights from computational social science. *Frontiers in Behavioral Economics* 3:1503793. https://doi.org/10.3389/frbhe.2024.1503793.

Banerjee, Sanchayan, Till Grüne-Yanoff, Peter John, and Alice Moseley. 2024a. It's time we put agency into behavioural public policy. *Behavioural Public Policy* 8 (4): 789–806. https://doi.org/10.1017/bpp.2024.6.

Banerjee, Sanchayan, Peter John, Brendan Nyhan, Andrew Hunter, Richard Koenig, Blake Lee-Whiting, Peter John Loewen, John McAndrews, and Manu M. Savani. 2024b. Thinking about default enrollment lowers vaccination intentions and public support in G7 countries. *PNAS Nexus* 3 (4): pgae093. https://doi.org/10.1093/pnasnexus/pgae093.

Bovens, Luc. 2009. The ethics of nudge. In *Preference change: Approaches from philosophy, economics and psychology*, 207–219. Springer.

Dunleavy, Patrick, Helen Margetts, Simon Bastow, and Jane Tinkler. 2006. New public management is dead—Long live digital-era governance. *Journal of*

Public Administration Research and Theory 16 (3): 467–494. https://doi.org/10.1093/jopart/mui057.

Hood, Christopher, and Helen Margetts. 2007. *The tools of government in the digital age*. Bloomsbury Publishing.

John, Peter, Graham Smith, and Gerry Stoker. 2009. Nudge nudge, think think: Two strategies for changing civic behaviour. *The Political Quarterly* 80 (3): 361–370. https://doi.org/10.1111/j.1467-923X.2009.02001.x.

Loewenstein, George, Cindy Bryce, David Hagmann, and Sachin Rajpal. 2015. Warning: You are about to be nudged. *Behavioral Science & Policy* 1 (1): 35–42. https://doi.org/10.1177/237946151500100106.

Marcuse, Herbert. 1965. A critique of pure tolerance. In *A critique of pure tolerance*. Beacon Press.

Nikoloski, Marjan, W. J. W. Botzen, Sanchayan Banerjee, and Julia Blasch. 2025. Clustering Dutch citizens into behavioural phenotypes to understand green energy investment preferences. *Economics Letters* 255:112566.

Oliver, Adam. 2018. Nudges, shoves and budges: Behavioural economic policy frameworks. *The International Journal of Health Planning and Management* 33 (1): 272–275. https://doi.org/10.1002/hpm.2419.

Oliver, Adam. 2025. Clarifying by declassifying: Removing the buzzwords from behavioral public policy. *Policy and Society* puaf010. https://doi.org/10.1093/polsoc/puaf010.

Reijula, Samuli, and Ralph Hertwig. 2022. Self-nudging and the citizen choice architect. *Behavioural Public Policy* 6 (1): 119–149. https://doi.org/10.1017/bpp.2020.5.

Sartori, Giovanni. 1970. Concept misformation in comparative politics. *American Political Science Review* 64 (4): 1033–1053. https://doi.org/10.2307/1958356.

Glossary of Key Terms[1]

Agency The capacity of individuals to act intentionally. Agency focuses on the ability to execute decisions, thus, having the power, resources, and competence to engage in well-endowed decision-making.
See also: Nudge+; Perspective transformation; Reflection; Competence

Anchoring A bias in which people's judgements are strongly influenced by the first number or piece of information they encounter, even if it is not relevant.
See also: Heuristics; Biases

Availability heuristic A mental shortcut where people judge how likely or important something is based on how easily examples come to mind.
See also: Heuristics; Biases

Autonomy The capacity for self-determination, making decisions based on one's own values, preferences, and reasoning rather than external influence. Autonomy focuses on the origin and ownership of decisions.
See also: Agency

[1] This glossary collects the main technical terms and concepts used in the book. Each entry provides a short, accessible, non-technical explanation to support readers who may not be familiar with the specialised language of behavioural economics and public policy. Cross-references are included so that related ideas can be easily connected.

© The Editor(s) (if applicable) and The Author(s), under exclusive license to Springer Nature Switzerland AG 2026
S. Banerjee, P. John, *Nudge+*,
https://doi.org/10.1007/978-3-032-13261-1

Behavioural economics A field that combines insights from psychology and economics to explain why people often make decisions that depart from the "rational actor" model.

See also: Homo economicus; Behavioural public policy

Behavioural public policy The use of findings from behavioural science to design public policies that work with how people actually think and act.

See also: Nudge; Nudge+; Think

Biases Systematic tendencies to make decisions that depart from rational calculation, such as being overly optimistic or sticking with the status quo.

See also: Anchoring; Availability heuristic; Overconfidence bias; Status quo bias

Boosts Competency building interventions that help people learn better skills or develop better capacities.

See also: Behavioural Public Policy; Nudge; Nudge+; Think

Choice architecture The way choices are presented or structured. Small design changes—like setting a default option—can significantly influence people's behaviour.

See also: Nudge; Defaults

Commitment device A tool people use to help stick to long-term goals, such as signing a pledge or setting up automatic savings, even when short-term temptations arise.

See also: Nudge+

Competence The cognitive and practical abilities needed to make effective decisions, including skills like statistical reasoning, self-control, and means-ends evaluation. A component of agency that can be enhanced through boosts.

See also: Boosts; Agency

Cost-benefit analysis A method of comparing the expected advantages and disadvantages of different policy options in order to guide decisions.

See also: Rational-actor model

Defaults Pre-set options that apply if people take no action. For example, automatically enrolling workers into pension plans unless they opt out.

See also: Choice architecture; Nudge

Deliberative Democracy A model of democracy emphasising reasoned discussion among citizens before decisions are made. Deliberative democrats argue citizens should actively engage in decision-making.

See also: Think; Mini-think; Mini-publics

Dual-systems theory A model of thinking that distinguishes between fast, intuitive responses ("system 1"/ "type 1") and slower, more deliberate reasoning ("system 2"/ "type 2").
See also: Think; Nudge+

Heuristics Simple rules of thumb people rely on to make quick decisions without weighing all the information.
See also: Anchoring; Availability heuristic; Satisficing

Homo economicus A theoretical figure in classical economics representing a perfectly rational, self-interested decision-maker.
See also: Behavioural economics; Rational actor model

Inconsistent time discounting A tendency to give much more weight to immediate costs and benefits than to future ones, leading people to undervalue long-term gains.
See also: Biases; Nudge

Libertarian paternalism The philosophy behind nudging: guiding people towards better choices while still allowing them freedom to choose.
See also: Nudge; Nudge+

Mini-publics Small groups of randomly selected citizens come together to deliberate on specific policy issues (e.g., citizens assemblies). Designed to be more representative than self-selected participants but more deliberative than mass voting.
See also: Mini-think; Think; Deliberative democracy

Mini-think A prompt or cue to encourage thinking in an individual.
See also: Reflection; Nudge+

Nudge A light-touch policy tool that steers people towards certain behaviours by altering the choice environment, without forbidding options or imposing large costs.
See also: Choice architecture; Defaults; Nudge+; Think

Nudge+ An enhanced form of nudge that incorporates a moment of reflection, giving citizens the chance to think about whether the nudge aligns with their own goals and values.
See also: Nudge; Think; Commitment device

Overconfidence bias The tendency for people to overestimate what they know, how skilled they are, or how likely they are to succeed.
See also: Biases

Perspective transformation A reflective process where people reconsider their assumptions and adopt new ways of thinking, leading to reflective empowerment.
See also: Think; Nudge+

Randomised Controlled Trial (RCT) Experimental method that randomly assigns participants to treatment or control groups to test intervention effectiveness while controlling for confounding variables. Considered the gold standard in experimental social science research.
See also: Behavioural public policy; Behavioural economics

Rational-actor model The assumption in classical economics and policy design that people always weigh costs and benefits carefully and act in ways that maximise their self-interest.
See also: Homo economicus; Cost-benefit analysis; Behavioural economics

Reactance A pushback that happens when people feel their freedom of choice is being restricted, often leading them to resist or do the opposite of what is intended.
See also: Nudge; Libertarian paternalism

Reflection The process of thinking about one's true preferences and beliefs. The process can be active or passive.
See also: Nudge; Perspective transformation

Satisficing Settling for an option that is "good enough" rather than the best possible, often to save time or effort.
See also: Heuristics

Sludge Excessive friction that makes beneficial choices unnecessarily difficult, essentially "negative nudging". Examples include complicated opt-out procedures, buried cancellation options, or lengthy forms for accessing benefits. While nudges make good choices easier, sludge makes them harder.
See also: Nudge

Status quo bias A preference for keeping things as they are, even when change could bring benefits.
See also: Biases; Defaults; Choice architecture

Think A deliberative policy approach that encourages citizens to reflect and engage with choices more deeply, often contrasted with nudges that work automatically.
See also: Nudge; Nudge+; Dual-systems theory; Perspective transformation

Index[1]

[1] Note: Page numbers followed by 'n' refer to notes.

© The Editor(s) (if applicable) and The Author(s), under exclusive license to Springer Nature Switzerland AG 2026

S. Banerjee, P. John, *Nudge+*,
https://doi.org/10.1007/978-3-032-13261-1

The manufacturer's authorised representative in the EU is Springer Nature Customer Service Centre GmbH, Europaplatz 3, 69115 Heidelberg, Germany. If you have any concerns regarding our products, please contact ProductSafety@springernature.com

Printed and bound by CPI Group (UK) Ltd, Croydon, CR0 4YY

17/09/2026

02218434-0003